Rabbit's Blues

Rabbit's Blues

The Life and Music of Johnny Hodges

CON CHAPMAN

OXFORD
UNIVERSITY PRESS

OXFORD
UNIVERSITY PRESS

Oxford University Press is a department of the University of Oxford. It furthers
the University's objective of excellence in research, scholarship, and education
by publishing worldwide. Oxford is a registered trade mark of Oxford University
Press in the UK and certain other countries.

Published in the United States of America by Oxford University Press
198 Madison Avenue, New York, NY 10016, United States of America.

CIP data is on file at the Library of Congress
ISBN 978–0–19–065390–3

9 8 7 6 5 4 3 2 1

Printed by Sheridan Books, Inc., United States of America

Stomp down those symmetrical after-beats, baby, so that Rab can smelt the melody to smoldering, and over the hush let's hear the broads in the back row whisper, "Tell the story, daddy."

—DUKE ELLINGTON, *Music Is My Mistress*

Contents

Rabbit's Blues

Prologue

HE WAS THEN, and is still now, a bit of a mystery.

The first name by which he is known does not appear on his birth certificate; his given name does not appear on his death certificate. Several sources state that he had a middle name—Keith[1]—but he didn't. A reviewer for a New York newspaper referred to him incorrectly as "Jimmy."[2] Some writers claimed that he got his own last name wrong or didn't know how to spell it, assertions belied by his signature. He went by at least seven nicknames and four pseudonyms.

His birth year is regularly cited as 1906, yet his birth certificate shows that he was born in 1907. One of his albums gives the year of his death as 1960, but it is a matter of public record that he died in 1970.

When his picture first appeared in a national magazine he was confused with Harry Carney, his boyhood chum and bandmate in Duke Ellington's orchestra for many years.[3] Two Chicago radio stations inexplicably insisted on mispronouncing his surname as "Hargus."[4] A newspaper in England praised his trumpet solos,[5] and on American albums he was listed as a trombonist[6] or a tenor saxophonist,[7] although he played none of those instruments.

His natural reticence didn't help; he was the Calvin Coolidge of the jazz world of his day, never saying three words when two would do. He was not an approachable person, rarely giving interviews and revealing little when he did; in the words of Stanley Dance, who got more out of him than any other writer, he "regarded his private life as *private*."[8] Rex Stewart, a trumpeter in the Ellington band, said of him that "little of his personality emerged from the cocoon of his imperturbability."[9] If, as Lytton Strachey wrote in *Eminent Victorians*, "ignorance is the first requisite of the historian," then the subject of this book provides the biographer with a fertile field to plow.

But the taciturn figure he struck on and off the stage was diametrically at odds with the sounds—by turns languorous and inflamed—that he produced when he played. Despite the ambiguities concerning the mundane details of the nearly three score and three years of his life, he could be immediately and positively identified, then and now, by that most ephemeral of things: a single musical note, one of the few musicians in the history of jazz about whom that assertion can be made as anything more than hyperbole.

This is Johnny Hodges's story.

1

A Sax Is Born

ON JULY 25, 1907, a boy named Cornelius was born in Cambridge, Massachusetts, to John H. and Katie Swan Hodges.[1] The boy's color was listed on his birth certificate as black; the other two choices on the form were white and mulatto. His last name was given as "Hodges"—not "Hodge," as some have claimed.[2]

There are several reasons for the uncertainty as to the spelling of the boy's last name: First, the father's name appears as "John H. Hodge" in the City of Boston's record of the couple's 1896 marriage[3] and in the 1880 census of Danville, Virginia.[4] Second, as an adult the son reportedly owned a stamp bearing the name "Hodge,"[5] and he would display a curious indifference throughout his life to the spelling of his surname; records of American Federation of Musicians Local 802, the union to which he belonged in New York, give the spelling as "Hodge" from 1928, when he first joined, until 1948, when it was corrected to "Hodges." Three years later, the former erroneous spelling returned, and it remained in the union's directories until his death in 1970.[6]

The birth certificate bears the marks of confusion on the part of either the canvasser, the local official who signed the document, or the person who supplied him with the information; on the first page the father's occupation is listed as porter, on the second as waiter. On the first page the canvasser identified the attending physician as F. W. Gilman and on the second as Dr. Lockhart, whose name is then crossed out and replaced with Gilman's. Perhaps, like many babies, Cornelius Hodges was born in the middle of the night and when the time came to record the birth, the person who reported the facts was groggy from lack of sleep.

The father's place of birth is given as Danville, Virginia, the mother's as Woodburn, Virginia. According to the parents' wedding records, John

H. Hodges was twenty-eight years old (and a waiter) when the couple was married on September 2, 1896, and Katie Swan Hodges was twenty-three years old (and a domestic). Thus, the father would have been born around 1868, and the mother around 1873. At the time of their marriage both husband and wife lived in Boston, but they would later move to Cambridge, across the Charles River. The father's parents' names are listed as John, who worked in a tobacco factory, and Bettie, whose occupation is listed as "Keeping house."[7] The wife's parents' names were James N., described in census records as a laborer, and Lizzie. It was the first marriage for both the father and the mother of the boy

Most sources suggest that Cornelius Hodges had only one sister, but the records of the Thirteenth Census of the United States in 1910 show three older sisters, and Massachusetts vital records confirm that John and Katie Hodges had three daughters. The first was born on February 24, 1897, also in Cambridge, and left unnamed at the time her birth was recorded, as was frequently the case in those days; she was subsequently named Claretta. The second was born on July 1, 1899, at the Boston Lying-In Hospital, and was also unnamed when the record of her birth was made; she would be called Daisy B. The family lived in Washington, DC, at the time of the Twelfth Census of the United States in 1900.[8] The third daughter was born on May 18, 1902, in Cambridge, and was named Cynolia. She would go by the name of Josephine.[9]

Her little brother would also go by a name other than that on his birth certificate. The name Cornelius was soon dropped, and by the time of the 1910 federal Census, when he was three, his family had reconsidered their christening choice; he is listed then as "John C. Hodges," and Johnny is the name by which the world at large would know him. The name Cornelius had peaked in popularity among Americans in the 1880s;[10] it was often given in talismanic tribute to business magnate Cornelius Vanderbilt (1794–1877), but it was a playground burden to boys whose parents hoped his Midas-like touch would pass to their sons in the manner of William Faulkner's Eck Snopes, who named his son "Wallstreet Panic" thinking "it might make him get rich like the folks" who caused the crash of 1929.[11]

Nicknames, unlike given names, are applied by one's family and friends— or enemies—*after* our features, characters, and personalities have developed a bit, and not at the baptismal font. As the narrator of Melville's "Bartleby, the Scrivener" says, nicknames are "deemed expressive" of the person or character to whom they are applied, and they imply "cherished disrespect and dislike" in "the form of merriment."[12] Hodges's next nickname was Rabbit, and several grounds for it have been proposed: the first was that Hodges was fast on foot, able to escape truant officers who pursued the errant student through the streets of Boston. This was the story Hodges himself told, perhaps because it satisfied a male ideal of athleticism and a boy's distaste for the tedium of the classroom. "They never could catch me. I'd go too fast," he said. "That's why I'm called 'Rabbit.'"[13] The second explanation (and the more likely, since it comes from an independent source, Harry Carney, a childhood friend), was that Hodges looked like a rabbit when he regularly nibbled on lettuce-and-tomato sandwiches.[14]

For a nickname to last, it must seem apt to successions of acquaintances who are unfamiliar with its origin, however, and in Hodges's case there was ample justification. According to Carney, Hodges was shy and skittish like a rabbit, for example, when it came to taking a solo, and he was known to bolt from interviews, bringing them to an abrupt conclusion. He was small, like a rabbit. His stage demeanor was impassive, and his face was a mask that camouflaged his emotions in much the same way a rabbit stands still against a natural background to avoid detection. Further, rabbits have historically been considered melancholy. For example, Prince Hal says to Falstaff, "What sayest thou to a hare, or the melancholy of Moorditch?"[15] in Shakespeare's *Henry the Fourth*, and Hodges would project an air of melancholy on the bandstand from youth until his last gig.

Tenor saxophonist Johnny Griffin adds another overtone to this chord, saying that Hodges "looked like a rabbit, no expression on his face while he's playing all this beautiful music."[16] Duke Ellington biographer Barry Ulanov claims that Hodges was born again as "Rabbit" after he joined the orchestra: "'Rabbit' they called him—because he looked like one."[17] This theory of a spontaneous rechristening strikes one as improbable; it seems more likely that Carney told his bandmates of Hodges's boyhood nickname and it stuck because (as Ulanov puts it) "of his amusing facial resemblance to a bunny."[18] His features were, at least to this writer's eyes, leporine, and this may account for the durability of "Rabbit" long after Hodges had progressed beyond lettuce-and-tomato sandwiches and footraces. Ellington trumpeter Rex Stewart concurs: "Let me presume it was because, straight on, he did look a little like a rabbit."[19]

In New York Hodges was known for a time as "Little Caesar," a name that may have occurred to one of his peers because of his short stature and sometimes brusque manner, after the mobster character played by Edward G. Robinson in the 1931 movie of that name. Used by musicians he encountered around the Rhythm Club (according to Rex Stewart), this was one name that didn't spread beyond the circle where it originated.[20] A name by which he was known during the period when he played with Chick

Webb's band, from approximately 1926 to 1928, when he was hired by Duke Ellington, was "Paulie,"[21] according to Russell Procope, who was a member of Billy Freeman's orchestra but would later join Ellington.[22] Again, this name apparently didn't stick.

Then there was "Jeep," as in some of his most popular numbers, "The Jeep is Jumpin'" and "Jeep's Blues." Some have expressed puzzlement as to the source of this name, but those familiar with the cartoon character Popeye will recognize its antecedent in Eugene the Jeep, a friendly animal of indeterminate species who was introduced by E. C. Segar to the comic strip on August 9, 1936. The character proved so popular that his name was adopted for the rugged four-wheel-drive vehicle used by the U.S. Army in World War II because, like Popeye's "jungle pet," it was "small, able to move between dimensions and could solve seemingly impossible problems."[23] This nickname was given to Hodges by Otto "Toby" Hardwick, a fellow alto in the Ellington band.[24] Eugene the Jeep is a doglike creature who walks upright, says little (just the word "Jeep"), and has an oversize head and a large nose, all traits shared by Hodges, and thus the moniker satisfies the principal purpose of a nickname; it is an affectionate put-down that points out an individual's flaws in a shorthand manner without rubbing them in too much. As to Eugene's personality, he is highly intelligent and helps get Popeye out of jams, just as Hodges provided his boss with a constant flow of musical solutions. "Give me a long slow glissando against that progression," Ellington once called out to Hodges at a recording session, and when the Jeep had filled in the musical blank, Duke said with satisfaction, "Yeah, that's it!"[25]

In addition there was "Squatty Roo," an invidious comment on Hodges's short stature that he applied by a sort of creative *jiu jitsu* to a jaunty number he played with small groups formed among Ellington's band members.[26] The song was a solo vehicle for him, and he seems to have used it to answer those who called him by that name for derisive reasons, as if to say that sticks and stones might break his bones, but you could stick that nickname in your ear.

Finally, there was "The Earl of Ellingtonia," which appears in one biographical sketch of Hodges but does not seem to have achieved any currency;[27] it has the ring of something dreamed up by a publicist or an overwrought journalist and not the spontaneous wit and insight that produces a nickname that lasts.

Like two of his sisters, the boy was born in the family's home, rather than at a hospital. At the time, home birth was considered the safer alternative for several reasons, one being the lower rate of infection for home deliveries than for hospital deliveries,[28] another being the undeveloped state of the nursing profession; as Lytton Strachey put it in his biography of Florence Nightingale, " 'nurse' meant then a coarse old woman, always ignorant, usually dirty, often brutal . . . tippling at the brandy-bottle."[29] The house was located at 137 Putnam Avenue in Cambridge, Massachusetts, in a residential area known as Cambridgeport. The neighborhood is bounded by the Charles River on one side, which explains the addition of "port" to "Cambridge."

The Hodges family is listed as residents of Ward 8, Precinct 13 of Cambridge in the 1910 census, when Johnny was reported to be two years old. The parents' choice of the neighborhood where their son spent the first years of his life may indicate that, coming from Virginia, they had high aspirations for themselves and their children in Massachusetts. In antebellum America, Cambridgeport was home to influential white residents sympathetic to the advancement of African Americans, including the journalist and antislavery advocate Margaret Fuller and the abolitionist William Lloyd Garrison, who published his newspaper *The Liberator* from his home there. Many blacks moved to Cambridgeport after the Civil War because they viewed it as a hospitable locale, and in 1868, the Howard Industrial School was opened on Putnam Avenue to provide shelter and training for newly freed slaves. Maria Louise Baldwin, who lived at 196 Prospect Street, became the first female black principal in Massachusetts; the school that she led from 1889 to 1922 became one of the best in the city, attended by children of Harvard professors and members of old families of Cambridge (including e. e. cummings).

One final aspect of the 1910 census data concerning Hodges's family is curious: all members are listed as white. Johnny was light-colored, his skin "like coffee with a lot of cream" according to Rex Stewart,[30] but his birth certificate lists him as black, and his parents are both listed as black in Boston marriage records. (Hodges's sisters are listed as black or colored on their birth certificates.) This error, unlike the misspelling of "Hodges" as "Hodge" in Boston marriage records, can't definitively be chalked up to a civil servant's negligence or personal assessment. Did Katie Swan Hodges hope that by claiming her children were white, she would give them a chance for a better life? (Her husband, according to census records, was gainfully employed during the entire year of the census, and so less likely to have been home to answer a census taker's questions.) Or did she, who was listed in the Loudoun County, Virginia, Registry of Births as "Colored female," not consider herself African American? In any case, all family members were later listed as "B" for black in the 1920 census.

The jazz critic and Ellington biographer Stanley Dance, who knew Johnny's mother, said that she was Mexican-Indian.[31] There is no evidence to support this claim, although more than one observer saw characteristic traces of Native American physiognomy in Hodges's appearance. Hodges himself apparently repeated this tale of his ancestry and was sufficiently invested in it that he contributed to Native American charities and studied Indian lore, though the extent of that study is not known.[32] Rex Stewart speculated that "perhaps unknown to himself," Hodges was a "descendant of an ancient Indian heritage, and I choose that particular lineage deliberately because . . . there's no other racial stock that can control emotions so completely or present such a stoic exterior to the world. Johnny had that kind of impassive face."[33] It is possible that an indifferent Virginia public official could have looked at a Mexican-Indian baby girl and her mixed-race parents and decided that the catch-all category "colored" was close enough for government work. Nonetheless, when Katie Swan decided to marry in Boston in 1896, she did not object to the entry "c" for "colored" by her name, so there appears to have been conscious intent in her designating her family's race as white fourteen years later.

A final thought on this curious item is that if Johnny's father self-identified as black and his mother did not, it would have been illegal for them to marry in Virginia, where they were born. Interracial marriage was barred by statute in Virginia until the United States Supreme Court struck down state antimiscegenation laws in 1967 in the coincidentally named case of *Loving v. Virginia*,[34] so it is possible that the two moved north in order to consummate a marriage that would have been forbidden in the South.

In 1920, when Johnny was twelve, his family moved within Cambridge to 10 Clarendon Avenue, Ward 11, part of Precinct 2, in the area known as North Cambridge, and they apparently remained there until they moved to Boston around 1922.[35] The Hodges family then disappears from census records as a unit: Daisy B. Hodges married Joseph Francis, a baker and a native of Antigua, British West Indies; Cynolia/Josephine married Don Kirkpatrick, a musician and arranger who lived in the New York area; the further fate of Claretta is unknown.

The address where the family settled in Boston, 32 Hammond Street, was located in the city's South End, like Cambridgeport a racially mixed neighborhood. The area was home to many young musicians, including Leonard Withers, a pianist, James "Buster" Tolliver, who played reeds, and Harry Carney, who lived, as Hodges recalled many years later, "about three blocks from me,"[36] and who would spend most of the rest of his professional life alongside Hodges in the Ellington sax section. The structures in which the Hodges and Carney families lived are listed in the city directory with the designation "h," meaning a free-standing house as opposed to a tenement apartment; the occupation of both John Hodges and Harry F. Carney, the heads of the households, are given as porter.[37]

As to why the Hodges family moved from Cambridge to the South End, the latter neighborhood had experienced a 38.4% drop in real estate values in the thirty years from 1875 to 1905, shortly before their relocation there. The initial cause was the financial crisis of 1873, but the South End's decline accelerated when Boston's "Back Bay" neighborhood was created by filling in the former tidal area located west and south of fashionable Beacon Hill; the assessed values of houses in the South End's Union Park neighborhood declined 8% in 1882, the year after the bay was filled in. As a result of this downturn in the South End's real estate values, the three-story houses that had been built to hold a single family were divided up into apartments, rooming houses (available by the week or month), or lodging houses (available by the night).[38] Thus, instead of becoming an urban refuge for the well-to-do, the South End became a place where housing was affordable to the masses, namely, young clerks and office workers, laborers who had risen as far in life as they would go, and those who had begun to succumb to despair. One single-room residence alluded to the latter problem by the sign on its door: "Friendly Lodging House for Sober Men, No Drunken Men Admitted."[39] It is thus likely that the six-member Hodges family moved to the South End in part for reasons of economy.

There was also the matter of convenience. The South End was closer to hotels and restaurants where Johnny's father could find employment as a waiter and to the Back Bay railroad station, where he could work as a porter. A 1913 study reported that a "large number of negro waiters, cooks and stewards, barbers, janitors, and porters" found rooms in the belt of territory that extended across the South End from the Back Bay Station to Tremont Street and the lower part of Shawmut Avenue—precisely where the family's new home on Hammond Street was located.[40]

In the decade before the Hodges family moved to the South End the neighborhood had taken an even further turn downward: the Boston Elevated Railway from downtown to the South End was completed, making it easier to commute to and from Boston but adding to the grime and noise that already marred the neighborhood. The stations at either end of the railway became dock pilings to which the barnacles of urban life—saloons, theaters, and pool halls—began to attach, and a "garish night life . . . 'turned night into day.'"[41] The Boston Brahmin poet Robert Lowell, who wrote about the more proper neighborhoods he frequented, could open his windows in the Back

Bay and "hear the South End / the razor's edge / of Boston's negro culture."[42] The neighborhood thus came to resemble a sort of permanent fair that an impressionable young boy with an ear for music might appreciate, and the music he would hear in the South End would not be the genteel sort that he would have been exposed to in Cambridge. "Johnny was into the big world," his neighborhood pal Howard Johnson noted would say, "but I was still in the little world. . . . He used to hang out nights, while I was more or less a home boy."[43]

Hodges may have attended the Hyde School on Hammond Street, which ran from kindergarten through the sixth grade, along with Carney, who told an interviewer in 1958 that he and Hodges were schoolmates.[44] Built in 1884, the school had a high student-teacher ratio—there were 51.3 students for every teacher at one point—that would have afforded Hodges ample opportunity to skip classes without detection, which is consistent with his account of himself as a truant.[45]

With the South End's increased density and poverty came an increase in crime. Prostitutes, pimps, and pickpockets walked the streets of the neighborhood, and the life of the roguish petty criminal must have appealed to a boy bored with school but forced to attend classes under the Massachusetts compulsory education law, the first in the nation.[46] "I think I was all set to be a crook, a mastermind crook," Hodges would explain in later years, "until I came under the spell of music[;] music was too strong."[47]

2

Young Man With a Sax

JOHNNY HODGES WAS first attracted to the saxophone, he said, because a particular soprano model he saw in a store window "looked so pretty." His father refused to buy one for him, so he did what boys have historically done when thwarted by paternal parsimony: he went to his mother. He told her that if she didn't buy the horn for him he'd get one the way "the bad fellers" did—by theft.[1] Perhaps fearful that he meant it, she agreed even though on her husband's pay and tips and her income as a maid earning $3.20 per day,[2] the purchase represented a luxury.

The Hodges family was a musical one—Hodges recalled that everyone played "a little piano for enjoyment"—and his parents encouraged him to learn how to play piano, but he wanted to play drums. "[He] beat up all the pots and pans in the kitchen."[3] His mother persisted; "My mother used to give me piano lessons but nothing ever happened."[4] On this point, Hodges is too modest; he learned enough to be able to develop musical ideas on the keyboard, a skill that would serve him throughout his career.[5] As a youth he was good enough to play piano at "house hops," dances with paid admission in private homes to raise money for the necessities of life—usually rent, hence the other name by which these affairs were known, "rent parties." According to Willie "The Lion" Smith, the profit from such an event could be substantial: the household would stock the party for as little as twelve dollars and could sell its wares for fifty times the cost.[6] For pianists, typical pay for such a night's work in the Boston area was $8 (the equivalent of around $100 today), enough to attract good players; one night Hodges was relieved by Bill (not yet Count) Basie, three years his elder, who was "in town with a show."[7]

Hodges liked to say that he taught himself the saxophone, but he received both informal musical schooling from friends and acquaintances and some formal instruction. Hodges described his education thus: "I didn't have any tuition (used in the archaic sense of instruction) and I didn't buy any books. A friend, Abe Strong, came back and showed me the scale just after I bought the horn, and I took it up from there by myself, for my own enjoyment, and had a lot of fun. So far as reading went, I took a lesson here and there, and then experience taught me a lot, sitting beside guys like Otto Hardwick and Barney Bigard."[8]

The lessons Hodges received were few, perhaps because he was naturally talented, perhaps because instructors cost money, perhaps because he was an impatient student. According to Rex Stewart, Hodges took lessons and "after about eight or ten sessions, the teacher asked, 'Show me how you do this,' and 'How did you do that?' So Johnny figured he knew more than the teacher and stopped."[9] The instructor in question may have been a Boston man named Bob Joiner, who, according to one source, told Hodges, "You're finished taking lessons from me . . . how about teaching me a few things?"[10]

Hodges also received lessons from Jerome Don Pasquall, who taught his neighbors Harry Carney and Charlie Holmes as well.[11] Pasquall was five years older than Hodges and received his early musical training in a boys' band outfitted by a fraternal order, as did Carney. He played with various groups in St. Louis and in 1921 began to work with Fate Marable's band on riverboats plying the Mississippi River, as Louis Armstrong had before him. He studied and gigged in Chicago before leaving in about 1923 to study at the New England Conservatory of Music in Boston. While a student there he played with local bands and in New York until June 1927, when he graduated and left Boston permanently to join Fletcher Henderson as lead alto.[12] This chronology means that Hodges began to take lessons from Pasquall when the former was perhaps as young as sixteen. Regardless of the details of his formal musical education, as a result of his limited training Hodges was not a quick study as a sight reader, and he relied on his ear and assistance from bandmates throughout his career to pick up new material.

Hodges benefited from the concentration of saxophonists in his neighborhood in the South End, which came to be known as "Saxophonist Ghetto"[13] because of the number of practitioners of the instrument who lived there. They included Carney, Holmes, and Howard Johnson, who, though younger than Hodges, had learned to play sax from his older brothers, Charlie and Bobby. Johnson recalled how Hodges used stealth to acquire some rudimentary instruction from him after Hodges acquired his first horn: Hodges sent another boy to invite Johnson to view his new sax, and when Johnson arrived he played a few scales on it. "That was what he wanted to know," Johnson said.[14]

There are the fundamentals, and then there is the style that a player chooses to adopt, and for that Hodges looked first to Sidney Bechet, who played frequently in Boston burlesque shows although, as Nat Hentoff put it many years later, "Sidney [was] not too fond of Boston."[15] In the early 1920s burlesque impresario Jimmy Cooper staged a mixed-race show in Boston and other cities called the Black and White Review, whose first act was performed by an all-white cast and the second featured "twenty Negroes." Cooper promised "complete separation" of the performers by race and "complete satisfaction to the audience."[16] Among those appearing in the second act was Bechet, a mixed-race Creole of color.

Hodges took in the show for two years running and finally persuaded his sister Claretta, who was ten years older than he and already acquainted with Bechet,[17] to introduce him to the great jazzman. Hodges brought his curved soprano saxophone to the theater "wrapped up in a cloth bag" made from a sleeve of one of his mother's coats.[18] The two siblings went backstage to see Bechet. "I had a lot of nerve," Hodges later recalled, "and I made myself known."

"What's that under your arm?" Bechet asked Hodges.

"A soprano," Hodges replied.

"Can you play it?" Bechet asked.

"Sure," Hodges replied, although he had reportedly owned the horn for only a few days.

"Well, play something," Bechet said, and Hodges responded with "My Honey's Lovin' Arms." Bechet expressed his approbation with a simple "That's nice."[19]

On June 30, 1923, Bechet's sound was captured for the first time on record as a member of Clarence Williams's Blue Five on "Wild Cat Blues" and "Kansas City Man Blues." Thanks to the technological innovation of the phonograph, Hodges became an early student of a form of musical self-instruction now well-established: learning by listening to an idol's recordings. "I used to enjoy going to Johnny's house because he had a very good record collection, and we used to borrow ideas from records and copy as much as we liked," Harry Carney would recall. "We had the old Victrola that you wind by hand, with the horn. It gave us the feeling of being sort of big-time musicians, being able to play some of the things that were on records, for instance by Sidney Bechet, who was our idol."[20] Hodges and Carney were electrified by Bechet's tone, and they wore the records out by playing them over and over.[21]

"Sidney Bechet is tops in my book," Hodges would later tell British jazz writer Henry Whiston. "He schooled me a whole lot," Hodges related. "If it hadn't been for him, I'd probably just be playing for a hobby, not even professionally."[22] Hodges would initially fashion his style from what he heard on records by Bechet and by Louis Armstrong. "I had taken a liking to [Bechet's] playing, and to Louis Armstrong's[,] which I heard on the Clarence Williams Blue Five records, and I just put both of them together, and used a little of what I thought of new," he told Stanley Dance.[23] In later remarks he would credit Frankie "Tram" Trumbauer, the C-melody saxophone player who recorded seminal jazz pieces with Bix Beiderbecke, as the third leg of the stool on which his fully developed sound sat.[24] At some point Hodges realized the alto's pre-eminence as "the determining voice among the saxophones as the violin is among the strings,"[25] and switched to alto, then he started to play both.[26] Eventually, his schoolmate Carney convinced him to switch from the curved soprano to a longer, straight model. "It was I who made Johnny buy a [straight] soprano," Carney said. "I thought he looked kinda sharp walking along the street with an alto case in one hand and a long soprano case in the other."[27]

The saxophone, a brass-and-reed hybrid, was invented in 1840 by the Belgian instrument maker Antoine-Joseph "Adolphe" Sax.[28] Because the sax came into being more recently than other instruments played in a jazz context—the first entirely new instrument to appear since the clarinet a hundred years earlier—there was no formal European style to impose on young players, who were free to create techniques that were in tune with twentieth-century fashions and mores.[29] When Hodges first picked up the instrument in the early 1920s it was still fairly new to the instrumentation of African American music; W. C. Handy claimed that his orchestra was the first to include a saxophone, a tenor played by James T. Osborne, in 1909.[30] Hodges, therefore, "had no extended saxophone tradition to draw upon, no foundation of techniques and styles comparable to that available to performers on the instruments that were . . . . traditional in jazz."[31]

In its infancy the saxophone was frequently attacked as risqué, a compromiser of moral virtue, an aid to seduction—"The Siren of Satan," as one composer put it. Self-appointed moralists with widely divergent claims to virtue—Nazis, Communists, imperial Japan, and the Vatican—condemned or banned it.[32] Like many positions that strike one as ridiculous at first, this one contains a kernel of truth if expressed in a slightly different fashion. The saxophone is capable of producing a sound that strikes the ears as seductive; a British critic referred to the reed section of the Ellington band, "spearheaded by Hodges," as "sexophones" when that band first toured England in 1933, and tenor Don Byas would later adopt that libel as a compliment.[33] If the aim of an advertisement or soundtrack today is to create a seductive mood, the instrument most likely to be chosen is thus a saxophone. Hodges would become the great master of this tone, and we are indebted to his mother for her willingness to expose him to the moral hazard of the instrument. He earned $11 from his first gig, and he turned it over to her in repayment of her trust.[34] According to one source, the band with which Hodges performed in this maiden professional engagement was an eight-piece group led by pianist Joe Steele.[35] Steele was born in Boston in 1899 and graduated from the New England Conservatory in 1924. He had moved to New York by 1926 and was playing and recording as part of the Savoy Bearcats with banjoist Henri Sapporo.[36] From 1927 to 1929 Steele led his own band, which included Charlie Holmes on saxophone, at the Bamboo Inn, and he eventually joined Chick Webb's band.[37]

In contrast to the difficulties he claimed to have encountered in learning the piano, on the saxophone Hodges was a *wunderkind*. Benny Waters, five years older than Hodges, noted, "I was influenced by three guys—first, Johnny Hodges," Waters said (his other models were Benny Carter and Earl Bostic). "I had the privilege of working with him when he was in Boston, when he was thirteen years old. I was eighteen. But he could play. I think he was playing more jazz then than he did with Duke."[38] According to Waters, Hodges had already developed the look of blasé indifference he would maintain throughout his career: "Johnny always had that bored look even when he was fifteen years old."[39]

Hodges gained experience by playing with local artists such as Danny Carey, a pianist "who looked like Fats Waller and whose specialty was playing in many different keys."[40] Hodges played high school dances, including one attended by his South End neighbor Charlie Holmes.[41] "I was about ten then," Holmes said of the first time he heard Hodges,

and I'd never heard a saxophone, but Johnny's name just spread all over Boston. I was amazed. I sat right up in front of the hall all night long, like he was God. He was nothing but a kid, but he was blowing saxophone then as well as he played it down through the years. I've never known anyone in my life just pick up an instrument and play it the way he did. I mean he was playing it—he wasn't just playing *with* it. And he didn't know a note as big as a house, but he had a hell of an ear. After dances, we'd go to them little house-rent parties.[42]

When he began to gig regularly, Hodges was still so young that he could only play afternoon dates such as Sunday tea dances, at which alcohol was sometimes served despite the genteel air the name suggests.[43] As Benny Waters put it, Hodges "had to work with permission of the government and with guardian as he was a minor."[44] He would nonetheless worm his way into nighttime gigs with grown-up groups, including one headed by Tom Whaley, a pianist who would later become a copyist for Duke Ellington. As Whaley recalled,

It was at the Avery [Hotel] that I met Johnny Hodges one day in 1920. He was about fifteen years old, and he came up the back steps and said, "Hey, can I play?" I said[,] "Sure, come on and play!" He had a C-melody sax, and he started playing, the same then as now—sweet, swinging. He's a gifted man, another genius.[45]

Hodges joined a group that Whaley put together to play at a Boston venue called The Lamp's Club that included Whaley on piano and Benny Waters on alto. That venue, according to Waters, was a place where "we could swing a little bit," unlike the hotels where groups organized by Whaley usually performed, which Waters described as "high class" places where they couldn't play jazz. "Johnny couldn't read then so we did some things by head, pop-ular songs and so [forth]," Waters recalled. "We played harmony together, Johnny could do that. He played so well. There wasn't anybody in Boston who could play that much jazz or blues. No-one had his tone." In addition to alto, Hodges and Waters played both soprano saxophone and piano. After that gig ended, Waters says, he and Hodges "played for Sunday afternoon Tea-party for the elite of Boston."[46]

Hodges began to travel as his reputation grew, though he was still in short pants, both figuratively and literally.[47] Pianist Earle "Nappy" Howard, who toured New England with his own band after playing in New York with Benny Carter,[48] described the sensation Hodges caused at a July 4 dance in York, Maine, in 1922:

That band was jumping and at that moment a little short guy was playing a gold soprano sax, and he had all the folks cheering him on. When the dance was over I went up and introduced myself. He appeared to be quite young, and he had knickers instead of long pants, and when he told me his age I understood why. He was just sixteen. His name was Johnny Hodges.[49]

Either Howard had his dates confused, or—what is more likely—Hodges was lying about his age; on July 4, 1922, Hodges would have been fourteen years old. Frances Jones, a flame from Hodges's youth in Boston, says he was playing clarinet in solo gigs in Boston when she met him at the age of fifteen; later, she says, he put together his own band, which played what Rex Stewart characterized as "burlesque" music. Among the musicians in that group was Louie Metcalf,[50] who was a member of Ellington's orchestra from 1927 to 1928, when Hodges joined.[51]

A few other Boston sightings of Hodges in his youth are recorded: Stan Harris, a member of the Boston black musicians' union, saw him play at the Alpini Restaurant in Kenmore Square.[52] Rex Stewart recalled meeting Hodges in "a little bistro around the corner from Shag Taylor's drug store" (the Lincoln Pharmacy at the corner of Tremont and Kendall Streets). "[T]his was a common meeting place for all musicians during those times, principally because Shag sold the best whiskey in town, never mind that we still had Prohibition,"[53] Stewart said. "This was my first visit to Beantown and I was playing with Leon Abbey's Savoy Bluesicians."[54] Silas "Shag" Taylor was a politically active businessman in Boston's black community who, in addition to a drugstore with a back-door liquor business, operated the Pioneer Social Club, an after-hours jazz club.[55] It was probably in this drugstore that Hodges was interviewed by Stanley Dance in 1960 on a return to his youthful stomping grounds. There, Dance found Hodges among old friends, "lolling back against the counter, apparently much concerned with the nickel's worth of peanuts in his hand," as they discussed the old neighborhood until three o'clock in the morning. Dance concluded that "the continuing *naturalness* of his music derives from the fact that fame and years of traveling haven't separated Hodges from his roots."[56]

According to Ellington biographer Barry Ulanov, Hodges would attend Boston-area performances by Ellington while he was "a short little boy still in knee pants." He would "stand around listening intently, sometimes with his growing excitement apparent, but more often with almost somber mien."[57] As to where Duke Ellington first heard Johnny Hodges, the most likely theory is that offered by Whaley. According to his account,

there was a nightclub on Washington Street near Dudley [Square, in Boston], and Walter Johnson had the orchestra there. That was where Duke first heard Johnny and told him to come on over to New York. Walter played piano, and his brother, Howard, played sax. All the Johnson family were great musicians. Bobby and George both played guitar. Walter had charge of all the music in Boston—all the big things.[58]

The night club in question was the Black and White Club, unrelated to the burlesque review at which Hodges first met Sidney Bechet. Walter Johnson (not the New York drummer of the same name)[59] was a pianist and bandleader who also played the role of booking agent from an office on Tremont Street in Boston. In the early 1920s he opened a night club, Walter Johnson's Social Club, that subsequently was called first the Phalanx Club and then the Black and White Club. Hodges played at the Black and White Club with a trio that he led and with Walter Johnson's band. His playing there impressed established bandleaders Ted Lewis and Phil Harris, who frequented the club when they were visiting from New York.[60] According to Stanley Dance, Ellington first tried to recruit Hodges to join his band while the latter was still living in Boston.[61] Apart from the Boston gigs that Hodges played where Ellington may have made his pitch, there would have been ample opportunity for the two to encounter each other on the Ellington band's regular summer tours of New England.[62] As Hodges would later recall, "Duke used to come to Boston every summer, and he would ask me to join him."[63]

Hodges would later leave Boston for New York, traveling what has been referred to as the "Boston–New York Pipeline" with a pianist named Bobby Sawyer.[64] Sawyer was a native of Roxbury, then as now the neighborhood of Boston with the greatest concentration of blacks. Hodges and Harry Carney played gigs in Boston with Sawyer's orchestra, and later, as Stewart recalled, they made weekend trips to New York with him to work there.[65] As to why Hodges would leave his hometown, good musicians generally left Boston for New York because of the greater opportunities offered by the latter. Jazz critic George Frazier, who went on to contribute to national publications after getting his start writing the first regular jazz column to appear in a big-city daily, the *Boston Herald*, derisively called Boston "the biggest small town in the country." To turn a line from the song "New York, New York" on its head and apply it to Boston, if you had only made it there, you hadn't made it anywhere. As Frazier said, "Boston may be great, but New York—New York is the varsity."[66]

One reason for New York's pre-eminent stature when it came to African American music was its demographic, an instance of a large quantitative difference producing a qualitatively different kind of music: Blacks have historically represented a small percentage of Boston's population—just 2% in 1910, increasing slowly to 2.6% by 1930.[67] By 1940, when blacks represented 6%

of New York's population,[68] African Americans still represented just 3% of Boston's populace, a figure so small that special steps were taken to count them in the 1940 census.[69] In New York, by contrast, the black population increased by 66% in the years from 1910 to 1920 and by 115% over the course of the following ten years. By 1930, shortly after Johnny Hodges joined Ellington's orchestra, there were 327,706 African Americans in New York, a number that would have represented 45% of Boston's population at the time.[70]

But there are other reasons why New York became a mecca for jazz while Boston remained a backwater. The New York musicians' union never excluded blacks by rule, and a black man, violinist Walter Craig, first joined the otherwise all-white union in 1886 without opposition.[71] In Boston, by contrast, black musicians split from American Federation of Musicians Local 9 in 1915 and formed their own union, Local 535, because of their perception that the white union discriminated against them, and the two groups didn't reunite until January 13, 1969.[72] Although aging members of the black local say they weren't expressly excluded from joining the white union, entertainment in the city was divided along racial lines so that only white musicians were allowed to play in upscale venues.[73] The pretext for this artistic segregation was that blacks couldn't read musical notation well enough to play in theatrical pit bands or in "class A" clubs, as one frustrated musician put it. "[W]hat existed was[,] they had clubs where only black played and places where only white played," recalled tenor saxophonist Andy McGhee.[74] This de facto segregation meant that there were fewer union jobs open to black musicians in Boston.

Where there is greater demand, greater supply arrives to satisfy it. In New York, colloquially known as "the city that never sleeps," alcohol could be served for consumption on licensed premises from 8 A.M. to 4 A.M. every day but Sunday, when drinks could be served starting at noon.[75] In Boston in the first decade of the twentieth century the law stating that "no liquor shall be sold after eleven o'clock P.M. [was] rigidly observed" in hotels and saloons. Dance halls would open "at eight o'clock and last till two A.M. or later"— but they could not serve liquor.[76] Thus, just as jazz flourished in Kansas City during the wide-open administration of Mayor Tom Pendergast, it prospered in New York's libertine atmosphere and failed to thrive in strait-laced Boston.

Further, white New Yorkers had been more open to black music than Bostonians since the early days of jazz, when Duke Ellington's orchestra performed before segregated all-white audiences at the Cotton Club. Boston has never had a black entertainment district comparable in size or focus to Harlem that would attract (as black writer James Weldon Johnson put it in

1933) "white sightseers and slummers . . . on the lookout for 'Negro stuff.' "[77] Perhaps Boston's Puritan heritage inhibited its residents (as Johnson wrote in *Along This Way*) from "dancing to a Negro band" in an attempt

> to throw off the crusts and layers of inhibitions laid on by sophisticated civilization; striving to yield to the feel and experience of abandon; seeking to recapture a taste of primitive joy in life and living; trying to work their way back into that jungle which was the original Garden of Eden; in a word, doing their best to pass for colored.[78]

That there was greater demand for African American music in New York when the music we now call "jazz" first began to emerge from its roots in ragtime is demonstrated by the letter of a white musician, one Eugene De Bueris, to the *New York Globe* on September 8, 1915. "Why does society prefer the Negro musician?" he writes plaintively. "The Negro musician is to-day engaged at most of the functions given by society, especially its dances. . . . Even the New York hotels are now beginning to discard the white musician for the Negro. It will not be long before the poor white musician will be obliged to blacken his face to make a livelihood or starve."

Johnson answered this self-pitying plea with the impolitic truth:

> Not only is modern American music a Negro creation, but the modern dances are also. . . . Mr. De Beuris is right when he says that white musicians can play ragtime as well as Negro musicians; that is, white musicians can play exactly what is put down on the paper. But Negro musicians are able to put into the music something that can't be put on the paper; a certain abandon which seems to enter in the blood of the dancers.[79]

This is not to suggest that New York was an idyllic environment where black entertainers were always treated with dignity; the demands placed on Ellington's band to play in a pseudo-African "jungle" style (which he subverted to his own creative ends) in a whites-only setting is evidence that New York was not necessarily more enlightened than Boston. Benny Carter noted that even with an integrated union some jobs were closed to black musicians in New York. In 1933, when 80% of the members of the American Federation of Musicians local in Manhattan were out of work, blacks suffered more, he said, because "radio staff and studio orchestras were closed to [blacks] and these were steadier jobs paying hundreds of dollars weekly at a time when union scale at places like the Savoy was thirty-three dollars."[80]

Two black violinists performed in the orchestra organized in Boston for the 1872 World Peace Jubilee, and pianist Rachel Washington became the first black graduate of the New England Conservatory of Music in the same decade,[81] before the New York musicians' union had its first black member, but these were advances in the field of European classical music, not jazz, America's indigenous classical music. The music of Czech composer Antonin Dvořák that was inspired by African American models was greeted differently by white audiences in the two cities. Dvořák accurately prophesied that "Negro melodies" would form the basis of a "great school" of American music, and in New York his American Suite (op. 98, 1894) was warmly received. In Boston, by contrast, Dvořák was reviled by one critic as a barbaric Slav who had a "negrophile" influence on native composers.[82]

It is to Boston's credit that its audiences did not expect black musicians to play in a concocted African style in a setting that recalled a southern plantation, as the owners of the Cotton Club required of Ellington's band. On the other hand, white audiences heard very little of Boston's black musicians due to the policy of apartheid imposed by both unions and performance venues, and as a result the city was bypassed or abandoned by many eager to create a new music in an African vein on American soil.

One of those was Johnny Hodges, who while he was still a Boston resident would travel to New York to play at a recording session that he said was put together by Jelly Roll Morton and included New Orleans musicians such as Barney Bigard and pioneering jazz cornet player Joseph "King" Oliver. According to Hodges, Oliver didn't play much that day because he had recently had his teeth fixed, but it still meant that Hodges had crossed a bridge that spanned both space and time: the distance between Boston and New Orleans, the city where jazz was born, and the years that separated him from the date of the music's birth.[83]

3

His Tone

A PARIS SYMPHONY conductor once stopped Johnny Hodges on the street, bowed respectfully, and asked him where he got his distinctive tone, to which Hodges replied, "I just lucked up on it, Bubber, I just lucked up on it.'"[1] British poet and jazz critic Philip Larkin described Hodges' tone thus: "So bland, so clear, so voluptuously voiced with *portamento* (gliding gracefully from note to note) and *glissandi* (gliding from one pitch to another but not continuously, unlike *portamento*) and yet so essentially hot, Hodges' alto tone sounds the reverse of accidental. But it is not unduly studied."[2]

The tone that a player achieves on a saxophone represents a combination of nature and artifice; nature, in that each human being possesses a unique embouchure and lungs, and artifice because the saxophone's "revolutionary acoustical design" allows "everyone who puts a saxophone to his lips" to produce "a unique sound." In the words of Coleman Hawkins, the father of the modern jazz saxophone, a sax player's tone is "the one thing nobody can take away from you."[3] Rex Stewart dissented in part from this view; a "person's tone on an instrument" could be duplicated, he said, with three exceptions: "No one has reproduced the saxophone sounds of Hodges, Bechet or Otto Hardwicke," another alto in Duke Ellington's band.[4] Whatever one decides regarding this question, it remains true that a succession of pickers on an electric guitar set to the same amplifier and instrument controls plucking a single note will, by contrast, sound much the same; electric enhancement reduces differences among human agents.

Hodges was a short man—five and a half feet, according to the estimate of Stanley Dance, who knew him well[5]—and from films we know that he changed the placement of the mouthpiece of his sax depending on the tone he wanted to produce; when he desired a softer sound or to release a note, he held it a bit off center, on the right side of his lips, and when he wanted to blow more forcefully or with the vibrato that characterized his most passionate flights, he'd edge it back to the middle. He would sometimes remove his instrument from his mouth at the end of an ensemble riff and "run his tongue across his lips, put it back, and sing out another line."[6]

The tone he drew from his horn may seem paradoxical given his size, but it doesn't take a large man to produce a rich sound on the sax; witness Hawkins, who was less than average height (five feet, seven inches) but produced a sound so virile, so "big" in jazz parlance, that fans who saw him for the first time were surprised by how short he was. "Tone has always been the first thing I look for in a musician," said Edward "Kid" Ory, an early New Orleans jazz trombonist. "Without good tone, nothing you play means anything."[7] Sidney Bechet expounded on the theme that tone, not virtuosity, came first, saying, "You put your whole body into your music. *Lean* into the note. The horn is you." Bechet disparaged the notion that virtuosity was paramount, telling neophytes to practice on a single note: "See how many ways you play that note—growl it, smear it, flat it, sharp it, do anything you want to it. That's how you express your feelings in this music. It's like talking."[8] Bechet's simile suggests a connection between the emotional and the verbal in the deep structure of the African American musical tongue, where sound and meaning coalesce to express both feeling and thought in a way that mirrors the sound and meaning of spoken language.[9]

The two great enemies of tone are speed and volume, which frequently—but not necessarily—occur together. (A fast passage may be played *pianissimo* and a melody performed at a slow tempo may be played loudly.) Both undermine tone, however, which was central to Hodges's distinctive sound. In his early years Hodges was known for his up-tempo playing. "Until Otto [Hardwick] left, if you notice, during those years, I very seldom played anything slow," he said. "They were all peppy and fast tunes."[10] Hodges gradually came to avoid upbeat tempi because he didn't need speed; he wasn't out to express an outpouring of harmonically complex ideas, as was his successor on the alto throne, Charlie Parker. When bandmates would tease him about his slow and steady pace, he would remind them of the fleet playing he was capable of in his youth, which was a matter of public phonographic record; witness "The Giddybug Gallop," from the early 1940s. "I played pretty fast on that," he would say of the breakneck speed of his solo.[11] The reason for the emphasis on speed in his early years may have been that, as a member of Ellington's Cotton Club Orchestra, he needed to play for dancing, either by customers or for the floor show.[12] It may also have been a case of the vigor of youth giving way to the calm of age; Count Basie is one of many jazz musicians who played fast when young and slowed down as he grew older. As a spokesman for the New Orleans school, Bechet advocated completeness of expression over rapid invention when it came to improvisation. "Always finish your idea," he said. "The trouble with most of these Northern players is they start a new idea before they finish the old one."[13]

Volume similarly detracts from tone, as Hodges's fellow alto and adolescent bandmate Benny Waters would testify. "I played too loud when I was young," he said, "and when you play too loud, you lose your tone."[14] As with speed, Hodges was a judicious user of volume, tending to limit it to ensemble play in the Ellington orchestra, when he was forced to play louder in order to be heard. According to Clark Terry, Hodges could play as loud as a trumpet, "and even when [he was] playing a harmony part in the section you [could] feel him through the whole band."[15] Later in life, when his powers might have been expected to fade, he remained powerful enough to be a formidable section mate. After Hodges teased tenor Norris Turney one night about how loudly the younger man was blowing on a particular passage, Turney fired back "Who can blow louder than you?"[16] Hodges remained in control of his tone even at high volumes, however.

Hodges once said that his technique included "different little tricks" that came to him without instruction, "when [he] really wasn't aware of it." Of his glissando, for example, he said "I may have been glissing, for instance, and started going from one note to the other—probably took it in two, then three, like that."[17] According to W. C. Handy, it was once believed that "no instruments other than the violin family and the slide trombone family were capable of perfect legato or glissando. Had it not been for the mistakes of the ignorant and illiterate, Gershwin would not have been able to write a two-octave chromatic glissando clarinet passage for his *Rhapsody in Blue*. . . . Theory made a mistake and had to be rewritten. Perfect glissandos now are made on the clarinet, sax and trumpets."[18]

A saxophone glissando was a jazz innovation not only because it was difficult, but also because it had previously been considered improper; glissando was "ruled out of European music as 'bad taste,'" but it was "an essential part of all other musical systems, including the African and Oriental, which recognize curves as well as straight lines of pitch," according to Frederic Ramsey Jr. and Charles Edward Smith. They continue:

> Thus in melodic as well as rhythmic sources, the hot jazz of the Negro proves its independence from the Western music of the white man. The glissando is an essential part of all vocal blues where the small

curves and subtle inflections are particularly expressive. We find in the accompaniments to blues singers some of Armstrong's most stirring and characteristic playing. Louis, who never adhered to the conventionalities of European music, is continually getting away from the diatonic scale and altering with chromatics the modal material often found in the blues.[19]

Hodges was an inadvertent translator of the glissando technique to American jazz: "Now take that famous gliss down that I had on 'Passion Flower,'" he said. "I wasn't looking for that. The only reason that happened—I just got tired. I'd been recording all day long and this was my last number. My lip was tired and I just had to release it. So I released it gradually—and there was 'Passion Flower.'"[20]

Barney Bigard, a New Orleans native who played beside Hodges in the reed section of the Ellington band from 1928 through 1942, and thus knew him from his earliest days through the development of his mature sound, confirms that at first Hodges "was a disciple of Sidney Bechet. . . . He had all those Bechet licks down, but then he developed that slurring, that tone of his own."[21] Hodges "transposed Bechet's methods to the alto saxophone and streamlined them," in the view of jazz critic Whitney Balliett. "He eliminated Bechet's operatic vibrato and his tendency to run the scales. He bottled Bechet's urgency and served it in cool, choice doses. He skirted Bechet's funky tendencies—his growls and squeaks and odd, bubbling sounds."[22]

Ellington had been entranced by Bechet's sound since he first heard him play at the Howard Theater in Washington in January 1923. Bechet was cast in a vaudeville review titled *How Come* as a Chinese laundryman so named who was also, improbably, a brilliant jazz musician. Bechet had acted professionally before, as part of a traveling show with Clarence Williams, and in talent contests in his childhood,[23] but his principal contribution to the show was musical, not thespian; he played a bluesy solo near the end of the sketch that, Ellington said, was his "first encounter with the New Orleans idiom."[24] It represented "a completely new sound and conception" to him. The tone, he recalled, was "all wood," and "*au naturel*, all soul, coming from the inside." It sounded as if Bechet was "*calling* somebody." He had never heard anything like it.[25] Ellington hired Bechet in 1924 to play dances on a summer tour of New England and found that he "fitted [the] band like a glove." He was, in Duke's words, a "gladiator" who relished competition with other musicians such as trumpeter Bubber Miley, with whom he would swap choruses, driving the band to greater heights.[26]

The Ellington band, though considered a product of New York, had become "a New Orleans band in disguise," as Balliett put it. "During the twenties and thirties, it used such New Orleans musicians as Wellman Braud [bass], Lonnie Johnson [guitar]," Bechet, and Bigard. "It used muted techniques brought forward by Joseph 'King' Oliver, and many of its brass players emulated Louis Armstrong."[27] Of Bigard, Ellington would say, "He was invaluable for putting the filigree work into an arrangement, and sometimes it could remind you of all that delicate wrought iron you see in his hometown."[28] "Mood Indigo," one of the band's earliest hits (1930), was derived in part from a song written by Lorenzo Tio Jr., Bigard's clarinet instructor in New Orleans,[29] and "Creole Love Call" was based in part on "Camp Meeting Blues" by King Oliver.[30] Ellington had his own theory about the two daughters that were formed from the division of the parent cell of jazz:

> The history of jazz, of course, begins with the rhythm coming to America from Africa. It . . . takes two courses: one . . . to New Orleans, and the other up the East Coast. The East Coast was inclined to favor strings—violins, banjos and guitars—while the . . . one that went to New Orleans and then up the Mississippi to Chicago, came out in the form of clarinets, trombones and trumpets. And then they all converged in New York and blended together, and the offspring was jazz.[31]

Ellington was no slavish admirer of all ingredients of the gumbo that was New Orleans jazz; he said that Jelly Roll Morton "played piano like one of those high school teachers in Washington; as a matter of fact, high school teachers played better jazz."[32] But there was thus a foundation within the Ellington band for an instrumentalist such as Hodges whose style was a product of New Orleans.

New Orleans musicians had historically learned to play by blowing to the winds, *en plein air* in a musical sense, marching in parades and funeral processions, playing for picnics and other social affairs, while New York players learned their trade by taking lessons, which they then put to use in clubs and theaters and at parties and dances. Earl Hines, a neutral third party aligned with neither New Orleans nor New York because he was born in Pittsburgh and cut his jazz teeth in Chicago, characterized the New Orleans approach thus: "As far as tone: you know, it's a funny thing about all those New Orleans guys. That's one thing they dwell on: the tone. Open, you know, not piercing."[33] New York musicians, on the other hand, had been "taught that notes came before music. . . . They wrote down what they heard but each time a little was lost. Somehow the notes were not the same as those the jazzmen played."[34] So there were "two separate bodies of instrumental technique," according to novelist, trumpeter, and jazz critic Ralph Ellison, "the one classic, widely recognized and 'correct'; and the other eclectic, partly unconscious and 'jazzy.'" To borrow a concept from Nietzsche, the former represented the realm of Apollo, the god of the rational, and the latter sprang from Dionysus, the god of the irrational.[35] When the "tension between these two bodies of technique" is periodically resolved in favor of Apollonian purity, the next innovation—Ellison calls each of them "technical discoveries of jazz"[36]—usually comes from an outbreak of Dionysian fervor that disrupts the prevailing norm.

Sometimes the dichotomy is expressed more generally as west versus east, as, for example, in the words of Ellington trumpeter Ray Nance: "Yardbird [Charlie Parker] had that western, soulful blues touch to his playing, you know. Everybody in Kansas City used to play like that."[37] Musicians from the two extremes of east and west recognized the difference and were chauvinistic about the merits of their respective regions. Bechet was involved in one legendary cutting contest between Hodges's model Sidney Bechet and Coleman Hawkins—born in St. Joseph, Missouri, but a scholar in the eastern mode who studied harmony and composition and played cello and piano as well as tenor sax. Hawkins had dared to say that "New Orleans musicians can't play, 'they ain't no hell.'" The fighting words were repeated to Bechet, who challenged Hawkins to a musical duel and thoroughly outplayed him. Bechet encountered similar hostility (or felt that he did—he was something of a paranoid) during his time with Ellington; he feuded with trombonist Charlie Irvis (born in New York) and trumpeter James Wesley "Bubber" Miley (raised in New York) and suspected they were making sotto voce cracks on the bandstand about his unschooled New Orleans musicianship.[38]

The animus flowed both ways; New Orleans musicians made invidious comparisons between their sound, which they sometimes referred to as "The Right Way," and the less robust tones produced by New Yorkers. Jelly Roll Morton said that New York bands didn't have a beat, and when one player goaded him—saying, "Jelly[,] what's that you say about New York musicians yesterday?"—he responded with an epic insult: "What I said yesterday and today and on Judgment Day and also my dying day, is that it takes one hundred live New York musicians to equal one dead police dog."[39]

Louis Metcalf, a trumpeter employed by Ellington during the latter half of the 1920s with whom Hodges played in Boston burlesque shows, said that musicians in the band

> almost came to blows in Harlem . . . about the two different styles of playing. Why, when I joined Duke Ellington at the Cotton Club, about 1925, I guess, the men in the band were always fighting about which was the better style, Eastern or Western. 'Course, when I say Western, I mean everything that came out of New Orleans, Chicago, St. Louis, Kansas City and places like that. The Western style was more open . . . open horns and running chords and running changes. With Ellington, it was the new men like myself and Johnny Hodges and Bigard against guys like Bubber Miley and Tricky Sam Nanton. They were playing wah-wah music with plungers and things. Actually, our coming into the Ellington band made them change somewhat.[40]

New Yorkers were better at sight-reading, which was considered one of Hodges's weaknesses, although Rex Stewart, again, challenges the conventional wisdom: "He was a very good reader," Stewart said, "and you don't learn that without studying."[41] A certain contempt for the written score was a badge of pride among New Orleans musicians. "Here is the thing that made King Bolden Band be the First Band that played Jazz," Willie G. "Bunk" Johnson wrote. "It was because it did not Read at all. I could fake like 500 [tunes] myself."[42] Bechet shared this primitive's aversion to written language and refused to learn musical notation, believing that he would lose his capacity for improvisation if he did.[43] According to New Orleans violinist Peter Bocage, Bechet "never had two weeks good schooling in his life,"[44] and there was an element of masculine emulation at work in his disdain for book learning. New Orleans trumpeter Henry "Red" Allen told Willie the Lion Smith that in his hometown, if "you read music, you're considered a sissy."[45] Bechet was a protean improviser despite his inability to read music, but as the Swing Era dawned it cost him jobs playing ensemble-style in larger groups, for which he was ill-suited anyway.

The end of Bechet's brief career as a member of the Ellington organization came one day when he arrived three days late to a gig and his only excuse was that his cab driver got lost. "Bechet was always a rover who wanted to see over the other side of the hill,"[46] according to drummer Sonny Greer. Ellington loved the man's tone, but couldn't abide his work habits, and finally had to let him go. He needed someone to bring Bechet's color to the collective palette of his orchestra, however, and he would find, at least initially, that "it took two skilled musicians to fulfil the role in his arrangements that Bechet alone had undertaken during his brief stay in the band. The two players were Johnny Hodges on alto saxophone and Barney Bigard on clarinet."[47] Bechet "was Johnny Hodges' inspiration," according to Sonny Greer. "He liked Johnny and Johnny studied him."[48]

Thanks to the technological innovation that allowed Hodges to hear musicians playing from far away, he was able to develop a New Orleans–based tone and style before he left his home fifteen hundred miles to the northeast as a young man. He would so fully absorb the sound of his adopted musical motherland that when he died the obituary distributed by United Press International stated that the man who grew up in Boston and spent most of his adult life in New York "was a member of the 'old school' of New Orleans jazz musicians who taught himself how to play."[49]

4

Scuffling in New York

THE DATE ON which Johnny Hodges first saw the Manhattan skyline is impossible to specify with precision. One source says he made his maiden trip to New York in 1923,[1] when he would have been fifteen or sixteen, although Hodges himself said he didn't reach the city until he was seventeen,[2] so 1924 is the more likely year. Hodges was energized by New York's bigger and better jazz scene. "Gee, New York was a real terrific town then—*really* a night-life town," he would recall. "All night long you'd go from one place to another. Nothing was expensive. You had a good time for just a little money. Everybody was happy—and no taxes!" There was, according to Hodges, "a club on every corner in those days—there were five clubs on 134th Street. There was Small's, Leroy's, The Owl and Fritz's, and Connie's—this was all in one block."[3]

Hodges began to make the trip to New York "every two weeks and stay over a weekend, or four or five days." He noted, "It was very easy to get a job then. You'd work in a dancing school and you'd go to a jam session."[4] The term "dancing school" was a bit of a pretext. As Willie "the Lion" Smith described one such operation, Drake's Dancing Class on 62nd Street, "they couldn't get a license to operate unless they taught dancing. . . . There were plenty of dancers but no teachers."[5] Benny Waters was more explicit: "Every dancing school had its girls. There was no law against a beautiful girl taking someone out after work. A guy could certainly date a woman in a dancing school for after work. I used to think of dancing schools as high class whore houses!"[6] The pay at a dancing school was "union scale, about twenty-eight dollars a week," according to guitarist Lawrence Lucie, "so a lot of people took the work until they could move on. . . . If you got a job paying more money, you would leave."[7]

The culture of the jam session was more organized than the name suggests. According to Duke Ellington, Small's Paradise was the site of a regular jam on Sundays, when the owner would "hire a guest band, the best he could get, and there'd be a regular jamboree." Elmer Snowden, the original leader of the Washingtonians who ceded that role to Ellington, did the hiring to put the groups together for a while, and "all kinds of musicians worked that job, Johnny Hodges, and guys from Chick [Webb]'s band and a lot of others. . . . The music would jump,"[8] Ellington recalled. Hodges jammed at Small's, a club called Mexico's,[9] and, beginning around 1924, at the Capitol Palace,[10] and he recalled them as fiercely competitive affairs: "They didn't call them jam sessions then, they used to call them 'cuttin' contests,'" he said, "and you would learn a whole lot from the different saxophone players, trumpet players, and trombone players who would come in and play all night long. You would get cut and when you got cut you went to 'school.'" Once "schooled," the neophyte Hodges would return to Boston and catch up with friends— Harry Carney, Charlie Holmes, and others—to show them "what was new in New York" and learn "what had happened behind in Boston."[11]

Jam sessions brought Hodges exposure, as related by Tommy Benford, a drummer who had played as a substitute in the Ellington orchestra.[12] "One night at the Hoofer's Club a kid named Johnny Hodges sat in, and Willie 'the Lion' Smith, who had the band, hired him on the spot. He didn't sound like anybody,"[13] Benford recalled. Smith remembered the sequence of events somewhat differently; he stated that he worked with Hodges at a predecessor of the Hoofer's Club, the Rhythm Club, located at 132nd Street and Seventh Avenue,[14] where Hodges and Bechet would later play together. The Rhythm Club, as Smith recalled in his autobiography,

> was a hanging-out place for musicians around 1924 and 1925. . . . Jazz men could come in at any time and play whatever they wanted without bothering with the usual singers or floor shows. It became the place where young musicians would go to learn and be heard. Many jazz fig-ures were first heard at the Rhythm Club and leaders like Henderson, Ellington, Elmer Snowden and Charlie Johnson would go there to hire their sidemen.[15]

After Smith finished his regular gig at the Capitol Palace at around three in the morning he would join the Rhythm Club's house band, which included Sidney Bechet on clarinet, Louis Metcalf on cornet, and Benford on drums. Musicians would get out their horns and line up to take their turns. A regular among the reed men, according to Smith, "was a seventeen-year-old kid from up near Boston named Cornelius Hodges. In later years," in Smith's opinion, "he became one of the greatest alto saxophonists of all time."[16]

Hodges soon graduated from dance schools and jam sessions to a regular job at Fritz's, "a little ol' cabaret at 135th Street," as he described it. He was paid $25 per week and made about $25 to $30 per night in tips.[17] Adjusted for inflation, that would amount to more than $2,000 per week today—a heady sum for someone whose first professional engagement earned him $11 (about $160 in today's money). According to Carney, Johnny was immediately in demand and liked to flaunt his new wealth. "He left home," Carney said, "and when he came back, a year or so later, he was a big-timer. He had a Mexican bankroll—that's a big bill on the outside that covers a roll of ones."[18]

The date on which Johnny Hodges changed his residence from Boston to New York is also not susceptible of precise determination. One source says that Hodges relocated in 1924, when he was sixteen or seventeen.[19] A more concrete indication that Hodges had moved permanently to New York occurred in the summer of 1925, when he began to share an apartment with reedman Cecil Scott on 135th Street; he would have then been seventeen or eighteen.[20] Until he made the move Hodges was a peripatetic practitioner for some time, shuttling back and forth between the two cities, seemingly indifferent to the greater financial rewards that the bigger metropolis offered. Hodges was less motivated by money in his youth than he was later in life, when he had a family to support. "I used to come from Boston just for pleasure and stay a week," he related. "I'd work almost up to pay-day, just get enough money to get home—and leave all the money. I wasn't particular about any money. Then I'd come back, probably three or four weeks later, join another band, get some new ideas, go back to Boston—and just have fun."[21] As this quotation suggests, any attempt to give a chronological account as to the order in which Hodges played with various bands in New York before he joined Ellington's group is a difficult if not impossible task.

This statement also paints a self-portrait of a young man unconcerned about money that is inconsistent with Hodges's portrayal of himself as the family breadwinner at an early age. When he gave his mother the $11 that he made on his first paying job on sax, she "was astounded," he said. "She didn't want me to work and had only thought of the sax as something to make me happy. But being the man of the family" after his father died, "I put my foot down. For her no more going out to work . . . in freezing cold weather to clean other people's houses, to come home late in the evening tired and weary."[22]

Cecil Scott played tenor sax and clarinet and was the younger brother of Lloyd Scott, a drummer. The two siblings played together in Lloyd Scott's

Symphonic Syncopators in Ohio, then Pittsburgh, and finally Harlem, where, in early 1926, they became the resident band at the Capitol Palace. "The Cotton Club closed at three or four in the morning," Cecil would recall,

> while we played till dawn and even past sometimes to seven A.M. . . . When the other clubs closed, one by one their band members and patrons would drift into our spot, and musicians . . . used to vie for the chance to sit in with us. We usually had a waiting line holding their horns against one far wall waiting turns. Fellows like Johnny Hodges, members of Fletch Henderson's gang, Fats Waller, Earl Hines, and fellows from Charlie Johnson's band, Luis Russell's band. . . . They were eager to blow since on their regular job they were restricted from right-eous playing because they would have to play stock arrangements for floor shows.[23]

According to one account, Hodges was a member of the Scott brothers' band for a time in 1926.[24]

Another group that Hodges worked with on a regular basis once he settled in New York was headed by drummer Walter Johnson,[25] who played with Fletcher Henderson during the thirties.[26] Johnson greatly expanded the role of cymbals in jazz drumming, which had previously been limited to in-termittent crashes for dramatic effect. Johnson is said to have been the first to use the high-hat (two cymbals on a pole clapped together with a foot pedal) effectively[27] and the first to "ride" cymbals to propel a song forward rhythmically. Hodges also gigged with groups led by Johnny Dunn, a trum-peter from Memphis who specialized in the use of the wah-wah mute,[28] and Henri Sapparo, who employed Hodges's fellow Bostonians Harry Carney and Charlie Holmes. Sapparo was a banjoist whom Joe Steele, the man who hired Hodges for his first paying gig on saxophone in Boston, played with in New York as a member of the Savoy Bearcats.[29]

Hodges and his former jam session colleague Tommy Benford would later become members of a band that Sidney Bechet put together. "It had Hodges and me," Benford recalled, "and we went into Herman's Inn. The first night, Hodges, who had been playing clarinet and alto, picked up Bechet's soprano and played it, and Bechet about went crazy. After that, Sidney encouraged Hodges on the soprano, and he even gave him one, which Hodges still had when he died."[30] Hodges remembered the chronology and the details some-what differently: He says that Bechet approached him when he was still playing at Fritz's while a nightclub Bechet would open was in the planning stages. "[Bechet] came by one night and approached me and said he wanted me in this band right away!" Hodges said. "That was my big chance so I quit 'Fritz and went to work for him."[31]

Looking back four decades later, Hodges would say, "[It was] the best thing that ever happened to me. . . . He would tell me to learn this and learn that. 'The old man won't be here long,' he'd say. I didn't know what he was talking about then, but he would go away and get lost, and I was supposed to play his part. At the same time, I was learning, getting an education." Playing with Bechet meant exposure as well. "They used to have midnight shows at the Lafayette Theater every Friday. All the clubs used to put on their shows for free," a practice sometimes referred to as "the ballyhoo."[32] It was, in Hodges's view, "Fantastic. We put on our show, and that's how I got to be known, through him. We played 'I Found a New Baby' in duet form. So I was a big guy from then on, playing a duet with Bechet."[33]

Hodges had been playing alto and clarinet, but he went back to playing soprano when he joined Bechet at his new night spot, the Club Basha (a phonetic rendering of the way Bechet wanted his name pronounced, BASH-ay),[34] on 145th Street and Seventh Avenue. "He had another soprano, a straight one, which he gave to me, and he would teach me different things in the duet form," Hodges recalled. "Then I learned all the introductions and solos, and if he was late I would take over until he got there. This was . . . before I joined either Chick Webb or Duke." Hodges and Bechet would play together "sometimes," Hodges would say, "but I don't think very many people would remember that."[35]

In other words, the point of bringing Hodges on board was not primarily to play duets with the bandleader but for Hodges to add the voice of his instruments to the band and to spell Bechet when the latter would "go away and get lost" with a woman or drink or both.[36] It is a measure of Bechet's ego that, for all the influence he had on Johnny Hodges's style, the man who was his most faithful acolyte is not mentioned once in Bechet's autobiography, *Treat It Gentle*.[37] Bechet was proud of his legacy and defensive as to where his influence ended and Hodges's creativity began. In 1951, when French trumpeter Pierre Merlin told Bechet he was delighted to hear him play the Johnny Hodges chorus on Duke Ellington's recording of "The Sheik of Araby," Bechet snapped, "He stole that from me!"[38]

The ever-volatile Bechet abandoned his nightclub abruptly and left America for Europe in September 1925, reportedly owing to a quarrel with his business partner over a belly dancer.[39] One source says that Hodges then returned to Boston,[40] but Willie "the Lion" Smith, who took over leadership of the band at that point, said that he promoted Hodges to first chair on soprano and the band continued as before, which is consistent both with Hodges's decision to take an apartment and his own recollection; Bechet "was getting ready to go to England," Hodges said. "He was gonna leave and he had to teach me everything."[41] According to Smith, in 1926 Hodges left to join Chick Webb's band and was replaced by a "young Benny Carter," at the time—in Smith's estimation—"just a fair C-melody [saxophone] player."[42] Hodges's gig with Webb would be his last steady job before he joined the Ellington orchestra, and the two men became close friends as well as bandmates.

William Henry "Chick" Webb was born in Baltimore on February 10, 1905.[43] He suffered from congenital tuberculosis of the spine, and was of short stature as a result.[44] He was selling newspapers on the streets of Baltimore by the time he was nine—a common fate for the disabled in that day—but he began to play the drums at the suggestion of his doctor in order to loosen up his stiffened limbs.[45] He bought his first trap set with his earnings as a newsboy and began to work on Chesapeake Bay pleasure boats. He moved to New York in 1925 with a guitarist named John Truehart,[46] who lived up to his name by sticking with Webb over the course of a long career while others deserted him for higher pay. After working with Edgar Dowell's Orchestra,[47] Webb and other musicians formed a group that got its first job at the Balconnades Room at Healey's, then moved to the Black Bottom Club for a five-month engagement in 1926;[48] by then the group included Webb, Truehart, Bobby Stark (trumpet), Hodges's brother-in-law Don Kirkpatrick (piano), and Hodges on alto sax and clarinet. Webb and Hodges were said to be cousins, a claim not supported by genealogical research; Ellington biographer Barry Ulanov says that although the two men resembled each other, they called each other "cousin" as a term of familiarity, and were unrelated.[49]

Drawing on skills he had developed in Washington, Ellington frequently acted as booking agent-cum-manager. "When some of the boys around downtown decided to open up a new joint, they would stop by and tell Sonny Greer and me, 'We need a band,'" Ellington recalled. "This particular night, a guy came in and said, 'Hey, we need a band! We're going to open up a place tomorrow night.' Sonny and I assured him everything would be all right. 'Don't worry about it,' we said. 'They'll be there.' We went uptown and hired five or six musicians, and Chick was one of them."[50] Hodges confirmed Ellington's account: "Duke started Chick, gave Chick his first band. Duke was working at the Kentucky Club, six pieces. Another club opened on 50th Street and Seventh Ave. I don't remember the name of it. But I wanted a band just like Duke's. So he asked me to have a band, and I didn't want any part of having a band (that is, of being a band leader). He asked Chick. . . . We got together with six pieces and tried to make it sound like Duke."[51]

The club where the group first began to play under Webb's name was the Paddock Club.[52] No one in particular was the leader of the newly formed group, but Ellington decided that "they might as well use Chick's name, though at that time Webb wasn't thinking anything about getting along on his own, his mind was all on the drums." Ellington told Webb, "Now, you're the bandleader."

"Man, I don't want to be no bandleader," Webb answered.

"All you do is collect the money and bring me mine," Ellington replied.

"Is that all I have to do?"

"Yeah."

"Okay, I'm a bandleader."[53]

No one else in the group objected, since no one else wanted the job. "We were hungry," Hodges said, "and Chick had to make the grade or we wouldn't have stood to listen to his stories again," referring to Webb's penchant for braggadocio.[54]

Barney Bigard described this sort of business relationship with legalistic clarity as a "subsidiary band."[55] Ellington had put the band together and found work for it so he was entitled to a cut, which could be substantial, as Ellington himself learned; Louis Thomas, a Washington pianist who would sometimes subcontract with Ellington when he had two dances to play at the same time, took $90 of the $100 fee for the gig that Ellington covered.[56] Ellington would later call on Webb to pay him a dividend not in money but in human capital, because he used the group as a musical farm team to build his own orchestra. The group "worked up a gang of arrangements even though they didn't use any music," Ellington said, adding that in those days "anything good just got memorized."[57]

According to Hodges, Webb's band was a success. "We did pretty good until we had . . . a fire," he recalled in a *DownBeat* interview in 1962. "During that time fire was common in clubs,"[58] he said innocently, with no editorial comment on the fact that club owners seeking to cut their losses often used arson to collect on their fire insurance; if they were considerate, they would tell the musicians to "take their instruments home" the night the deed was to be done.[59] Afterwards, Hodges said, the band "went up to the Savoy for two weeks, stayed about six months."[60] The Savoy Ballroom was a Harlem dance

hall known as "The Home of Happy Feet" that became the first truly integrated building in America.[61] Ellington said that Webb's band started at the
Savoy "shortly following its opening. They only had eight pieces and couldn't
read a note of music, but that was a band."[62] Webb and his group, which
started out as the Harlem Stompers and became the Chick Webb Orchestra,
would hold court at the Savoy for the rest of his playing days.[63]

Rex Stewart recounted that "it was a sight to see and hear [Webb] and
young Johnny [Hodges] arguing about how a saxophone riff should be played.
This happened frequently up at the old Savoy Ballroom and it amused us because they were both so serious. Verbally, they would square off at each other
like a pair of bantam cocks. However, they were really pals." According to
Stewart, Webb couldn't read a note, which made Hodges—with his limited
sight-reading ability—a one-eyed king among the blind. Webb "possessed a
phenomenal ear and a very retentive memory," Stewart said. He "would sing,
whistle or hum his arrangements, note for note. At rehearsals Chick took full
charge and told his arrangers how the routines should go." Hodges "really
enjoyed baiting Chick by telling him that he was wrong, which would make
[Webb] furious."[64]

A review in the *Amsterdam News* (New York) in early 1928 of a broadcast by Webb's group over radio station WPAP (for "Palisades Amusement
Park")[65] reported that

> in this outfit "Chick" plays a "doggy" drum, Elmer Williams is the
> tenor saxophonist; Bobby Stark, the cornetist, and Johnny Hodges,
> the feature saxophone soloist. All of the members of the group are
> vocalists of no mean ability as well. . . . They contributed a wonderful
> hour, dashing back to Loew's Lincoln Square Theatre from which they
> have begun a vaudeville tour.[66]

It may surprise some to read that Johnny Hodges sang at one point in his
musical career, but Willie "the Lion" Smith had urged Hodges to be versatile.
"It was the Lion's policy to give the yearlings tips on how to make it in show
business," he said. "I used to tell them to learn to sing and dance. They could
starve if they depended too much on just being a good instrumentalist."[67]

Only one recording of a Webb group with Hodges as a member is known
to exist: "Low Levee—High Water," recorded August 25, 1927, at Brunswick
Studios in New York but never released.[68]

Even after the Harlem Stompers had a steady gig at the Savoy, there were
still "hard and hungry times,"[69] according to Stanley Dance. Webb never

prospered the way his competitors did, a fact that can perhaps be traced to his lack of physical appeal; most successful bandleaders of the swing era, black and white, were conventionally attractive men, and Duke Ellington was tall with matinee idol good looks. In addition, Webb was never able to pay his men enough to keep them from leaving for higher-paying jobs with other bands, a fact of his life as leader that gave him an air of resignation. Whenever he saw Fletcher Henderson at the Savoy, for example, he would ask, "Well, who do you want this time?"[70] But Webb was his own worst enemy as well; a perfectionist, he would turn down jobs rather than alter the line-up of his band for a prospective customer, and "there were lean times when the band wound up sleeping all in the same room and missing meals."[71]

When Webb was short of work Hodges would play with Luckey Roberts, with whom he had gigged off and on since his early days in New York.[72] Charles Luckeyeth "Luckey" Roberts began his career in show business as a child acrobat, but learned piano at an early age and started playing in Baltimore "barrelhouses," small establishments that served beer not from bottles but straight from the brewers' wooden barrels. The jazz played in these places had a rocking, spontaneous air, and "barrelhouse" piano refers to a style of play marked by a hard touch and emphatic swing so as to be heard above the noise of crowds. An estimable ragtime pianist, Roberts is said to have influenced James P. Johnson, and he was a transitional figure between ragtime and the New York "stride" pianists. From these rough-edged beginnings Roberts developed a "society" band that played functions in fashionable locales such as Nantucket, Massachusetts, and Palm Beach, Florida,[73] and Hodges would play with groups put together for these dates; it was perhaps on one such job that Hodges first heard Benny Carter in Saratoga Springs, New York. Roberts eventually had his own club—Luckey's Rendezvous—to which Ellington's arranger and songwriting partner Billy Strayhorn would retire late at night when other clubs had closed.[74] According to Willie "the Lion" Smith, the club failed because Roberts was too willing to provide free drinks to friends and show business acquaintances.[75]

Two events then combined to create an opening in the Ellington band: First, around the turn of the year to 1928, Rudy Jackson, clarinet and tenor saxophonist, was fired by Ellington, in part because of his unreliability[76] but also because of a copyright controversy. Jackson had played with King Oliver in Chicago and taken a melody from Oliver's "Camp Meeting Blues" that is heard in the third chorus of "Creole Love Call." Oliver sued Ellington (unsuccessfully) and Ellington, angry at Jackson for the trouble he'd caused, replaced him.[77] In his typically diplomatic fashion, Ellington said in his auto-biography merely that Rudy Jackson "left."[78]

Since Jackson played clarinet and tenor, not alto, his departure was a necessary but not a sufficient condition for Hodges's hiring; Ellington still had Barney Bigard, who played clarinet and tenor, and Otto Hardwick, who played alto, soprano, and baritone saxes, giving him several combinations with which to orchestrate particular numbers. Then Hardwick, who was lead alto in the band, went through the windshield of a taxicab in an accident, cutting his face extensively. "Had his face all cut up, and I had to go to work for him," Hodges said.[79] Hardwick had been an undependable employee even before the accident. "Otto was the worst" of the Ellington band's drinkers, according to Bigard, who said that Hardwick "would sometimes not show up and be off for days."[80] Hodges would recall that Hardwick's nickname in the band was "Professor Booze" (pronounced, with sarcastic grandiloquence, "Bou-*zay*").[81]

Ellington had made two prior offers to Hodges, who turned both down, saying he wasn't ready; according to drummer Sonny Greer, these offers were extended during the Ellington band's summer tours of New England in 1925 and 1926, but "Hodges declined both offers because he had found work with Lloyd Scott's band at the Capitol Palace."[82] Hodges had even substituted for Hardwick before, in the fall of 1926 when Hardwick returned to Washington for a family funeral.[83] Ellington redoubled his efforts now that his lead alto was out of commission for an indefinite period. Hodges said, "Duke offered me a job. I still wouldn't take the job, kept putting it off and putting it off.[84]

The reasons for Hodges's reluctance were several; the first was his genuine affection for Webb. According to Barney Bigard, Hodges "loved Chick so much and [was] so faithful to him that Duke had to practically get on his knees" to get him to leave. Webb eventually added his own voice to those encouraging Hodges to move on. "Finally Chick himself told [Hodges] to take the job because he was able to see that it would better [him] in the long run," Bigard said. Hodges would "get a better chance to express what he wanted to do with [Ellington] than with [Webb]" because the latter "played mostly ensembles. There were very few solos."[85] Webb said the same thing to Ellington: "Chick came to me," according to Ellington, "and said he thought Johnny would be better in our band where he would have more freedom of expression."[86]

Second, Hodges hesitated because Ellington's group was, in Bigard's phrase, a "reading band," meaning that they played from written arrangements. "Johnny was scared when he first joined us," Bigard said.

I guess we all were at first because most of us had never before played with a large orchestra that was beginning to get somewhere. Naturally you get a funny feeling, and you're fighting to do good all the time until you can relax yourself. Its [*sic*] kind of a challenge and it scared Johnny plenty.[87]

Thus Hodges could no longer get by, as he did with the Webb band, playing "head" arrangements and depending on his ear. "Johnny Hodges couldn't read so well at that time. Johnny could blow like hell though. He was a natural musician," Bigard said.[88] "Natural" in this context means, as Benny Waters—who had known him from his Boston days—explained, that Hodges "could play in any key without knowing what key he was in."[89] Carney and Bigard helped Hodges make the transition; they "would take him in hand and if Duke had written a new orchestration with a sax ensemble [they] would go over it with Johnny until he had it down pat."[90] Hodges later confirmed that Bigard and Otto Hardwick, once he recuperated, were "very helpful" in getting him acclimated to the Ellington organization's regimen.[91]

The final ground for hesitation on Hodges's part was monetary. "The bread was good," he said of the money he made playing with Roberts, but it wasn't steady. Roberts was a one-man entertainment conglomerate, writing scores for musical comedies, composing popular songs, and playing concerts at Carnegie Hall and Town Hall. Roberts's society bands were just one division of his empire, however, so Hodges couldn't depend on him as a regular source of income. "Thought it would last forever," he said after he'd been wooed away by Ellington, "So I kept gigging and gigging and gigging."[92]

Ellington had been known to lure musicians away from higher-paying jobs with promises of greater things to come and little else; the most extended account of such a seduction is given by Bigard, whom Ellington hired in 1927. At the time Bigard was playing with Luis Russell, whose band had a regular booking at a New York after-hours club. When the two got together for final negotiations, Ellington's offer "turned out to be a smaller salary than I was making," Bigard said, "but the more the man talked, the more I liked him. He was very ambitious, even then." Part of the appeal was artistic: "I noticed he kept talking in the plural," Bigard noted. "'Our band,' 'We can stay there,' and liked that from the start about him. He thought of the band as a unit and I dug him."[93] And while Ellington's music might sound scripted, the finished work one heard was frequently the product of what could be called, without paradox, composed improvisation. "He would write a whole darned arrangement on a number of his own," Bigard recalled, "and tell me, 'OK. When you get to there, just take it.' That was how he made you feel at ease. Like you belonged in there."[94] Ellington would eventually use the same approach with Hodges, and may have held out such freedom as an inducement.

Hodges's reservations were eventually overcome by a pressing personal concern: as Bigard recalled it, Hodges "was married at the time he joined the band," to his first wife, Bertha, "and had a baby."[95] He needed a steady pay-check, not the spotty cash flow he took in when playing for Chick Webb and Luckey Roberts. Hodges did not specifically mention his family when he recalled his decision to join Ellington, although there is a suggestion that he made the move for more than mere aesthetic reasons: "Everybody was trying to talk me into taking it," he said. "So I finally took it. And here I am."[96] Ellington's persistence was a function of his long-held desire to add Hodges to his roster and his knowledge of Webb's weak spot, namely, his inability to hold a band together. "Chick was always dogged by bad luck, and never man-aged to work steady for long," Ellington said. When he had "a lay-off . . . some of the guys would have to take work somewhere else."[97]

Bigard claimed that the decision to hire Hodges was a communal one. "The way it worked from the inside of Duke's band, at that time at least, was like this. We would all get together to decide who would be best to hire as a replacement and then we all made our suggestions. After a while a decision was made and Duke would go talk with the guy in question. That's how it was with Johnny Hodges. Harry Carney knew Johnny from Boston[,] which was the home town of both of them. He suggested that we get Johnny into the band and practically everyone agreed that he was the man for the job."[98] Bigard's support for Hodges may have been colored by self-interest; at the time, the band was also thinking of adding a clarinet, and Buster Bailey was under consideration.[99] Bailey was a big name, having played with Fletcher Henderson and King Oliver. He was the first academically trained clarinetist to become successful in jazz—he had studied under Franz Schoepp of the Chicago Symphony, who would later teach Benny Goodman.[100] Hodges, by comparison, was just a journeyman on Bigard's instrument; he recalled his days playing clarinet with Webb's band with self-effacing amusement, saying that when he played "Someday Sweetheart" in the low register, he would do it "with a squeak every four bars." So it was natural for Bigard to advocate for "the little ol' boy from Boston."[101] Ellington seconded Bigard's account; ac-cording to the bandleader, after Jackson left "we had a meeting of the band to decide whether to get Buster Bailey or Johnny Hodges. Buster was regarded as just about the top clarinetist at that time, 1928, but Barney Bigard voted him out and Johnny Hodges in!"[102]

Thus before he had turned twenty-one, Hodges joined the Duke Ellington band.[103] "I didn't really settle down until 1928 when I joined Duke," Hodges would say. "And I consider that a very lucky break for me, too. After all, if I hadn't been with Duke in '28 they'd probably have never heard of me. He's helped a whole lot, you know."[104] Although this may be false modesty on Hodges's part, the Ellington organization represented a significant step up for Hodges both artistically and in terms of professionalism. One objective measure of the improvement in Hodges's status is that before joining Ellington's organization, he had somehow avoided joining Local 802 of the American Federation of Musicians. Ellington's outfit was more successful than any of the bands he had previously played with, and as such couldn't run the risk of labor problems.

And so in the Diary & Directory of the Associated Musicians of Greater New York for the year 1928, for the first time appears the name "John C. Hodge" of 2187 7th Avenue.

5

The Competition

AS JOHNNY HODGES became acclimated to the New York jazz scene he began to make the rounds to see where he stood in the pecking order of alto sax players. One night in 1927 at a basement club on 7th Avenue, he heard a man whom he had met in 1925 at Saratoga Springs, New York, when they were both in that resort town playing summer gigs. Hodges was impressed enough to tell Charlie Holmes, a fellow altoist he knew from Boston, to go to Small's Paradise and "hear the greatest alto saxophone player in the world." He was referring to Benny Carter, whom most would rank as Hodges's only genuine rival on the alto over the next two decades.[1]

Holmes had played oboe with the Boston Civic Symphony Orchestra but later gravitated to jazz. He moved to New York with Harry Carney in 1927 and played with Chick Webb, among others. He spent the bulk of his career with the Luis Russell Orchestra, including the years when that group functioned as Louis Armstrong's backup band.[2] He was thus in a position to offer an informed opinion of the man whom Hodges had singled out for such high praise, but when he heard Carter he was unimpressed. Hodges insisted that Carter was supreme, and Holmes would later revise his view after hearing Hodges and Carter play together one night.[3]

Over the course of their careers, Carter and Hodges would frequently be linked. Benny Goodman listed the two as the top altos of the day; Ben Webster, whose mature style was formed in part by imitation of Hodges, ranked Carter first among saxophonists, "then Hawk (Coleman Hawkins), then Johnny Hodges (the 'most feeling')."[4] They may have been together at the top, but they were different. Carter was better trained musically, but his tone was thinner, less viscous than that of Hodges, and so while Carter's solos are models of harmonic development, they pack less of a wallop (to this author's ears) than does Hodges's emotional punch. If Hodges was the quintessential

Dionysian New Orleans western alto, Carter—born in Harlem—was his Apollonian New York eastern counterpart.

Who was better? It is largely but not entirely a matter of taste. Carter was "the most admired alto saxophonist of the thirties," wrote Whitney Balliett, "but that was hardly surprising" since in his view "Johnny Hodges didn't draw himself up to his full height until 1940."[5] Jazz scholar Martin Williams expressed his preference by saying, "Johnny Hodges can play the blues; Benny Carter not."[6] French critic André Hodeir handed down an even harsher judgment: "I feel that Johnny Hodges" had a "more valid" approach to the instrument, he wrote, but it might be only because he was "closer to [Hodeir's] own temperament." Hodeir went on to say that in terms of

> absolute value Benny Carter may well be Hodges's equal—though not [Charlie] Parker's of course—but he undoubtedly has certain failings; a flair for accents and their correct placing would have enabled him to produce a swing worthy of his musicianship. Such as he is, Benny Carter often disappoints me; sometimes he even bores me. If it comes to a showdown, I have to admit that I don't think his music as a whole will stand the test of time.[7]

Carter was Hodges's superior in terms of melodic invention and harmonic complexity. Benny Waters, who knew both men well, recalled a late-night cutting contest among Hodges, Carter, and Jimmy Dorsey, a popular white alto player who was three years older than both of his rivals and a more established figure than either, having played with Paul Whiteman.[8] On the night in question "Jimmy Dorsey . . . came up to Harlem to jam with the best black alto saxmen" at the Melody Club, a place just around the corner from the Rhythm Club and a "real place for jamming," according to Waters.[9] Dorsey cut Johnny Hodges because, as Waters put it, Dorsey "knew a little bit more harmony than Johnny. Johnny, in his harmony, wasn't too advanced." Then

> somebody said, "Call up Benny Carter." So Benny came around there with his own piano player. . . . Benny started playing "Georgia Brown," and here's what Benny was doing: Benny played along with Jimmy, and every four bars he'd move into a different key.

Waters said that Dorsey "got all red in the face and practically hauled up and walked out—looked like a drowned rat,"[10] leaving Carter—whose nickname was "The King"—the winner. Victory in a sax battle is won not just by stamina; it is primarily a test of creativity, of a player's ability to produce new musical figures, either from memory or invented on the spot. By this standard Carter, with his more extensive knowledge of music, was at the time better equipped than Hodges to last through the night.

Although Dorsey cut Hodges that night, with Carter's encouragement he came back to win a rematch:

> Johnny was very upset, but Benny Carter told him not to worry, he'd get him the next time he showed up. Sure enough, when Dorsey came back the next week, Benny took him on. They did "Tiger Rag" and Benny suggested they do four choruses, taking it through the keys. When they got to B major [five sharps], Jimmy got his ass kicked.[11]

Perhaps Hodges developed his facility playing in the key of B at house-rent parties in Boston, where, Charlie Holmes would recall, the pianist was expected to play "in either F sharp or B natural. That's all they'd play, on all the black notes, you know. And Johnny would take his horn out, without knowing about the keys, and just blow in any key."[12]

Dorsey's ego may have been bruised by his encounters with Carter and Hodges, but Hodges nonetheless admired him. In a 1955 interview Hodges said that in his early days Dorsey, like Frankie Trumbauer, had attracted his attention when he was starting to create his own style because Dorsey was "kickin' up a fuss"[13] with his playing.

Hodges went on to become the first among equals in the Ellington orchestra, taking three solos to every one that the Duke gave to any other musician. Benny Carter, on the other hand, made the fateful decision to spend the years 1935 to 1938 in Europe. He ultimately decided to return to America for artistic reasons, saying, "I don't hear enough decent music to inspire me at all and I think what keeps me going now is the anticipation of my return to America. I really don't want to get too far behind for when I come back I intend to have the greatest band ever."[14] Like many other expatriate American jazzmen, Carter found the more congenial racial attitude and higher acclaim given to jazz musicians overseas to be a tonic, but at the same time he began to thirst for the purer springs of his chosen art form back home.

Over the years Hodges frequently expressed his admiration for Carter's style, along with that of Willie Smith, who played the bulk of his career with Jimmie Lunceford (eleven years) and spent a brief period with Duke Ellington, taking over when Hodges struck out on his own in 1951. Leonard Feather praised Smith for his "buoyant, happy tone and rhythmic style," while noting that he used fewer glissandi than did Hodges.[15] *New York Times* jazz critic John Wilson assessed Smith as "one of the triumvirate of great jazz alto saxophonists before Charlie Parker arrived," the other two being Hodges with his "fat, luscious tone" and Carter, who struck him as "a model of clean, pure-toned playing." In stylistic terms, Wilson said that "Smith fell between Carter and Hodges for he combined some of Carter's clarity and singing directness with a variant of Hodges' gut sound."[16]

But it was Carter with whom Hodges was most frequently compared during his playing days, and not always to the latter's advantage. As a result, there are signs that Hodges ultimately developed feelings of professional envy toward Carter. Hodges was omitted from *Jazz Masters of the Thirties* because Rex Stewart didn't think Hodges's work was significant enough to be included, while Carter was covered in a chapter of his own, "The Benny Carter I Knew." Stewart died before the book was published, and Martin Williams, the jazz scholar who wrote the foreword, said he was "sure that had Rex Stewart lived to prepare this collection for publication there would be more here" on Hodges,[17] but this is speculation. At the end of his career Stewart accused a number of people of plagiarizing his works, including Hodges, whom he implicated in the alleged theft of his tune "Finesse," credited to Ellington and Hodges under the name "Night Wind."[18] So there was bad blood on Stewart's side that may have led him to deprecate Hodges's work.

Because Carter was not only a musician but also a successful arranger, composer, and bandleader, he achieved something Hodges didn't, namely, independence, both artistic and financial, from a bandleader. Jazz aficionados who rated intellect above emotion tended to favor Carter, as evidenced by some doggerel comparing the two that appeared in the January 1942 issue of *Swing* magazine over the nom de plume "Snooty McSiegle":

> *Johnny Hodges*
> *Sounds gorgeous.*
> *He knows how to jump it.*
> *But Benny Carter*
> *Is smarter.*
> *He doubles on trumpet.*[19]

Carter was deferential to Hodges in some areas, such as the slow numbers in the Ellington repertoire; in 1977 at a performance in London, for example, Carter stopped the pianist when he played two choruses of "Sophisticated Lady." Afterwards, he said, "I didn't like to play that particular Ellington so closely associated with Johnny Hodges because the audience was expecting to hear it as Johnny did it. I knew I couldn't satisfy those who wanted it played as Johnny would have done it. And to do it that way would not have satisfied me."[20]

In the late 1960s Hodges and Carter played together in the Jazz at the Philharmonic tours when Ellington's orchestra was one of the established units called upon to back other performers, and in 1968 they appeared at the Newport Jazz Festival along with Ellington and his rhythm section. Like many all-star aggregations, this one didn't live up to its promise. Ellington and Carter shared a dressing room, which Hodges entered before the performance to ask, "What are we going to play?" Ellington answered, "I don't know," and after Hodges left, Carter asked the same question. Ellington gave the same reply. Ellington faced a looming deadline for an Italian magazine article, and after musing to himself, turned to assembled writers including Stanley Dance and said, "Write this down for me, please: 'When a symphony man wants to know about jazz, he goes to Benny Carter. When a jazz man wants to know about the symphony, he goes to Benny Carter.' "[21]

Ellington would use the same words to introduce Carter a few moments later, but as the three stood in the wings before going on, he repeated to Hodges and Carter that he didn't know what they would play. Once they were on stage, Ellington called for "Satin Doll," then "Take the A Train." Carter looked mystified and played in a somewhat confused manner. Ellington then called for a blues on which Carter and Hodges traded riffs, but when it was done Hodges yelled "Rollin'," signaling that he was done, and then, "Bye, Duke!" As was often his practice, Ellington refused to let his sideman off easy and instead called for "Passion Flower" and "Things Ain't What They Used to Be." The set ended with a new number that Ellington's small group had begun to play recently on which Carter acquitted himself ably with the help of a hastily produced lead sheet.[22]

The set was, in the words of Amy Lee, jazz writer for the *Christian Science Monitor*, "the height of ineptness." Ellington gave more solo time to Hodges, whose playing was luscious as usual, but this meant that Carter had to stand around on stage with nothing to do. Carter, known for his gentlemanly demeanor and unwillingness to say anything negative about another jazzman, living or dead, "displayed unfailing poise and forebearance [*sic*] in a cruelly thoughtless gaffe," Lee wrote.[23] "Carter's sound was like crème de menthe . . . but the spirit wasn't there as it should have been," according to Ira Gitler in *DownBeat*. Backstage reports portrayed Carter as unhappy, and Gitler went further: "This cavalier treatment of such a distinguished musician was shameful."[24] It also may have been the case that Ellington used a façade of indecision to allow Hodges—who was more familiar with his repertoire—to outshine Carter, as he had done on other occasions to protect his musicians from unfavorable comparisons with guest artists who appeared with his band.

Carter was, as always, courtly and conciliatory, saying, "Puzzling things occasionally take place on the bandstand when mixed units are put together hurriedly. . . . I just try to play my part without worrying about anything else. I don't think Duke or Johnny meant to be rude."[25] Stanley Dance would later downplay Hodges's role in this incident; Carter biographer Morroe Berger, he wrote, "didn't realize that he was unjust to Hodges. It is particularly unfortunate that this judgment was made in a book about Benny Carter."[26] Whatever the reason, Ellington seemed to have ambivalent feelings about Carter. Although he publicly praised him, when it came time to write his autobiography, he mentioned Carter only once, left him off a list of innovators on the saxophone, and didn't include his band among fourteen groups other than his own that "led the way" in the development of swing.[27]

Hodges may have been innocent in that incident, but he seemed guilty of rudeness toward Carter on another occasion, when the latter replaced Russell Procope at an Ellington engagement in Reno, Nevada, in 1968. Harry Carney was ill and Procope was assigned to cover for him on baritone, which meant that Ellington needed an alto to replace Procope. He called Carter and asked him (perhaps disingenuously) if he knew of anyone who was available.

"When do you need him?" Carter asked.
"This evening," Duke replied.
"Well, how about me?" Carter asked.

Ellington demurred, saying he couldn't afford him, but Carter said he'd do the gig "for kicks" if Duke would cover his travel and hotel expenses.

And so Carter rejoined the Ellington band for three nights after a forty-two-year absence (he had spent a few weeks with Ellington in 1926, before Hodges joined the band in 1928). He was received cordially by everyone—except Hodges. As Carter took his seat Hodges gave him a grudging hello, then turned his back "and never said anything else," according to Carter's biographers.[28]

Hodges was known for being taciturn and proud, but his chilly reaction to the presence of his principal competitor on that job may have instead reflected tensions between him and his boss; Hodges was persistent in demanding better pay, and Ellington's choice of Carter as a temporary stand-in may have been intended to tweak the ego of his resident diva—or so Hodges may have thought.

But thirty-five years after their first encounter in Saratoga Springs, Hodges's admiration for Carter endured. Asked by Stanley Dance in 1960 which alto players he especially admired, Hodges emphatically named Willie Smith first.

And whom did he consider second after Smith?

Benny Carter.[29]

6

The Partnership Begins

MAY 18 WAS a date of familial significance in the life of Johnny Hodges because one of his older sisters, Josephine *née* Cynolia, was born on that date in 1902. His son would be born on the same date in 1947, and he would use these occasions to mark another milestone in his life: the day he joined Duke Ellington's band. "I joined Duke in '28. It was on my sister's birthday, May 18th, which is also my son's birthday, a day to remember,"[1] he would recall.

Hodges's first gig with Ellington was at the Cotton Club, where the "Cotton Club Show Boat" revue had opened on April 1, 1928.[2] The first of Hodges's many road trips with Ellington took place on May 23, when the band traveled to Brunswick, Maine, to play a dance at Bowdoin College, then back to New York for Hodges's first recording session with Ellington on June 25, 1928, in which he played alto and soprano sax as well as clarinet.[3] Seven takes were recorded: two of "What a Life!" although neither was released; three of W. C. Handy's "Yellow Dog Blues," with Hodges soloing on soprano; and two of "Tishomingo Blues" by Spencer Williams, a New Orleans native who also composed the jazz standards "I Ain't Got Nobody," "I Found a New Baby," and "Basin Street Blues."[4] On "Tishomingo Blues," Hodges solos on alto.[5]

Stanley Dance said that Hodges's solo on "Yellow Dog Blues" betrayed some "nervousness,"[6] but his chorus on "Tishomingo Blues" was uniformly pronounced a success. With only the rhythm section playing behind him, Hodges's attack recalls Sidney Bechet's, and he finishes his sixteen bars with "the kind of glissando that became one of his trademarks," according to jazz scholar Gary Giddins, who ranks this chorus as "one of the most impressive recorded debuts in jazz history."[7]

Although Dance suggests that Hodges adapted easily to his new job with Ellington,[8] this view is undercut by the testimony of his colleagues. Barney

Bigard recalled that "Johnny was scared when he first joined" the band,[9] and he sought to compensate for his feelings of inadequacy by trying to appear older and more worldly than he really was; long-time Ellington guitarist Freddy Guy said Hodges was "a sickly kid who'd smoke cigars to make himself feel more grown up."[10] In addition to normal new-guy-on-the-job jitters, there were two substantive sources for Hodges' anxiety: first, he was nervous that his sight-reading skills were inadequate for the Ellington organization, which worked from written rather than "head" arrangements; and second, the man he replaced, Otto Hardwick, was a highly competent performer who played a major role in the orchestra. Hodges said of Hardwick that there "was no man in the world I know who could master the high notes like him . . . hittin' off them and slidin' off them, so what happened was that Duke threw it all on me and I had to go rehearse this thing and try to get as close to him as I possibly could."[11] Hodges practiced diligently to fit into the tight-knit cloth that the Ellington orchestra wove, and with his bold tone he eventually began to stand out from the fabric of the band as a whole.

At the time of these early recordings Ellington and trumpeter James "Bubber" Miley sought to create an idealized aural counterpart to the jungles of Africa for all-white audiences who sought the safe *frisson* of watching and listening to an all-black show at the segregated Cotton Club. As the English composer-musician and jazz writer Spike Hughes put it in *Melody Maker*, "Why they do not move the Cotton Club down to the Forties [i.e., to mid-town Manhattan from Harlem] I cannot imagine. It would save many an expensive taxi-fare. On the other hand, the unimaginative American business man and his peroxide stenographer might not feel that they were being 'wicked' if it were located in the mid-town section."[12] Miley used a rubber plumber's plunger as a mute to produce growls and wah-wah sounds on his horn that mimicked human speech.[13] In addition to his proficiency on his instrument, he was responsible for establishing a fundamental principle of Ellingtonian music theory: "If it ain't got swing, it ain't worth playin', if it ain't got gutbucket, it ain't worth doin',"[14] he would say, which Ellington's manager Irving Mills would shorten to "It Don't Mean a Thing If It Ain't Got That Swing" in the lyrics he added to an Ellington melody.

Ellington would characterize Hodges's sound as "physical" in contrast to the "clean" style of trombonist Juan Tizol, who played without "smears and slides,"[15] but it was nonetheless "a piquant tonal contrast to the bizarre sounds Miley conjured up to depict the jungles of his and Ellington's imagination," in Dance's view. "Yet what Hodges played became every bit as much a part of these jungles: a different voice crying beneath tall, moonlit trees, sensual, seductive, often mysterious, sometimes sinister."[16] Like the man playing the reed instrument who charms the nude woman in the jungle of Henri Rousseau's painting *The Dream*, Hodges provided an erotic element to the dense vegetation of the Miley-Ellington sound. "Dark, tropical and warm fulfillment seems to lie in his sound," wrote the German music critic Joachim Berendt of Hodges's play.[17]

Miley was quite fond of liquor and thus undependable, and he was soon gone, participating in his final recording session on January 16, 1929. He was replaced by Charles "Cootie" Williams, who abstained from liquor entirely. By replacing first Hardwick on alto, then Miley on trumpet, the Ellington band eliminated the problem described thus by Barney Bigard: "Every time some big shot who could help the band would come down to the club, either one or two of them would be gone. Duke would get so mad that when they came back he would tell them, 'Well, you all did a great job. We had some very important people in here to listen to you and you weren't here. That's great for the future of the band, isn't it?' "[18] Both Bigard and Hodges would, according to the former, "drink a little" but never to excess.[19]

The same session that was Hardwick's last was the first at which Hodges performed a piece composed by Ellington with him in mind: "Flaming Youth." According to one source Hodges plays both alto and soprano sax on the song; according to another, only alto.[20] In March of that year Hodges would be credited for the first time as co-composer with Ellington on "Rent Party Blues." As with many tunes labeled "blues" that he would record in his career, the song is blues-infused but not a blues per se. In the words of Gary Giddins, it "uses blues intervals" and "is blueslike in its simplicity and directness," but it is a blues "in name only. . . . Again there are echoes of Bechet, but only echoes. Hodges is his own man and with one of his stabbing notes he can make the same point as effectively as Bechet with less effort. Bechet used a broadsword, Hodges a rapier."[21]

Hodges' reputation grew both locally, among the patrons of the venues where the Ellington orchestra played and, thanks to nightly radio broadcasts on the CBS network that began in February 1929, nationally. The band was heard in the early evening on Mondays and Thursdays, and later at night on Wednesdays.[22] Drummer Sonny Greer described the impact that the earlier broadcasts had on the lives of the people who began to listen to them:

From the Cotton Club, we used to broadcast . . . from 6:00 to 7:00. . . .
Everybody was waiting for that from New York to California and coast

to coast was waiting for that. Of course, you know, that's suppertime.…
Didn't anybody get anything to eat until we came off. Cats working all
day, starved to death until we get off.[23]

Greer's claim may seem like hyperbole today, but in the days before taped
performances and reruns one heard a program live or not at all.

A session released on the Victor label in May 1929 yielded "Cotton
Club Stomp," a composition credited to Ellington, Hodges, and Harry
Carney on which Hodges solos on soprano and employs an embellishing
technique known as a turnback, a "faster, more complex series of chords
that comes in the last two bars of a blues or the [final] A section of an
AABA form,"[24] according to one definition. "This was a common tactic by
the late '30s, but not in 1929," noted Giddins. "Hodges was not usually an
adventurous or an experimental player; he was simply a jazz genius who
established early in his career a style that was ahead of its time."[25] While
credit for this stylistic touch may be due as much to the song's arranger as
to Hodges, it is nonetheless evidence that he was on the forefront of jazz
innovations at the time.

Like many jazz artists, Ellington and his subgroups were sometimes asked
to perform inferior pop material by the business interests that backed him,
in his case Irving Mills, the man who aggressively promoted the bandleader
commercially at the same time that he encouraged him to pursue the highest
artistic standards the market would bear. Hodges's first fall from aesthetic
grace in pursuit of lucre was "When You're Smiling," recorded in March 1930.
As he would throughout his career, he performed the saccharine number
with commendable reserve, stopping short of bathos and elevating technique
over sentiment. Yet Hodges's creative fire could not be doused by even such a
bland number, as he spars for the first time in a "chase chorus," a musical version of the African American game of verbal one-upmanship known as "The
Dozens," trading riffs with Cootie Williams. Hodges would mix his solos with
those of others rarely, perhaps because he was such a purist of tone and *egoist*
of his instrument: six years later he and Williams would again play in this
fashion on "In a Jam"; in 1940 he and Lawrence Brown would do so on "Me
and You"; and much later (1959) Hodges would lock horns in lick-swapping
matches with Dizzy Gillespie on "Squatty Roo" and with Gerry Mulligan on
"18 Carrots for Rabbit."

In the summer of 1930 the Ellington band was in Hollywood filming *Check
and Double Check*, and Cab Calloway and the Missourians took their place at
the Cotton Club. Calloway was a hit with club patrons, and Ellington and

his band were thus free to go on the road where he could make more money than he could at the Cotton Club.[26] The club's owners—believed by some to include criminal elements[27]—had a contract that gave them options to book Ellington so that, in the words of his son Mercer, "as his popularity increased he couldn't always take advantage of lucrative outside dates."[28] Money was probably the foremost reason for the change from a house band to a touring one, but there were others. Ellington, a man proud of his race who read accounts of slave revolts,[29] must have chafed at the atmosphere of the Cotton Club, which was decorated in the style of a southern mansion with waiters dressed in red tuxedos, like butlers. "I suppose the idea was to make whites who came to the club feel like they were being catered to and entertained by black slaves," Calloway would surmise.[30] A composer at heart, Ellington also grew tired of taking requests from drunken patrons and performing background music for floor shows. Playing week-long engagements in movie theaters along with an occasional nightclub gig gave him greater artistic latitude, at least until the band produced the roster of hits that became known as "the dreaded medley," which was in high demand by audiences but dulled the creative instincts of the orchestra as a whole.[31] Regardless of the cause, the decision meant that Ellington and Hodges would, except for brief periods, remain musical nomads for the rest of their lives.

In 1932 Hodges would reunite with Bechet for a week in Philadelphia to work on "The Sheik of Araby," a number that Bechet would record in a noteworthy fashion nine years later, playing six instruments on different tracks that were layered on top of one another, a technological novelty for the time.[32] It is not clear who instigated the reunion, but Ellington "had been urging Hodges to contribute more on his soprano."[33] A perfectionist, Hodges said the soprano sax "was a funny instrument. . . . You just can't pick it up today and put it down tomorrow and go back and play it." Bechet made Hodges "play it over and over, until finally [they] recorded it." [34] The result was a thirty-two-bar solo based on "a spectacular chorus that Sidney usually played."[35] As Ellington's son Mercer would later note, it "commanded a lot of attention at the time."[36]

On January 16, 1938, Hodges took part in Benny Goodman's historic concert at Carnegie Hall, along with fellow Ellingtonians Harry Carney and Cootie Williams. The concert was advertised as "the first concert of swing music in the history of Carnegie Hall,"[37] the premier venue for the performance of European classical music in New York, but it was more important because it brought together, on stage and in the audience, blacks and whites in a dignified atmosphere to hear America's indigenous classical music. As the reviewer from the *New York Age*, a black newspaper, wrote of the Goodman concert,

> Some of the leading white citizens sat in evening dress next to some of our highly respectable colored citizens, who were also in evening clothes. No color line was drawn in any part of the house, both white and colored occupying boxes. . . . Yet no calamity occurred.[38]

As for the performers, whereas racially mixed groups of musicians in studio sessions had become accepted, the thought of a live multiracial group still represented in some minds an improper mixing of the races. A narrow exception was recognized for features in which a black musical personality would be brought onstage for a novelty number in an otherwise all-white performance, as when Fats Waller appeared with Ted Lewis's band in 1931. Goodman's music may today sound dated to ears used to listening only to rock and jazz from the fifties onward, but he was in fact a pioneer who brought black and white musicians together at a time when he ran real financial and reputational risks for doing so. The Ellingtonians were suitably impressed by the significance of the event: "Cootie [Williams] and Harry [Carney] were exhilarated by the occasion," according to Helen Oakley, who worked for Ellington's manager Irving Mills, and "Johnny Hodges shared in the excitement," though "true to form he maintained a cool demeanor."[39]

At the Carnegie Hall date Hodges played soprano sax on Ellington's "Blue Reverie" and alto during an extended jam session on "Honeysuckle Rose."[40] Hodges's introduction and coda in the former are representative of his more rococo moments, but his solo is bluesy and more fluid than that heard on the earlier recorded version of the song. The applause that Hodges received when he finished was so loud it obscured the first bars of the following solo by Jess Stacy, Goodman's pianist. Ellington attended the concert but declined to join his sidemen. Some said he did so out of pique because he had wanted to be the first jazz bandleader to perform at Carnegie Hall. While maintaining his typical air of composure, he "was furious," according to a friend who saw him there—"He was just livid."[41] Others, such as Ellington scholar John Edward Hasse, view the bandleader's reaction as more calculating than bitter: "It was Goodman's concert," Hasse notes, "and Ellington probably did not want to get second billing; or he may not have wanted to be categorized as swing, or lumped together with groups that operated on an aesthetic level different from his."[42]

"Honeysuckle Rose" was not a new number to Hodges; he had been a member of the studio group that backed Mildred Bailey when she recorded the song in 1935.[43] After solos by Lester Young, Count Basie, and Buck Clayton, Hodges played three choruses to appreciative applause. His name was not listed on the cover of the album of the concert despite the number and quality of his contributions, however; instead, he was lumped together with those in the anonymous category "Many Other Great Jazz Artists" after seven named musicians, including Cootie Williams. In his characteristic self-effacing style, Hodges never made much of his participation in the memorable event. Goodman, on the other hand, was uncharacteristically effusive: "I know that our 1938 concert in Carnegie Hall would have lost a lot if we didn't have the cooperation of fellows like Johnny Hodges, who is the greatest man on alto sax I ever heard."[44]

The process by which Ellington's sidemen—and not Duke himself—ended up playing at the concert involved a bit of intrigue on the part of Goodman and Helen Oakley, who had arranged the first meeting between Goodman and Ellington in her Chicago apartment.[45] Goodman's attitude toward the Ellington orchestra was, first, that of a business competitor, with artistic admiration second. He asked Oakley to persuade Harry Carney, Cootie Williams, and Hodges to perform at the concert; Oakley agreed, and she asked Ellington if he would mind if she spoke to his musicians. According to Oakley, Ellington was too proud to object, and she successfully accomplished her mission. Afterward Ellington was told that Oakley's request was the first step in a plan to persuade the three musicians to leave his band for Goodman's, and he was suspicious of her until she denied having such an intention.[46] He had what he believed to be legitimate cause for concern, for he knew her to be an avid admirer of Hodges's talent, and one who had sought to promote him in a manner that would have been at the expense of the band as a whole.

7

Women and Children

IT IS NOT surprising that Johnny Hodges, a man whose working hours began when the sun went down, would favor women from the night life; he would marry and have children by two, carry on a youthful affair and have a daughter by a third, and have at least one overseas fling that produced another child.

On July 29, 1927, Hodges wed Bertha B. Pettiford, a hostess at the Savoy Ballroom, in a civil ceremony in Manhattan.[1] Hodges was twenty-one at the time, and Pettiford was eighteen. The witnesses were Hodges's mother and the bride's father.[2]

Bertha was short, like Johnny. Al Sears, a fellow Ellingtonian, said, "They were the cutest couple you ever saw in your life. Johnny wasn't over four feet—you know I'm exaggerating—but she was smaller." According to Al Hibbler, who sang with the Ellington orchestra, Hodges and Bertha had a daughter.[3] Bertha apparently traveled with Hodges when he played; Mercer Ellington reports that she was among seven or eight band members' wives who made a trip to Chicago in 1932.[4] They would remain together for ten years, but by 1937 the marriage had fallen apart and Johnny had begun to be seen in public with Edith Louise Fitzgerald Cue, a dancer in the chorus at the Cotton Club.[5]

Fitzgerald was born on September 4, 1913, in Paducah, Kentucky, to Ellis Fitzgerald and Genevell Wallace Fitzgerald. In 1938, when she was twenty-five, her name appeared as Edith Louise Cue in Social Security records, presumably because of a marriage, and she would come to be known simply as "Cue" thereafter. On January 10, 1944, Hodges and Cue were married in Chicago, when Johnny was thirty-six years old and Edith thirty. In one picture she appears to be slightly taller than Hodges, at least in the shoes she was wearing at the time. The couple gave Chicago as their place of residence, a claim that was probably untrue; they may have decided to marry in Chicago because the waiting period in Illinois was only twenty-four hours.[6] The couple was subsequently remarried on July 26, 1968, in a religious ceremony at St. Paul's Church in New York in order for Cue to obtain recognition for their marriage by the Catholic Church.[7]

The couple had a daughter, Lornar (familiarly, Lorna), and a son named John C. Hodges II. Lorna, whose married name was Mafata, died on May 29, 2018. She was born on June 3, 1942, before Johnny and Cue Hodges were married. At the time of Hodges's death in 1970 she was awarded $5,000 from his estate, as was her brother. She was the holder of the copyright in 112 compositions by Hodges. She danced at the African Village at the 1964 New York World's Fair in Flushing Meadows, New York, and had her own dance troupe, Mafata Dance Company.

John C. Hodges II, born on May 18, 1947, would come to be known as "Brother." When asked how his son acquired that nickname Hodges replied, "My mother used to call me 'Brother,' too."[8] The son, a drummer, would join his father on live dates while still a teenager, substituting for Sam Woodyard in 1964 and 1965 at concerts in Philadelphia, Washington, DC, and Latham, New York, and one in Copenhagen, Denmark, when Woodyard missed the band's plane.[9] He can be heard on the 1965 album *Everybody Knows Johnny Hodges* on "Mood Indigo" and "Little Brother," and on the Hodges–Wild Bill Davis collaboration *Blue Pyramid*. At the time of his father's death in 1970, John II was living in Hollywood, California.[10] He died on January 14, 1984, at the age of thirty-six, and is buried in Flushing Cemetery in Queens, New York, along with his parents.

Everybody Knows Johnny Hodges was a family affair; in addition to the father on alto and the son on drums, Cue collaborated with her husband as co-composer on "Little Brother" and "Sassy Cue." In an interview with British jazz writer Max Jones, Hodges would say that the album "turned out pretty nice." When it was recorded, Hodges's son was fifteen years old and had his own quartet. "He has tenor, bass and piano with him," his father said.[11]

By all accounts Hodges's second marriage was a happy one. In his 1946 biography of Ellington, Barry Ulanov reports that Cue often traveled with her husband; he places her on a typical train trip, playing cards with Hodges and other band members.[12] In 1966, when Hodges was playing a date apart from Ellington with organist Wild Bill Davis in Atlantic City at the age of fifty-eight, she danced with fellow Ellingtonians Buster Cooper and Russell Procope, and the latter's wife as they celebrated Procope's birthday. Hodges was comfortable enough with the sight of another man dancing with his wife to smile down on the impromptu conga line with a look of happiness that rarely crossed his face when he was playing a job.[13]

According to one anecdote, Cue Hodges was a fierce defender of her husband's reputation. Norris Turney, the alto player whom Ellington hired as an insurance policy in 1969 after Hodges had to be replaced several times due to failing health, was supposedly awakened by a knock on his door one night. Turney's wife Marilee answered the door to find Johnny's wife, referred to in the tale as "Tootsie" and described as having been drinking heavily. "You ain't nothing. You can't play like Johnny," Hodges' wife supposedly said to Turner. Marilee Turney claimed that she "threw her ass out of there."[14] This tale may be apocryphal, but it is consistent with the sharp tongue that Cue displayed in at least one other instance. According to Ellington himself, it was Cue who gave him the nickname "Dumpy," and it stuck; it may have been a sarcastic variation on "Dumplin'," a nickname that Cootie Williams' wife had coined for the bandleader.[15]

The couple experienced the usual domestic issues, such as spending. On a tour of South America, for example, Cue went shopping with Mercer Ellington's wife and a singer in the band. When they returned Johnny was seen wandering about the lobby, as if in a daze. "I had a dream," he said of the aftershock of his wife's purchases as he waved some Brazilian paper currency before him. "I had a dream I had some money!"[16]

Although his daughter Lorna remembered Hodges as "kind, gentle and a good listener if somewhat uncommunicative," she lamented that he spent so much time away from home. "We didn't have much time together," she told Stanley Dance. "I can't remember him being around for my birthdays and he wasn't around for my wedding. A lot of major events passed, and he just wasn't there."[17] Hodges would phone home regularly and bring his children presents when he returned from the road, but he was nonetheless an absentee father. Moreover, since Cue accompanied him on the road as much as possible— probably to make sure he was faithful—the children spent long periods of time under the supervision of their father's mother in New York.[18] Although Hodges got along well with the children of others, he was apparently less comfortable with his own, according to Dance. When his son first showed an interest in music Hodges bought him a saxophone, then a drum set, and this shared interest brought them closer together. "Sometimes [Junior] gets in one of those [jazz history] books and says: 'Well I never knew this or that,'" Hodges told one interviewer. "I say: 'Well, there it is—right there.' He's always wondering why I don't have a lot to say about past happenings."[19]

He didn't have a comparable bond with his daughter Lorna, however. When she spent time with her father, she said, "he didn't open up freely. We'd just talk about the things in life—'your report card was good, you're going to do that,' you know. He would listen to whatever you had to say, but he wasn't a very talkative individual." It may have been that the characteristic reserve Hodges maintained toward people generally was too chilly for his relations with his children. "My ambition is to give them everything they need, not what they think they need," he once said.[20] That is not a bad philosophy of child-rearing, but it is one that may have struck a daughter who rarely saw her father as insufficiently supportive. "He didn't know how to handle a daughter or what to say or how to relate to her," Lorna told Dance.[21] She developed an interest in music and dance and attended the Juilliard School of Music, but even this potential avenue of communication failed him. "We had a lot of music theory that we were exposed to then, and he was not trained as a classical musician," she would recall.

> I would come to him and ask things about music, and he would say, "Well, I don't know that. I play or I feel things. I do not know what you're talking about technically." But then he would call up musicians and have them talk to me on the phone and give me answers to my questions. He was proud of that part.[22]

Before Johnny Hodges knew Bertha or Edith, he was involved with Frances Vivian Jones, a small woman about five feet tall, who met Hodges when she was in her mid-teens. At the time he was playing solo clarinet in Boston clubs and later led a group of his own. They started seeing each other, and she became pregnant and gave birth to a daughter, who was named Rosa Mae Hodges, though her parents never married.[23]

When she turned eighteen (and her daughter was six months old) Jones became a dancer at the Eagle Theater on Washington Street in Boston, which had been the scene of a thriving entertainment district until first radio and then television reduced the demand for live performances. The northern end of the street was the Scollay Square area, which included burlesque and vaudeville theaters. Jones was coached by Bill "Bojangles" Robinson, who taught her how to dance up and down stairs, as he did with Shirley Temple in the film *The Little Colonel.* She performed with Bessie Smith, Mamie Smith, and Lena Horne and danced in a chorus line with Josephine Baker. Jones didn't travel with Hodges when he was out on the road with the Ellington band because she had her own career and a child, but she would bring their daughter with her to see her father play when she could. "Everyone in Duke's band knew Johnny's little girl," she recalled.[24] These words, though they paint a picture of a fond if distant relationship, may be Jones's attempt to put the best face on an unhappy situation, as Hodges went on to fame, a degree of fortune, and two wives, while she was left behind.

There was at least one other child as well. Pianist-arranger Jimmy Jones recalled a trip to Sweden with the Ellington band and the wives of some members, including Cue Hodges. The orchestra had toured the country the previous year, and the band's plane was met by a number of women carrying babies with them. At a concert in Stockholm a woman whom Hodges "had been going with the year before"[25] was waiting in the wings on one side of the stage, while Cue Hodges stood offstage on the other. Drummer Sam Woodyard saw them and, according to Jones, said, "Watch this, I'm going to get a new drum boy." He then put Hodges busily to work as his assistant, changing the drums around until it was time to go back on. Hodges never left the stage between concerts as Woodyard spared him an embarrassing confrontation.[26]

There were doubtless other women in Hodges's life; it is a fact too commonly known to require mention that women are attracted to men in the performing arts. Still, Hodges had disadvantages to overcome in his wooing and winning. He was short, and thus by convention the range of females available to him was smaller than that which a taller man might choose from. "He was among the short musicians of our era, about my height,"[27] noted his bandmate Rex Stewart, but this is too generous; in a group photograph of the Ellington orchestra taken in 1934 Hodges is a head shorter than Ellington, half a head shorter than Barney Bigard, Cootie Williams, and Tricky Sam Nanton, and a bit shorter than Stewart. Hodges also had a grave mien, not generally considered an advantage when pitching woo; two writers found grounds to compare him with Sir Cedric Hardwicke, the British stage and film actor who frequently portrayed stuffy, formal characters. Jazz critic and novelist Albert Murray said of a local black man whom he asked for advice on lodgings in formerly-segregated Atlanta that "he smile[d] an old Joe Louis unsmile and wink[ed] an old johnny hodges sir cedric hardwick [*sic*]—cool things-aint-what-they-used-to-be unwink."[28] In a review of a 1947 Ellington concert that he found lacking in energy, a jazz critic for *Metronome* magazine wrote that the performance would have been improved "if Johnny Hodges didn't look disconcertingly like Sir Cedric Hardwicke playing the saxophone."[29] And his looks were average; not handsome but passable, as a Parisian prostitute once said of A. J. Liebling—"Tu n'es pas beau, mais t'es passable" ("You are not handsome, but you are passable").[30]

Hodges's tone was sensual, and the mesmerizing effect it had on female members of an audience was noted by multiple contemporaries; it was so seductive, according to one musician's wife, that she told her husband "never to leave her alone with him," because "whenever she heard [him] play she wanted 'to open up the bedroom door.'"[31] Jazz critic Dan Morgenstern recalled that when "the Ellington band was in residence [at the Apollo Theater], one waited for the moment when Duke would introduce Johnny Hodges. The always expressionless alto genius would slowly make his way to the solo mike (not that he needed it). When that first golden, glissandoed note issued forth, all the ladies would utter a collective sigh."[32] Ellington, never one to let a stray inspiration go to waste, told jazz critic Nat Hentoff that when "Hodges soloed . . . inevitably a sigh would come from one of the dancers, and 'that feeling . . . would become part of our music.'"[33] Rex Stewart said the band members "couldn't help noticing that he had a special something which was irresistible to the ladies. They oohed and aahed when he played and would have willingly gone home with him if he had beckoned."[34]

Hodges was, as one intimate of the two men put it, "rude" to Ellington "time and time again," and the reason may have been that, while Hodges was responsible for the orchestra's most sensuous sounds, it was the leader of the band who profited most from them. Hodges may have thought in his more bitter moods that, in the words of the old blues song, he was fattening frogs for snakes,[35] or playing John Alden to Ellington's Miles Standish. Both of Hodges's wives are known to have traveled with him while he was on the road, while Ellington generally had several girls in every port.[36] When Hodges was not accompanied by a spouse, he was rumored to have used the services of prostitutes, although anecdotes to this effect are understandably difficult to verify. The possibility that Ellington ever paid for sex cannot be ruled out entirely, but with his taller stature, good looks, and position as leader of one of the best-known jazz bands in the world, it is unlikely that he had to make a regular practice of it, especially once he achieved his first fame.

Outside the Ellington Constellation: The 1930s and 1940s

THE NAMES "J. Harjes" and "Cue Porter" mean nothing to the most learned jazz fan today, but the man who used them as camouflage was well known when those fictional sidemen appeared on recordings. The man behind these pseudonyms (and others) was Johnny Hodges, performing on dates with musicians including Earl Hines and Billy Strayhorn.[1]

After he joined the Ellington orchestra in 1928, Hodges would regularly record outside of Duke's auspices, sometimes when he was free to do so, at other times when he was prohibited by contract and thus forced to play incognito. Ellington would sometimes be accused of unfairly taking legal credit for works his musicians had created, but he was magnanimous in allowing them to earn extra money by playing with others. Several Ellingtonians benefited from this liberal moonlighting policy, but it was Hodges who was in greatest demand for a bandleader or producer looking to add the high gloss of his finish to a recording.

Hodges was a sideman on several sessions in the 1930s with Teddy Wilson, the pianist whose reserved but rhythmic style helped create the subcategory of jazz known as swing. On December 3, 1935, Hodges played with Wilson and singer Billie Holiday on three songs for the Brunswick label, "These 'n' That 'n' Those," "You Let Me Down," and "Spreadin' Rhythm Around." These are among Holiday's first recordings; she was young (twenty), and her sense of rhythm was buoyant. Recalling the sessions, Wilson told an interviewer, "I might have been more excited about working with Johnny Hodges [than Holiday]. He was an idol of mine. Those records are unique because every one of those men became a household word in the jazz world, though in those days we were all unknown, except for Johnny Hodges . . . and Benny Carter."[2]

On June 30, 1936, Hodges joined Wilson and Holiday to record four songs, two Tin Pan Alley numbers typical of the inferior material she was saddled with early in her career plus "These Foolish Things" and "I Cried for You," the first standard she ever recorded. On the former Hodges improvises behind Holiday's vocal in a sort of swing counterpoint, and on the latter he takes an extended introductory solo of the kind that would become characteristic of his style, hewing closely to the melody but embellishing it in a restrained manner.[3] "He gets an idea, thinks up a countermelody, and you end up with a whole new song," said trombonist Lawrence Brown. "Yet nobody seems to recognize him as the composer he is."[4] On March 31, 1937, Hodges, Carney, and fellow Ellingtonian Cootie Williams on trumpet were present for a Wilson-led session in which, among other numbers, they backed Holiday on "Moanin' Low,"[5] a bluesy vehicle that Hodges and Holiday resuscitated from the near-death experience it suffered at the hands of Libby Holman, the Broadway torch singer for whom it was written.

Two months later Hodges would play on four more songs with Wilson and Holiday, including two written for the Judy Garland film *Thoroughbreds Don't Cry*. The musicians assembled by John Hammond for this session were drawn from the bands of both Count Basie (including Lester Young) and Duke Ellington, and they do what they can with mediocre pop songs. "I'll Get By" and "Mean to Me," on the other hand, are worthy objects for Hodges and Young to sculpt away at; Hodges introduces "I'll Get By" and Young does the honors on "Mean to Me," with Hodges playing peek-a-boo behind Holiday's vocal as he had done in their previous collaborations.[6]

In all of these songs Hodges provides a tasteful complement to Holiday's singing, and Wilson features him as the principal soloist behind her. One is left to wonder what might have been had Otto Hardwick not flown through the window of a taxi in 1928, creating an opening in the Ellington orchestra. Hodges could have developed into a sensitive partner for Holiday on the alto comparable to Lester Young on the tenor, but he had steady work at good pay with Ellington's orchestra, an enterprise with recurring revenue from song royalties that offered him financial stability. He thus had no reason to take a chance as backup musician for a solo artist.

On April 29, 1938, Hodges was busy with Wilson again, recording with a group that included Bobby Hackett on cornet for recordings of "You Go to My Head," "I'll Dream Tonight," "Jungle Love," and "If I Were You."[7] On the last number, a Rodgers and Hart song,[8] Hodges is used in a manner that is typical of his gigs as a sideman: he provides an introductory sixteen-bar solo, hands things off to Hackett for eight bars, then returns for eight bars before yielding to a now-forgotten vocalist.

In late 1936 Wilson and Hodges backed vocalist Mildred Bailey as members of a drummerless combo arranged by producer John Hammond under the name "Mildred Bailey and Her Alley Cats." Bailey was a big woman with a Betty Boop–like little girl's voice that she used in a coquettish manner. Her first significant job was with Paul Whiteman, who featured her on ballads; she became so closely identified with Hoagy Carmichael's "Rockin' Chair" that she became known as "The Rockin' Chair Lady."[9] Hodges is featured on "Willow Tree," a New Orleans–style blues; "Honeysuckle Rose," on which he plays tag with Bailey as she sings the melody, then solos for sixteen bars; the Waller–Clarence Williams blues "Squeeze Me"; and "Down-Hearted Blues," by Alberta Hunter and Lovie Austin.[10]

Wilson was sufficiently pleased with Hodges's contributions to use him as the possible target of a retaliatory strike against Ellington. In 1942 Barney Bigard heard that Hodges had an offer to leave Ellington, and said, "I figured that I wouldn't be so happy if Johnny went," so he gave notice that he was quitting. Many big bands suffered financially during World War II, but Bigard wasn't motivated by money. "We were still getting the same salary with Duke, war or no war," he said, but he was tired of touring after fifteen years on the road.[11] Duke began to look for a replacement and fastened on Edmond Hall, who was playing with Wilson at the Downtown Café Society club. According to *DownBeat* magazine, "Hall refused the offer, and Wilson, possibly in retaliation, offered Hodges a job at the café."[12] Hodges turned it down, but the seed had been planted in his mind that there was life for him beyond Ellington's ducal manor.

Vibraphonist Lionel Hampton called on Hodges for several New York small-group recording dates in April 1937 that produced two noteworthy features for him. On "I Know That You Know"[13] Hodges—who, in the view of some, had no real precursors on alto sax in a jazz context—pays homage to Joe Poston, a Louisiana reedman who played with Fate Marable and who later became a member of Jimmie Noone's Apex Club Orchestra in Chicago. In that group he, like Hodges, was known to stick to the melody, allowing Noone to play counterpoint.[14]

The other song was "On the Sunny Side of the Street," the hit credited to Jimmy McHugh (composer) and Dorothy Fields (lyrics) but which some say Fats Waller wrote and sold in order to finance his lifestyle. The song had already been recorded by Louis Armstrong in 1933, and Satchmo's stamp on a tune was ordinarily sufficient to make further interpretations superfluous, but Hodges's rendition set a new standard among jazzmen, although it is not included in one list of noteworthy recordings of the song.[15] Hodges discovers in the melody what others had missed: a latent sadness that may be traced to a melancholy subtext, one detected by comedian and bandleader Steve Allen in his mystery novel *The Talk Show Murders*. It is that the lighter "sunny" side of the street referred to the benefits that could be enjoyed by a black person who could pass for white, a truth known to Waller if not Fields.[16]

The 1937 session with Hampton made a deep impression on Jess Stacy, the group's pianist, on loan from Benny Goodman. "His tone, and his phrasing— I was transfixed," he said of Hodges. "I was flabbergasted to be in the same room with him." Stacy wrote Hodges a fan letter saying "what a pleasure it was to work with him and how wonderful it sounded."[17]

In 1944 Hodges and three other Ellingtonians—tenor Ben Webster, trombonist Juan Tizol, and trumpeter Ray Nance—approached bandleader and clarinetist Woody Herman about the possibility of recording with him. According to Herman, their stated reason was that they "were unhappy about not getting enough attention" with Ellington. Herman felt that the complaint was unjustified. "I knew how Duke operated," he would later write. "If there had been reason for anybody in his band to get more attention, he would have made it possible. He was that kind of guy. They were unhappy nonetheless. . . . It didn't bother Duke. He told me[,] 'If you can make a buck, go ahead.' I jumped at the opportunity." And so on April 5, 1944, Hodges, Nance, and Tizol recorded four songs with Herman's band, including "Perdido," which Tizol had written.[18]

A month later Hodges joined Eddie Heywood Jr., one of his favorite pianists,[19] for a trio session, along with Shelly Manne on drums. Heywood first achieved notoriety on the New York jazz scene in 1939 with Benny Carter's band, but his career was interrupted in 1947 when he suffered partial paralysis in his hands; he recovered and returned to playing in 1951.[20] The songs on the album include "Flamingo," a Hodges-Heywood collaboration, and several standards.[21] As the only horn in the session, Hodges has ample opportunity to stretch his legs; the tempos of all the songs are moderate, the moods subdued. Heywood provides the rhythmic tracery for Hodges's figures, which are colorful but restrained, as with the best stained glass.

On April 26, 1944, Hodges would join a group led by Earl Hines that recorded for the Apollo record label.[22] Hines was forty years old and an elder statesman of jazz, having made some of the most important early recordings in the history of the genre sixteen years earlier with Louis Armstrong. His style was characterized by percussive octaves played with his right hand that enabled him to be heard without amplification over his band—"they could hear me out front," he would say.[23] The sound he got from his instrument was likened to a trumpet, and it served him well as a bandleader. A consummate professional, Hines had not been impressed with the discipline of the Ellington band when he had substituted for Duke earlier that year when the bandleader came down with a bad throat;[24] he noted, however, that "when they did get together they could tear the roof!"[25] The date with Hodges was a rebound attempt by Hines, who had recently lost Charlie Parker and Dizzy Gillespie to Billy Eckstine's newly formed big band.[26] Hodges's solos are relaxed and unhurried—at the age of thirty-seven, he had begun to settle into a jazz man's middle age.

Over the course of many years Hines had developed a lasting admiration for Hodges's playing. "You ever drink any cool, clean spring water?" he said.

You can add things to it, make lemonade, beer, coffee, or what have you, but when you're thirsty it's hard to beat it just as it is. And it's probably better for you than the kind hyped up with chlorine. Well, to me, Johnny was like that spring water—the real thing, unadulterated. He didn't change either. Maybe he added ideas as he went along, but he was always true to himself.[27]

Hines and Hodges would subsequently collaborate as co-leaders when Hodges's stature had risen to the lofty height that Hines then occupied.

In August 1944 Hodges was part of a group that recorded with bassist Billy Taylor as leader. Taylor started out with Elmer Snowden—a sax and banjo player who was a member of the Washingtonians, the group Ellington belonged to when he first moved to New York—then joined pianist Charlie Johnson's band and McKinney's Cotton Pickers. He switched to string bass from tuba and played with Fats Waller, then became a member of the Ellington orchestra in 1935.[28] The group went by the name "Billy Taylor's Big Eight" for the recording; Hodges plays on four songs, including "Night Wind," a lush vehicle written by him and Ellington that Rex Stewart claimed was based on his song "Finesse."[29] Because of contractual restrictions Hodges is identified on the cover as "Harvey the Rabbit," an allusion to the imaginary six-foot-tall rabbit featured in the 1944 play *Harvey*, later made into a movie featuring Jimmy Stewart.

In November 1945 Hodges and Harry Carney played on a small group recording with trombonist Sandy Williams as leader.[30] Williams had taken some lessons from Ellington's trombonist Juan Tizol when he was young and, after scuffling in his early years, played with both Horace and Fletcher Henderson before a long stay with Chick Webb.[31] The session is billed in the reissue's liner notes as a "small band pick-up date" that was "an important release, providing comparative freedom and soloing room, a contrast to the tight discipline of 'section' work."[32] This is less true of Hodges than of the other contributors, since he had ample time in the spotlight with his regular employer, but the four numbers provide him with the sort of ballads and jump blues that were comfortable vehicles for him.

9

The Small Groups

IN THE ANNALS of jazz there may be more unlikely encounters than the one between Duke Ellington and Helen Oakley in January 1934, but there can't have been many.

Oakley was a young woman from a wealthy Canadian family. As a girl she had been educated by English governesses, then sent to Switzerland for finishing school. She attended two private colleges without earning a degree and then "came out" to society at a debutante ball. Afterward, she traveled to London—a trip overseas being the traditional culmination of the debutante process—where she attended an Ellington concert in June 1933. A jazz enthusiast, Oakley realized she was not cut out for high society and persuaded her family to let her pursue a career as a singer in Detroit. They agreed, on the condition that she report periodically to a chaperone. When Ellington came through town she sent a note backstage that included a fabricated reference from a British jazz writer—"This girl is very knowledgeable"—and a request for a meeting. Ellington saw through the ruse but decided to see "the little debutante" anyway.[1] The two were simpatico, and it was the beginning of a relationship that bore much fruit.

Oakley eventually abandoned her musical ambitions and in 1934 moved to Chicago, turning to journalism and promotion. She founded a club for jazz enthusiasts, produced recording sessions, and organized performances for listening, not dancing, by artists such as Earl Hines and Billie Holiday. It was in this context that she brought together the Benny Goodman Trio—Goodman on clarinet, drummer Gene Krupa, and pianist Teddy Wilson.[2] This combination of musicians was important because it represented (in Goodman's words) "the first time . . . white and colored musicians had played together for a paying audience in America."[3] It marked a musical turning point as well.

Jazz ensembles had grown in scale from small groups to big bands in order to attract larger audiences, thereby making more money for promoters and musicians. Size had been an attraction, but it became a fiscal hazard as band payrolls grew; small-group jazz brought down the cost of a jazz performance or recording and at the same time allowed for effects more subtle than those allowed by a full orchestra. Goodman's trio and quartet ensembles (adding Lionel Hampton on vibraphone) had enjoyed success on the smaller scale, and Irving Mills, Ellington's manager, took note. There were other historical forces that created demand for small-group recordings, as well. When Prohibition was repealed in December 1933 roadhouses proliferated, and with them jukeboxes. Jukebox owners didn't want to pay high prices for music, and Ellington's records on the Brunswick label were expensive at seventy-five cents each. Recordings on competing labels cost thirty-five cents retail and about nineteen cents wholesale to jukebox operators. Ellington's band was priced out of this new market.[4]

Oakley (who would marry jazz critic Stanley Dance in 1947) on Ellington's recommendation. "Bring her to New York. Put her in the office. We need her," Ellington said.[5] In early 1937 Mills hired Oakley, and she soon orchestrated a jam session to introduce his new low-priced Variety records. The event was such a success that Mills put her in charge of recording dates for the label.[6]

Mills had pioneered the "band within a band" concept in about 1928, taking subsets of musicians from bands he managed and recording music by them (often under pseudonyms) that was hotter than the product of the parent group. According to Mercer Ellington, it was Oakley who persuaded Mills to make recordings by Ellington satellites (and price them at thirty-five cents apiece), while still recording the full orchestra and pricing those discs at seventy-five cents, but this overstates the case a bit since Ellington and Mills had used the small-group concept before she arrived.[7] For example, there was a 1935 recording by Duke Ellington's Sextet and a December 1936 recording by Rex Stewart and His 52nd Street Stompers, and Oakley said that she wasn't responsible for a March 1937 session by Cootie Williams and His Rug Cutters.[8] (Johnny Hodges played on the latter two sessions.) She may have had a hand in a March 25, 1937, session by the Gotham Stompers on which Hodges appeared, playing (among other tunes) "My Honey's Lovin' Arms," the song he played for Sidney Bechet when they first met.

What is clear is that Oakley was an advocate for Hodges. It took some effort to persuade Ellington that small-group recordings wouldn't undermine his "stature as composer and arranger acclaimed throughout the world." He "feared that the reduction of his palette might adversely affect his reputation," but there were other concerns, and they were specific to Hodges's growing popularity. Oakley said that the prime reason for the delay of Hodges's promotion to small-group leader was the concern that if he led off the series of recordings, he "would run away with the whole thing." If others went first, on the other hand, he would need to "live up to something."[9] Second, Hodges was usually the highest-paid musician in the band, in terms of both his weekly draw (which was sometimes more than Ellington's) and of piecework such as recording sessions.[10] So Ellington had to think of his other employees: "Duke knew there'd be no end to it if he gave in," Oakley wrote. "He had to show Johnny that the other guys were valuable too."[11] Thus Hodges was featured after Rex Stewart, Cootie Williams, and Barney Bigard. "Hodges' fans waited not too patiently," Oakley said, "since by now the Variety releases were creating a stir."[12]

The first session recorded under Hodges's name as leader took place on May 20, 1937. According to Oakley, decisions as to personnel on small-group dates were made jointly by Ellington and the session leader. "Johnny would have had a bit of say. But Johnny was sweet, too. He didn't like throwing his weight around. And he didn't want to hurt people's feelings."[13] The results were disappointing, primarily because of the material, which consisted of three sentimental pop tunes and "Peckin'," a number that trumpeter Harry James allegedly took from Cootie Williams's trumpet solo on "Rockin' in Rhythm."[14] As Stanley Dance put it, they were mostly "dog tunes,"[15] as were those chosen for Hodges's second session, which took place on January 19, 1938.

Then, in Oakley's view, came "the triumph of all triumphs": Hodges playing the blues. "They were mine," she would declare in a burst of forgivable (if somewhat excessive) pride. "All those things—Jeep's Blues—I mean, they were all mine . . . in the sense that they all knew that this is what I loved, and identified myself with." To Oakley, Hodges was "Mister Blues, so you had to do blues. . . . What a waste otherwise."[16] "Jeep's Blues" (originally titled "Johnny's Blues"),[17] a twelve-bar lament with Hodges on soprano, became a jukebox hit,[18] converting the streets of Harlem into a stereo corridor, according to Oakley:

When he made those things, Jeep's Blues, and all those titles which you must know as Johnny Hodges hits, Harlem rang with them. Corner after corner there were jukeboxes. And you could go forty blocks up Harlem and never stop hearing Johnny Hodges. It was gorgeous.[19]

And so Hodges had his first success under his own name. "Jeep's Blues" would remain part of the Ellington band's book even after Hodges's death, and it was recorded numerous times, both by others and again by Hodges on alto when he left Ellington in the early 1950s. Hodges also played it at the 1956 Newport Jazz Festival concert that revived Ellington's then-faded fortunes, in what turned out to be an unsuccessful effort to calm down an ecstatic crowd.

"Jeep's Blues" was backed with "Rendezvous With Rhythm," with Hodges getting the bulk of the solo time after a piano introduction by Ellington. Singer Mary McHugh is heard on the other two numbers recorded at this small-group session—"If You Were in My Place" and "I Let a Song Go Out of My Heart"—and in the view of jazz critic Nat Hentoff, she "sang with all the passion and dynamics of [U.S. Supreme Court] Justice William Rehnquist." McHugh had been imposed on Ellington by Irving Mills, who reasonably believed vocal numbers were more likely to be jukebox hits. When Oakley apologized for the concession to commercial considerations Hodges defended McHugh, saying, "She's kind of cute"—leading Hentoff to muse, "Who knows what makes for inspiration?"[20] According to Rex Stewart, "I Let a Song Go Out of My Heart" was based on "a riff that Johnny [Hodges] played behind the melody of the song 'Once in a While.'"[21] In 1940 the chord changes "were recycled for 'Never No Lament[,]' which in turn begat 'Don't Get Around Much Anymore.'"[22] Whatever Hodges's contribution was, he received credit for neither branch of the tree that grew from his seedling, both of which became hits for Ellington.

The first session, "with its mix of a slow blues, two ballads and a danceable mid-tempo tune," became the template for others that followed.[23] The August 24, 1938, date produced several numbers of note: "The Jeep Is Jumpin'," jointly credited to Ellington and Hodges but probably based primarily on a riff by the latter, is a miniature masterpiece that was widely recorded by others, including Ben Webster and Gene Krupa. Another song that bears discussion is "Krum Elbow Blues," jointly credited to Ellington and Hodges. The song is a "musical satire,"[24] in the words of Ellington scholar Steven Lasker, on the sensation created when "Negro pastor Father Divine moved in as President Roosevelt's neighbor"[25] on property formerly owned by Howland Spencer, an eccentric socialite farmer.

Spencer hated Roosevelt as a traitor to their class, and he hoped to embarrass the president by turning over his family's 425-acre estate, called Krum Elbow, to a multiracial cult profiled in the *New Yorker* article "Who Is This King of Glory?"[26] Spencer and Roosevelt had sparred over whether a resident on the west bank of the Hudson was entitled to use the name Krum Elbow, among other differences, and Spencer retaliated.[27] "I've given [Roosevelt] the first neighbor he's had in years, in Father Divine, who's not on relief,"[28] Spencer said, tongue deeply in cheek. Father Divine claimed to be an embodiment of God in human form; upon taking title to the property he painted "PEACE" in giant block letters on a building visible from Roosevelt's property across the river.[29] "Krum Elbow Blues" alternates between a snarling chorus that echoes the "jungle music" of Ellington's early years, a musical mimesis of the feud between the upper-crust combatants, and a lilting New Orleans–tinged verse by Hodges, a reflection of Father Divine's sweet disposition and his vague message of universal peace. It was a rare excursion into political controversy for Ellington and Hodges.

A further composition from the small group sessions, "Good Queen Bess," is noteworthy for the portrait it paints of Hodges's mother, Katie Swan Hodges, who was sixty-seven when the song was recorded.[30] "Good Queen Bess" was her nickname, perhaps given to by her grandchildren, whom she lived with and cared for when her son was on the road with his wife. The tune is genial, the rhythm comfortable, like a *hausfrau* bustling about her kitchen. "She was the one with little anecdotes and things," Hodges's daughter Lorna Hodges Mafata recalled near the end of her grandmother's life. "You'd think she was 60. She could not relate to [being] 94."[31]

Oakley's appraisal of the series of small-group blues recordings a half century later was that "it was a real peak there,"[32] and Hodges was the summit; more were recorded under his name (forty-six) than under the names of Cootie Williams (thirty-five), Barney Bigard (twenty-six), or Rex Stewart (nine). According to Oakley, the format for the sessions was loose:

> Nothing was ever planned, nor even dreamed up beforehand. Duke would seat himself at the piano, confident and relaxed. Johnny Hodges's insouciant attitude, adopted for the occasion, would alter Duke's expression, summoning a smile, and Carney would smile back. "Where do we go from here?" Duke might inquire mildly. . . . A few chords on the piano and Johnny would pick up his horn.[33]

Sometimes the inspiration came from an idle riff that one of the assembled sidemen tossed off. "Very little was written out," Oakley claimed. "Duke would reminisce at the keyboard until one or another of the men contributed a phrase. 'Crazy,' he might comment, with a smile, and all of a sudden, as though of itself, a theme would evolve."[34] Cootie Williams dissented from this romantic view of the musicians' creative process, however: "Most of the small group recordings were rehearsed beforehand and not made up in the studio," he said in a 1976 interview.[35] Hodges himself explained how the band, and he in particular, could play apparently complicated pieces with only little or no written music visible to an outsider such as Oakley:

> Say like [Ellington] would call a rehearsal at twelve o'clock [midnight] . . . and he'd probably rehearse some number of his, a brand new arrangement nobody [had] seen, nobody knows nothing about it. And he would rehearse it until probably three o'clock in the morning. Well, the first show, you would know . . . whether he was gonna play that and you'd probably have a solo to step out front and you'd have to play your solo, then you'd memorize your part. . . . So to keep from being embarrassed you'd learn that arrangement as quick as you could, that's the reason why nobody hardly ever used any music.[36]

The truth, as usual, probably lies somewhere in between, for the genius of the mystical body of the Ellington organism was its ability to synthesize composition by one or a few men and improvisation by the many.

The small-group sessions kept the Ellington organization grounded in the blues and connected to their African American roots. As the orchestra developed into an instrument for Ellington's more ambitious works, Cootie Williams noted, "Our type of music wasn't really for black people; most of everything we played was for white. While we were on tour we were playing mostly for white audiences. The rich, upper class of blacks would come but mostly we would be playing for whites. Yes, we did play the Savoy Ballroom but only for a night at a time, never for a weekly engagement. In the 1930s we played dance music for the aristocrats—waltzes and things like that—but when we broadcast it would be jazz."[37] The same distinction applied to the band's recordings; although there was great music to be heard on the seventy-five-cent recordings of the full orchestra, the earthier product—bluesy and hot—could be had for the poor man's price of just thirty-five cents.

10

Swee' Pea

ON DECEMBER 2, 1938, a young man arrived at a theater in Pittsburgh, Pennsylvania, to present himself to Duke Ellington. The meeting was arranged by friends who thought the neophyte—Billy Strayhorn—was a talented pianist who just needed a break to make it in the world of music. Short, neat, and bespectacled, Strayhorn had originally hoped to become a composer and pianist in the European classical mode. He was so dedicated in pursuit of his ambition that while still in grade school he got a job in order to earn money to buy a piano that his parents could not afford.[1]

He received a good musical education in high school and began to perform and compose ambitious pieces such as a Concerto for Piano and Percussion. Upon graduation he wanted to continue his formal musical education, but his family couldn't afford college and he wasn't offered financial aid by any school he looked into. Given the year (1934) and his race—he was African American—this was not surprising.[2]

Strayhorn continued to work until he'd saved enough to attend the Pittsburgh Musical Institute. He began to take classes there in 1936 but left in the spring of 1937 when an instructor whom he held in high regard died of a heart attack. He was introduced to jazz by friends who bought him an Art Tatum record. If any pianist was capable of persuading a classical music devotee that jazz offered as much potential to a would-be composer, it was Tatum, whose elaborations on pop melodies and jazz standards were works within works, like the interiors of Fabergé eggs. Strayhorn "literally wore [the record] out and had to buy another one," according to one friend. He came to admire the graceful, less ornate style of Teddy Wilson as well.[3]

After sitting in the audience while the band played its first set, Strayhorn made his way to Ellington's dressing room with William "Gus" Greenlee, the owner of two Pittsburgh night clubs. That Strayhorn met Ellington and not the leader of another band was a matter of chance; Greenlee was persuaded to help Strayhorn by his nephew, and Ellington's band happened to be the next one scheduled to play one of his clubs. Greenlee agreed that if he could set up an introduction with Ellington he would do so, and otherwise he'd "wait a week and introduce him to the next bandleader" he had booked, Count Basie.[4] (One wonders what would have happened to both men's bands had the timing been different.) Greenlee introduced Strayhorn, and Ellington, lying back with his eyes closed while he had his hair treated, said "Let me hear what you can do."

Strayhorn played "Sophisticated Lady" then "Solitude"—two familiar Ellington numbers that the band had just performed—twice each. The first time he played them as Ellington's band had, but the second time he added harmonic enhancements and key changes of his own that were distinctively different. Ellington was impressed. Harry Carney was summoned to listen after Strayhorn finished one number, then Carney was dispatched to bring Johnny Hodges and vocalist Ivie Anderson to hear the young phenomenon.[5]

Strayhorn played some of his own works for the assembled group: a then-untitled piece that became "Something to Live For"[6] and "Lonely Again," a song that was later rechristened "Lush Life."[7] Not sure how Strayhorn could be used on a full-time basis, Ellington began to give him piecework—assignments to write lyrics for an Ellington melody and a vocal arrangement for Anderson. Ellington paid Strayhorn twenty dollars for the latter, then left for New York after telling the young man he would "have to find some way of injecting" him into his organization.[8] When Strayhorn heard nothing from Ellington for about a month, he decided to track him down and, after a few unsuccessful attempts, managed to catch him right before he went onstage in Newark, New Jersey. Ever the diplomat, Ellington told Strayhorn he had just instructed his manager to locate him, and hired the young man without the usual formalities—no contract, title, or job description. "I don't have any position for you," Ellington said. "You'll do whatever you feel like doing."[9] Thus began a relationship that would change not only the sound of the Ellington orchestra but also the style of the man who would become its most famous soloist, Johnny Hodges.

Strayhorn first worked for Hodges on "Savoy Street,"[10] a joint Hodges-Ellington composition. Ellington ordered up an arrangement of that tune (along with "Like a Ship in the Night") for a February 1939 small group session to be recorded the next day at 10:00 A.M. Strayhorn had never dealt with such a tight deadline and an unfamiliar group of musicians. He worked through the night at the dining room table in Ellington's New York apartment. "What could I do?" he said with professional resignation. "I did it."[11] It is not clear where the border lies between the composers and the arranger on "Savoy Strut," a delicately bouncing tune, but when Ellington heard the final product he "didn't change a thing, and he was delighted," according to Helen Oakley. Strayhorn was given the responsibility for arranging most of the band's small-group recordings. "Oh, he did a little, but turned almost all of them over to me," Strayhorn said. "I had inherited a phase of Duke's organization."[12]

Strayhorn set to work while the orchestra left for a tour of Europe. He studied Ellington's scores, trying to decipher the method of his new master. As he would later describe this creative technique, "Each member of his band is to [Ellington] a distinctive tone color and set of emotions, which he mixes with others equally distinctive to produce a third thing, which I like to call the Ellington effect."[13] Strayhorn initially applied this approach to Hodges in "Day Dream" (credited to Strayhorn and Ellington), one of a number of works that he would create over the remainder of his life that gave the altoist a new canvas on which to paint his tonal colors, melodies fraught with melancholy, poignant and purgative. The American equivalent of *lieder* (German art songs), they produce—in the words of "Lush Life," Strayhorn's greatest lyric—smiles tinged with sadness. Hodges, whose dour demeanor concealed a romantic soul, became Strayhorn's instrumental voice of choice.

Strayhorn "had a wonderful way of scoring the band for ballads, especially behind Johnny," trombonist John Sanders would recall.[14] The Ellington "book" was already full of popular numbers when Strayhorn joined, so it took a while before he would hear his original works performed because the band had to satisfy audiences' expectations for a familiar repertoire, built up over many years. The playlist from the band's November 7, 1940, dance date in Fargo, North Dakota, reveals not a single Strayhorn composition, for example.[15] On January 3, 1941, the Strayhorn tune "Passion/A Flower Is a Lovesome Thing" was played for the first time at a concert by the Ellington orchestra in California,[16] and it would become a regular feature for Hodges over the years. This work, like "Day Dream" before it, was an early indication that Strayhorn could bring out a side of Hodges that had lain dormant before; Hodges's tone was plush, as were Strayhorn's harmonies, and Hodges began to wrap himself in new garments cut from Strayhorn's cloth.

There was, to give another early example, "Ballad for Very Tired and Very Sad Lotus Eaters," perhaps named after "The Lotos-Eaters," by Alfred, Lord Tennyson, which Strayhorn, who read widely in English literature, may have been familiar with. That poem speaks of music of the sort that Strayhorn would write for Hodges:

> *There is sweet music here that softer falls*
> *Than petals from blown roses on the grass,*
> . . .
> *Music that gentlier on the spirit lies,*
> *Than tir'd eyelids upon tir'd eyes;*
> *Music that brings sweet sleep down from the blissful skies.*[17]

Hodges and Strayhorn were similar in some respects: They were both short; they both used diminutive versions of their names, "Billy" and "Johnny," into adulthood; they shared a fondness for pretty scents;[18] and they both came to resent Ellington's giving them less credit for compositions (and less money for them) than they felt was their due. In Strayhorn's case, the purloined pieces included "Mood to Be Wooed," "The 'C' Jam Blues," and the "Sugar Hill Penthouse" movement of "Black, Brown and Beige,"[19] in Hodges's case the many blues riffs that Ellington transformed into complete songs, sometimes paying for them, sometimes crediting Hodges as co-composer, sometimes neither. In the words of Ellington's son Mercer, Hodges at first "sold his rights to songs for $100 or $200. . . . When Pop turned some of these songs into hits, Rab wanted the deal changed, and when he was refused he became unhappy. That explains why he would sometimes turn toward the piano onstage and mime counting money."[20] Both men would leave the Ellington fold at one point in their careers seeking more independence—and both would return.

Considered from other angles, the two were quite different. Strayhorn and Ellington were more friendly than not, while Hodges's relationship with his boss was often strained.[21] Strayhorn was a self-made intellectual, sophisticate and aesthete, and homosexual; Hodges was heterosexual, a no-nonsense type who prided himself on his journeyman's approach to his trade, planting his feet in a just-so manner before every solo, rejecting excessive complexity in arrangements, and disdaining the hubris he detected in Ellington's tone poems and other self-consciously "classical" works. One piece that Strayhorn composed exemplifies how the two men harmonized their difference in this regard and how Ellington trumped them both.

The tune was originally titled "Pretty Little Girl," a nod to the theme of flirtation that Hodges's music would explore throughout his career, released on a 1955 album titled *Creamy*. When Ellington was commissioned to write a work inspired by Shakespeare for the 1956 Stratford (Ontario) Music Festival he was, as usual, scurrying at the last minute to complete it. The man who said, "I don't need time. What I need is a deadline" called Strayhorn, who was writing new music for the work that would represent Romeo and Juliet, and told him to "steal from himself" using "Pretty Little Girl," which he had composed two years earlier. The song was accordingly incorporated into the larger work, *Such Sweet Thunder*.[22] When Jimmy Hamilton, who had played tenor sax and clarinet on the original version, heard the piece, now retitled "Star-Crossed Lovers," he said to Strayhorn, "You think nobody's going to remember this? Nobody going to forget this[,] man. This is the most beautiful thing you ever wrote." Strayhorn shrugged and said, "When Ellington has insisted, you know what we must do. We must do what we must do."[23]

Strayhorn acquired the nickname "Swee' Pea" after the baby who appeared in the Popeye comic strip and animated cartoons. Accounts differ as to who connected the man with the fictional character. Otto Hardwick had previously tagged Johnny Hodges with the name "Jeep" after another Popeye character, so he is one suspect; Ellington thought drummer Sonny Greer was responsible; and jazz critic Leonard Feather believed it was tenor Ben Webster.[24] As with Hodges's Popeye-based nickname, Strayhorn's moniker was apt: Swee' Pea is adopted by Popeye after the child is left on his doorstep, the way Ellington took Strayhorn in when the latter presented himself to the older man on the road, musically homeless. And Swee' Pea, like Strayhorn, is gentle and mischievous.[25]

In addition to their work on the small group sessions, Hodges and Strayhorn began to record together, beginning with *Creamy* in 1955, which featured Strayhorn's "Passion/A Flower Is a Lovesome Thing" and "Pretty Little Girl/Star Crossed Lovers," as well as two compositions by Hodges, "Honey Bunny" (the inevitable play on his principal nickname) and "No Use Kicking," which might be taken as a shorthand summary of Hodges's stoical philosophy of life. Hodges's wife Cue contributed "Scufflin.'"

The following year the two were involved in *Ellingtonia '56*, which combined numbers by the entire orchestra (excluding Ellington on piano) as well as smaller groups, in each case arranged by Strayhorn. Among the big band numbers is Strayhorn's "Snibor," named after Fred Robbins, a jazz disc jockey whose "Robbins Nest" program on various New York radio stations was a favorite of Strayhorn's ("Snibor" being "Robbins"—more or less—spelled backwards).[26] In 1956 *Duke's in Bed* brought Hodges and Strayhorn (on piano) together as "The Ellington All-Stars Without Duke," along with seven other Ellingtonians. In his liner notes jazz critic Bill Simon says that the record is "primarily a 'blowing' session," with Hodges featured but all of the musicians getting "plenty of room to solo." The album also included the first recording of Strayhorn's "Ballad for Very Tired and Very Sad Lotus Eaters," which, Simon wryly noted, doesn't require one "to be a lotus eater to appreciate."[27]

In 1957 Hodges and Strayhorn joined forces with fourteen other Ellington associates on *The Big Sound: Johnny Hodges and the Ellington Men*. Hodges was sole author of five of the twelve numbers: "Segdoh" (read it backwards for an instance of Hodges's love of wordplay, which belies his reputation as an illiterate); "Dust Bowl," for an area of Las Vegas that is known colloquially by that name and which Hodges, an inveterate gambler, may have known well; and "Little Rabbit Blues," "Gone and Crazy," and "Early Morning Rock," bluesy compositions that Hodges created off the top of his head but which in the hands of the classically inclined Strayhorn were transformed into works of greater harmonic subtlety. Strayhorn could write the blues (witness "Walkin' and Singin' the Blues," which he co-wrote with Ellington and vocalist Lil Greenwood), but the complaint against him by hard-core jazzbos was that he produced pretty stuff that wasn't black enough to be jazz or blues. That the two strains of music could be cross-pollinated to form a hybrid that lost the essential character of neither is demonstrated by this collective effort.

On April 14, 1959, Hodges and Strayhorn flew under a false flag to make *Cue for Saxophone,* an album on which both played but which could not bear Hodges's name because at the time he was under contract to producer Norman Granz. Hodges accordingly went by the *nomme de sax* Cue Porter, after his wife Cue and perhaps one of his father's occupations; along with five other musicians they were called the Billy Strayhorn Sextet. The record was one in a series of albums that Leonard Feather produced for a subsidiary of Decca Records; the genesis of the Hodges-Strayhorn edition was a conversation Feather had with Al Celley, Ellington's road manager, as the two sat in a cafeteria waiting for the band bus to arrive. When Feather said he was looking for artists who fit the description of "mainstream," Celley said, "Why don't you use some of our guys? They would like the money."[28] Strayhorn agreed despite some lingering hard feelings toward Stanley Dance, who would be writing the liner notes, for the latter had criticized his early work with Ellington as un-jazzlike with its "obsession for tone colour and voicing." According to Oliver Jackson, "Stanley and Billy, you know, I'd say kept away from each other. Billy and Rab (Hodges) were so close, man, that's the only reason Billy did the date."[29]

When told of the nature of the project, the two principal musicians pronounced themselves mystified by the concept of "mainstream" jazz, then went to a bar. They returned with a back-of-the-napkin arrangement of "Gone With the Wind" and a Hodges-Strayhorn original, "Watch Your Cue." They would add another of their co-compositions, "Cue's Blues Now," along with four other numbers. The irony is that the finished product, under Strayhorn's name, received high critical praise, earning the Grand Prix du Disque de Jazz pour Petit Orchestre (grand prize for small-group jazz record) from the Hot Club of France, while so many of his efforts for the full Ellington orchestra went unsung and uncredited. As drummer Oliver Jackson put it to the pianist, "Hey, Strays, isn't this something, man? All those things you did for Duke, and all the people think Duke did 'em? And here there's finally a record with your own name on it, and it's really Rab's!"[30]

Strayhorn had become estranged from Ellington for reasons both artistic—he began to chafe at the fact that he often received no public credit for pieces he worked on—and financial, because he had learned some fundamentals of the music business from Leonard Feather and concluded that he'd been deprived of royalties that were rightfully his.[31] As a result, he seemed indifferent to the task at hand and the plaudits that the record received. "I don't think Billy put very much into it. It was more like Johnny's kind of record," Cue Hodges said, and Jackson concurred: Strayhorn "showed up late, and he didn't have anything planned. He knocked off whatever arrangements we used off the top of his head."[32]

In 1961 Hodges and Strayhorn would collaborate on a full-length album for the last time, *Johnny Hodges, Soloist, Billy Strayhorn and the Orchestra*—"orchestra" referring to the band directed by Ellington, who went unnamed because of restrictions in his Columbia Records contract.[33] Neither Ellington nor Strayhorn plays on the album; Jimmy Jones handles the piano chores, and Strayhorn is referred to in the original liner notes as arranger and musical director. The music includes two Hodges originals: "Tailor Made" and "Juice A-Plenty," a "head" arrangement that, as Stanley Dance quips in the liner notes (unable to resist a pun), Hodges produced "as easily as some magicians produce rabbits from a hat."[34]

Hodges and Strayhorn must have enjoyed working together in the studio because the shy Strayhorn, who disliked performing in public, joined Hodges for a rare nightclub engagement in early 1958, along with a drummer and bassist.[35] The four were dubbed "The Indigos" in a discreet but hopeful allusion to "Mood Indigo," one of Ellington's most popular numbers. The group was resident at the Golden Strand Hotel in Miami Beach for two months, playing a mixture of Strayhorn compositions, features for Hodges, and standards. "They had a good little group," Cue Hodges said. "Swinging. The people enjoyed hearing them. Johnny liked his breaks from Ellington, and so did Billy."[36] During Hodges's leave of absence Ellington used Bill Graham, who would also play with Count Basie and Dizzy Gillespie in his career, on alto.[37]

Strayhorn would die at the age of fifty-one on May 31, 1967, and Ellington, though he may have taken advantage of his musical partner in the early years of their relationship, was duly and sincerely distraught. "Poor Little Sweet Pea," he wrote on that day,

> the biggest human being who ever lived, a man with the greatest courage, the most majestic artistic stature, a highly skilled musician whose impeccable taste commanded the respect of all musicians and the admiration of all listeners. His audience at home and abroad marveled at the grandeur of his talent and the mantle of tonal supremacy that he wore only with grace.[38]

As an orchestrator and arranger, Strayhorn soothed the savage breast of Ellington's "jungle" music, whose harmonies were regularly described as weird, and which were intentionally constructed to defy convention. When composer Percy Grainger invited the Ellington orchestra to play before a class at New York University, he compared Ellington to Bach and Frederick Delius, and Ellington admitted candidly, "I'll have to find out about this Delius."[39] Strayhorn surely would have known the man and his work. As a composer Strayhorn's legacy has grown dramatically since he died because his contribution is no longer obscured by the nimbus that surrounded the figure of Ellington while they lived.

Beginning three months after Strayhorn's death, Ellington began to put together a tribute album to his late collaborator titled . . . *And His Mother Called Him Bill,* which consisted exclusively of compositions by Strayhorn or joint Ellington-Strayhorn works. Hodges, the vessel for which Strayhorn mixed some of his most haunting melodic cocktails, pours out as libations solos on "Day Dream" and the Strayhorn compositions "My Little Brown Book," "Snibor," "After All," and "The Intimacy of the Blues." Finally "Blood Count" is heard. The song is Strayhorn's last feature for Hodges, which he revised as he lay dying and which was delivered to Ellington shortly before its premiere at a 1967 concert at Carnegie Hall.[40]

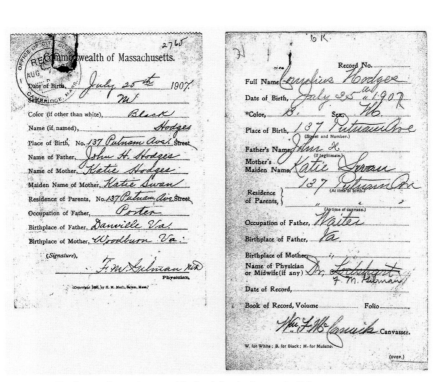

PLATE 1 Birth certificate showing Hodges's birth date to be July 25, 1907, contrary to accounts that he was born in 1906. His given name is Cornelius, not John.

PLATE 2 The house at 137 Putnam Avenue, Cambridge, Massachusetts, where Cornelius Hodges was born.

PLATE 3 The Duke Ellington band on the set of *Belle of the Nineties* starring Mae West, Los Angeles, California, March, 1934. The only band member who is shorter than Hodges is trumpeter Freddie Jenkins, and Hodges is a full head shorter than Ellington. Left to right, lower row: Snakehips Tucker, Juan Tizol, Arthur Whetsol, Ivie Anderson, Wellman Braud, Ellington, Fred Guy, Jenkins, Barney Bigard, Hodges, Lawrence Brown, Sonny Greer. Upper row: top, Joe Nanton; middle, Harry Carney; right, Otto Hardwick. (MPTV Images.)

PLATE 4 Hodges in a 1945 publicity photo, which was used in advertisements for Buescher saxophones. (Gilles Petard/Redfern/Getty Images.)

PLATE 5 Hodges performs at Cleveland's Sky Bar on May 27, 1951, a few months after breaking away from Duke Ellington. The date was billed as a jam session with a group dubbed "His All-Stars"; Sonny Greer on drums, Lloyd Trotman on bass, Lawrence Brown on trombone, and Al Sears on tenor sax. Two musicians are obscured; the trumpeter was probably Emmett Berry or Nelson Williams, and the pianist Leroy Lovett. Joseph Lauro collection, all rights reserved.

PLATE 6 Hodges was an avid gambler but in this photo he is merely kibitzing as Django Reinhardt joins Ellington band members on October 30, 1946, at the Aquarium Club in New York. Left to right: (unknown), Al Sears, Shelton Hemphill, Junior Raglin, Reinhardt, Lawrence Brown, Harry Carney, Hodges. (William P. Gottlieb/Ira and Leonore S. Gershwin Fund Collection, Music Division/Library of Congress.)

PLATE 7 Hodges (right) and tenor Al Sears, October 1946, at the Aquarium Club in New York. Sears would manage and play in the combo that Hodges put together when he left Duke Ellington in 1951 and would be featured on the group's biggest hit, "Castle Rock." (William P. Gottlieb/Ira and Leonore S. Gershwin Fund Collection, Music Division/Library of Congress.)

PLATE 8   Album cover by David Stone Martin for *Norman Granz' Jam Session # 1*, 1952. Appearing with Hodges on the album were Charlie Parker and Benny Carter, the other two leading alto saxophonists of his era. Hodges is depicted in the lower right-hand corner, below tenor Ben Webster (The David Stone Martin Estate.)

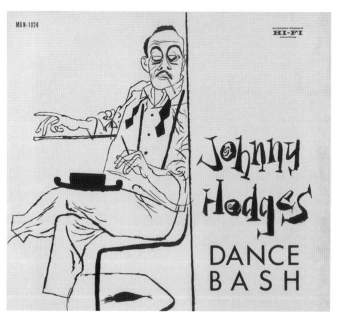

PLATE 9   Album cover by David Stone Martin for Hodges's *Dance Bash*, 1955. (The David Stone Martin Estate.)

PLATE 10 Photo by Esther Bubley of the July, 1952 jam session at Radio Recorders studio in Hollywood, California, produced by Norman Granz, which yielded music for two albums. Depicted left to right: Benny Carter, alto; Barney Kessell, guitar; Flip Phillips, tenor; Charlie Shavers, trumpet; Ray Brown, bass; Charlie Parker, alto; J.C. Heard, drums; Oscar Peterson, piano; Ben Webster, tenor; and Hodges. The closeness of Hodges to Webster is plain, as Hodges' arm is draped over Webster's thigh. David Stone Martin used this picture as the model for his album covers for the jam sessions, and Hodges' album "Dance Bash." (c) Jean Bubley/Estate of Esther Bubley/CTSIMAGES.

PLATE 11 Hodges in the Brasserie Lipp, St. Germain des Pres, Paris, watching as a waiter pours him a glass of white wine (probably sauterne) after he had given up hard liquor, November 1958. (© Herman Leonard Photography LLC/www.hermanleonard.com.)

PLATE 12 Harry Carney (baritone sax), Hodges, and Ellington at the Radio Recorders studio in Los Angeles, June 20, 1960. Carney's forty-two-year tenure with Ellington was the longest of any member of the orchestra. (Michael Ochs Archives/Stringer/Getty Images.)

PLATE 13 Trumpeter Cat Anderson, left, with Hodges, going to a gig. When the band traveled by bus Hodges would regularly claim what he considered to be the best seat, the first one on the right-hand side, which he felt was his due as the top soloist in the band. (Herb Snitzer/The LIFE Images Collection/Getty Images.)

PLATE 14 Johnny Hodges plays with his sixteen-year-old son John Hodges II, while Duke Ellington mugs for the camera at the April 1964 National Association of Broadcasters convention in Chicago. (Courtesy Johnson Publishing Company, LLC. All rights reserved.)

PLATE 15 Ellington, Benny Carter, and Hodges at the Newport Jazz Festival, July 6, 1968. The session was marked by confusion and what some considered favoritism toward Hodges by Ellington, but Carter brushed off the perceived slight in his characteristically gracious manner. (Tom Copi/Michael Ochs Archives/Getty Images.)

PLATE 16 A weary-looking Hodges displaying his sax to a young fan at a concert at the War Memorial Auditorium in Fort Lauderdale, Florida, February 8, 1969. (Public domain, State Archive of Florida, Roy Erickson, photographer.).

PLATE 17 Hodges's widow, Edith Cue Hodges, at his funeral in May 1970, with Russell Procope.

THE CITY OF NEW YORK
VITAL RECORDS CERTIFICATE

CERTIFICATE OF DEATH

JOHN HODGES 21

Certificate No. 156-70-110245

1. NAME OF DECEASED (Type or Print) — JOHN First Name — HODGES Last Name / Middle Name

MEDICAL CERTIFICATE OF DEATH (To be filled in by the Physician)

2. PLACE OF DEATH — a. New York City — b. Borough MANHATTAN — c. Name of Hospital or Institution. If not in hospital, street address — HARLEM HOSPITAL

3a. DATE AND HOUR OF DEATH — (Month) MAY — (Day) 11 — (Year) 1970 — 3b. Hour 4:30 PM — 4. SEX MALE — 5. APPROXIMATE AGE 62 YRS.

6. I HEREBY CERTIFY that, in accordance with the provisions of law, I took charge of the dead body
OFFICE OF CHIEF MEDICAL EXAMINER ... on ... 12: day of MAY 19 70
at 520 FIRST AVENUE, N. per above examination (with autopsy that in my opinion, death occurred on the date and at the hour stated above and resulted from (natural causes) and that the causes of death were:

PART 1
a. Immediate cause — HYPERTENSIVE CARDIOVASCULAR DISEASE.
b. Due to or as a consequence of — CARDIAC HYPERTROPHY.
c. Due to or a consequence of

PART 2 — Contributory causes

M.E. Case No. 4125 — Signed ... (Associate) (Medical Examiner) M.D.
MICHAEL BADEN

PERSONAL PARTICULARS (To be filled in by Funeral Director)

7. USUAL RESIDENCE — State New York — County Manhattan — City or Town New York City — d. Inside city limits (specify Yes or No) Yes
Street and house number 170 West End Ave. — f. Length of residence or stay in City of New York immediately prior to death. 42 Yrs.

8. SINGLE, MARRIED, WIDOWED or DIVORCED (Write in word) Married — 9. NAME OF SURVIVING SPOUSE (If wife, give maiden name) Edith Fitzgearld

10. DATE OF BIRTH OF DECEDENT — (Month) 7 — (Day) 25 — (Year) 1907 — 11. AGE at last birthday 62 Yrs. — If under year mos. days — If LESS than 1 day hrs. min.

12a. USUAL OCCUPATION (Kind of work done during most of working life, even if retired.) Musician — b. KIND of BUSINESS or INDUSTRY Band — 13. SOCIAL SECURITY NO. 111-07-0409

14. BIRTHPLACE (State or Foreign Country) Mass — 15. OF WHAT COUNTRY WAS DECEASED A CITIZEN AT TIME OF DEATH. U.S.A.

16. ANY OTHER NAME(s) BY WHICH DECEDENT WAS KNOWN — Johnny Hodges

17. NAME OF FATHER OF DECEDENT — John Hodges — 18. MAIDEN NAME OF MOTHER OF DECEDENT — Katie

19a. NAME OF INFORMANT Edith Hodges — b. RELATIONSHIP TO DECEASED Wife — c. ADDRESS 170 West End Ave.

20a. NAME OF CEMETERY OR CREMATORY Flushing Cemetery — b. LOCATION (City, Town or County and State) Brooklyn, N.Y. — c. DATE of Burial or 5/15/70

21a. FUNERAL DIRECTOR Wallace L. Jones — b. ADDRESS 1893 Amsterdam Ave. New York City

BUREAU OF RECORDS AND STATISTICS — DEPARTMENT OF HEALTH — THE CITY OF NEW YORK

Steven P. Schwartz, Ph.D., City Registrar

R 0 0 1 6 5 6 4 3

The City of New York

PLATE 18 Hodges's death certificate.

PLATE 19 Ellington and Hodges are depicted in a mural titled "Honor Roll" by Jameel Parker on the exterior of the Harriet Tubman House in Boston's South End, where Hodges grew up.

Originally composed as the first movement of his three-part work *The North by Northwest Suite* and titled "Blue Cloud," the piece was renamed to refer to a common laboratory test used to detect cancer and monitor its treatment. Strayhorn died of esophageal cancer, which is associated with the consumption of alcohol and tobacco, both of which he used heavily,[41] and he must have become familiar with the procedure as his life wound down. It was the second work with a medical theme he would compose, the other being "U.M.M.G." (for "Upper Manhattan Medical Group," the business entity through which Arthur Logan, Ellington's personal physician, practiced).[42]

That "U.M.M.G." came before "Blood Count" is apparent from the downward trajectory in the emotions expressed by the two songs: Composed in the early 1950s,[43] "U.M.M.G." is a hopeful enough tune to be played with a bounce even if it contains an undercurrent of sadness; listen, for example, to the Dizzy Gillespie version recorded in 1960, which moves at the stride one might expect of a man leaving his doctor's office who is thankful he still has, in the words of the Strayhorn song that became Ella Fitzgerald's favorite, something to live for. "Blood Count" is a darker piece, with forebodings of death, but free—in the words of one of Strayhorn's "Four Freedoms"—from self-pity. The song parallels Strayhorn's life in miniature: an ambiguous beginning and a struggle upwards; a peaceful plateau, then a modulation to a higher plane; a song of innocence that is a return to the man-child he was his whole life, then a climactic blaze of glory and a fade-out that ebbs away on a tide of resignation.

It has been said before, without stretching the truth, that when listening to their joint works, it is impossible to tell where Ellington left off and Strayhorn began. It can be said with equal accuracy that, when Hodges interpreted a Strayhorn tune, he became the embodiment of another man's artistic ideal, and the final product was a whole whose component parts could no longer be distinguished. To borrow a line from Yeats, you could no more separate the alto sax player from the man who composed with him in mind than you could separate the dancer from the dance.[44]

Blanton, Webster, and the Forties

IN THE AUTUMN of 1939 Billy Taylor, with whom Johnny Hodges would record in a small group five years later, had the misfortune to be the incumbent Ellington bassist when the orchestra played an engagement in St. Louis. Several members of the band, including Hodges, decided to visit an after-hours place known as Club 49, a favorite spot of jazz musicians passing through town. There they heard a bassist named Jimmie Blanton,[1] and Hodges went to the hotel, where Duke was already in his pajamas, and persuaded the bandleader to come hear the twenty-one-year-old musical find.[2] At the time, Blanton was employed by Fate Marable. Ellington sat in with his band and, when Marable asked, "How do you like my bass player?" Duke replied, "I was just going to ask you the same question. He's my bass player now."[3] When the St. Louis job ended and the Ellington orchestra headed for Chicago, Blanton went with them.[4]

Blanton had limited big band experience, but Ellington didn't care. "We wanted . . . that sound, that beat, and those precision notes in the right places." Ellington talked Blanton into joining the band for a few numbers the next night, and would later write that he "was a sensation, and that settled it. We had to have him . . . although our bass man at the time was Billy Taylor, one of the ace foundation-and-beat men." So Ellington had two basses until one night in Boston when, in the middle of a gig, Taylor packed up his instrument, saying, "I'm not going to stand up here next to that young boy playing all that bass and be embarrassed."[5]

In January 1940 Ellington dispatched Richard "Jonesy" Jones, man-of-all-work with the title "band boy," to find Ben Webster, a tenor sax player who was then a member of Teddy Wilson's group, and ask him to come see Duke. By his own account, Webster was drunk when the invitation was extended, but he said, "The news sobered me up in a second." He later recalled, "I immediately felt twenty years younger." When he reached Ellington's dressing room the bandleader casually asked, "Why don't you come to the rehearsal tomorrow morning?" by which Webster understood that he was being asked to join the band.[6] He played his first date with Ellington in Boston, although the particular date and venue are a matter of dispute.[7]

Webster had played with Ellington on an occasional basis since 1935 and had been angling for a permanent position with him even longer. "Every time I'd run across some of Duke's men I would ask for a job, because it was my ambition to join Duke," he recalled. When the invitation finally came, Webster said, "I just got so excited, it was a dream come true."[8] And so began a phase of the band's development that, though brief (Blanton would die on July 30, 1942, and Webster would leave in 1943),[9] is deemed deserving of its own musico-archaeological period: the Blanton-Webster Band.

The particular chemistry of the Blanton-Webster molecule was the product of multiple musical atoms: in 1939 Ellington had reached his fourth decade and had begun to achieve a corresponding level of maturity as a composer with works such as "Jack the Bear," about the folklore character who "ain't nowhere,"[10] and "Ko-Ko," his fierce rendering of Congo Square in New Orleans, where the African roots of jazz first sprouted green shoots in America. Webster was both an admirer and an imitator of Hodges, and he described his style as an "alto approach to the tenor" because he liked "Johnny [Hodges] and Jeff [Hilton Jefferson] and Benny [Carter] so much. [He'd] listened to them for so long. . . . [He took] each guy for what he [did]."[11] Webster began to mold his style after Hodges, noting, "I sat beside 'Rab' for four years, and he had so much feeling. To sit beside a man for four years must rub off on you."[12]

Just as the band hit its stride with the addition of Blanton and Webster, Hodges—with both Ellington and Billy Strayhorn composing numbers for him—accelerated to the head of the alto pack. In December 1939 *DownBeat* had declared him "certainly one of three top ranking altoists,"[13] but in 1940 he was ranked number one on the instrument in the *DownBeat* Readers Poll for the first time, a distinction he would earn for ten consecutive years. Webster, a proud man given to drink, would ultimately prove to be too much trouble even for Ellington's famously indulgent temperament and he was fired, although he claimed that he quit.[14] After Webster left, Hodges "was more or less completely in charge of ballads," according to Mercer Ellington. "He began to be featured after intermission at concerts, traditionally the prima donna spot in bands. The format normally featured one man per number, but it got so Johnny would always play three or four—whatever the audience demanded."[15]

One number that became a regular feature for Hodges was "Warm Valley," which he proclaimed one of his personal favorites.[16] Hodges's role in "the Ellington troupe," in the view of one critic, was "to talk of love, usually in a detumescent, floating phrase,"[17] and in the case of "Warm Valley" this judgment was especially true; the inspiration for the song was the fruits of the female groin, as recounted by trumpeter Rex Stewart, who was sitting next to Ellington as they rode in a train through "a succession of undulating, gently molded hills . . . [and] Duke remarked[,] 'Look at that! Why, that's a perfect replica of a female reclining in complete relaxation, so unashamedly exposing her warm valley.'"[18] The song was first recorded in October 1940 during a particularly creative period for Ellington as a composer and the band as a whole.[19] Billy Strayhorn participated in the writing process, but his contributions, for once, went unused. "We wrote reams and reams and reams of music on that," he said, "and he threw it all out except what you hear. He didn't use any of mine." When Hodges left the band in the early fifties, his solo was given to tenor Paul Gonsalves. "You see we wouldn't give it to another alto to play," Strayhorn said.[20]

World War II was being fought during the first half of the decade, and on April 1, 1944, Hodges, along with several other Ellington band members, was classified 1-A, meaning that they were eligible to be drafted into the armed forces.[21] He was never called up, but he had an impact on at least one member of the Allied forces, a young English sailor named Ray Bonner, whose ship was torpedoed in the Atlantic. While staying in New York he went to hear the Ellington band play at the Hurricane Club and said, "It was during this set that Johnny Hodges played a long solo on a slow number which sent shivers up my spine and influenced my appreciation of instrumental jazz for the rest of my life."[22]

During the 1940s Ellington would realize his ambition to play Carnegie Hall, beginning with a concert in January 1943 at which he introduced *Black, Brown and Beige*, his "tone parallel to the history of the Negro in America." A song from this work called "Come Sunday" represents his people's church-going side, whose importance could be measured, as Ellington once explained, by the fact that Harlem has "more churches than cabarets."[23] It became a feature for Hodges. Rex Stewart, whom critic John Hammond had panned for a lack of feeling, said that "the first time he heard Hodges play the glorious 'Come Sunday' theme . . . tears came to his eyes."[24]

Around the time of the first Carnegie Hall concert Hodges began to employ more frequently "the exaggerated *glissandi* and slurs which were to become associated with his playing from this period onwards," according to

G. E. Lambert. The advent of this "sinuous, smoother manner," in contrast
to the "concise phrasing of his early solos,"[25] sometimes attracted the critique
that his style had turned *schmaltzy*, from the German word for rendered
poultry fat, a term that (since the mid-1930s) has come to refer to art that
is excessively sentimental.[26] This was a charge that would dog Hodges until
the end of his days, especially after he recorded an album with sweet music
bandleader Lawrence Welk in the 1960s, despite his continued use of blues
themes and techniques and his association with hot numbers such as "The
Jeep Is Jumpin'."

Ellington's aspirations for classical composition were criticized by some
on the grounds that they represented a denatured form of jazz. Paul Bowles of
the *New York Herald Tribune*, for example, wrote that

> between dance numbers there were "symphonic" bridges played out of
> tempo. This dangerous tendency to tamper with the tempo within the
> piece showed far too many times in the evening. If there is no regular
> beat, there can be no syncopation, and thus no tension, no jazz. The
> whole attempt to fuse jazz as a form with art music should be discour-
> aged. The two exist at such distances that the listener cannot get them
> both into focus at the same time.[27]

The criticism would be repeated over the years. Of the fourth Carnegie
Hall concert in January of 1946, reviewer Howard Taubman wrote, "Some of
the sections from the extensive suites prepared for concerts . . . come perilously
close to being a bore, and that's not what you expect from Ellington. The great
virtue of jazz is its sense of spontaneity[;] there are times when Ellington's
band 'arranges' the freshness out of it."[28] By contrast, Hodges's playing in the
most prestigious venue for classical music in America was singled out for
praise, with one critic saying that the alto "once again creamed the crowd dry"
at the fifth Ellington concert there in November 1946.[29]

John Hammond claimed that Ellington had "spent most of his recent
years escaping from the harsh reality that faces even the most secure among
Negroes" and that the praise of critics had caused him to try to "prove . . . he
could write really important" music "far removed from the simplicity and
charm of his earlier tunes."[30] Ellington's sin, in Hammond's view, was to produce "material farther and farther away from dance music," for which "blues
and other folk music had been his primary source of inspiration."[31] Hodges
may have been thinking the same thing; he had seen Cootie Williams, Rex
Stewart, Barney Bigard, and Otto Hardwick leave Ellington for more money

or to pursue their particular muses, and a few years later he would decide to do the same.

Hodges's stature continued to grow despite the artistic controversy that his boss's musical ambitions generated. *DownBeat* reviewers regularly found his playing to be "brilliant,"[32] "breath taking,"[33] "superb,"[34] "magnificent,"[35] and "lovely."[36] Of his playing in *Jump for Joy*, one of Ellington's several unsuccessful attempts to write a musical, a reviewer wrote, "Hodges came through with some marvelous soprano saxing. It's a mystery why this man wasn't spotted [i.e., put in the spotlight] more often."[37] The show was a high-minded attempt by Ellington to "take Uncle Tom out of the theater, eliminate the stereotyped image [of blacks] that had been exploited by Hollywood and Broadway, and say things that would make the audience think,"[38] but Hodges couldn't save it. It closed after eleven weeks and 101 performances.

In recognition of his status as the orchestra's premier soloist, Hodges's name began to be highlighted in advertisements for the band's dates. He received top billing in ads for a show at Chicago's Regal Theater on May 25, 1945, and for a one-week engagement in the summer of that year at New York's Apollo Theater.[39] In 1946, 1948, and 1949 he was listed first for dates in Washington, New York, and Chicago, in one instance with his last name in capital letters.[40]

During this period *Esquire* magazine was both a reporter on the jazz scene and a tastemaker, producing rankings of musicians on the various instruments of jazz orchestration. In 1943 Hodges placed first on alto sax ahead of Benny Carter and James Ostend "Pete" Brown, who led a group of his own and played as a member of trumpeter Frankie Newton's band.[41] *Esquire* would broaden its sample in 1944, asking sixteen aficionados, including Leonard Feather and John Hammond, which player they thought was the best on the saxophone generally, without regard to pitch. Hodges finished a distant second to tenor Coleman Hawkins, with Benny Carter a close third.[42] Hodges appeared in the Second Annual *Esquire* All American Jazz Concert on January 17, 1945, at the Los Angeles Philharmonic and the Third Annual *Esquire* All American Jazz Concert at the Ritz Theater in New York. He would also play as a member of Leonard Feather's *Esquire* All Americans on a January 10, 1946, recording session for Victor in New York.[43]

Metronome, the long-running music magazine that shifted its focus to jazz with the coming of the swing era, was also a booster of Hodges during the 1940s. In May 1945 Leonard Feather and Barry Ulanov, writing under the pen name "Two Deuces," found Hodges's rendition of "Mood to Be Wooed" to be "seductive alto saxology at its best."[44] A reviewer in January 1946 praised his solos on "The Wonder of You" and "I'm Just a Lucky So-and-So" as "first-rate . . . tasteful, in handsome tone."[45] In June of that year the maga-zine reported that Hodges "brought down the house with his liquid sax work on Magenta Haze," performed at a concert at the Watergate in Washington, DC.[46] On December 17, 1946, Hodges recorded "Sweet Lorraine" and "Nat Meets June" with the *Metronome* All Stars for Columbia in New York, along with Harry Carney and Lawrence Brown.[47] And in March 1947 *Metronome* described Hodges's "typical scooped pitch . . . alto" as "another decorous presentation of the most practiced of all jazz musicians in the gentle art of innuendo."[48]

DownBeat provided Hodges and his Ellington bandmates with compa-rable recognition during the second half of the decade beginning in March 1945, when Hodges won the gold award for alto sax, while Lawrence Brown and Harry Carney took silver on their instruments and Ellington won the swing band award.[49] These awards were followed by a concert at the Civic Opera House in Chicago in January 1946 at which Hodges and Carney re-ceived trophies for preeminence on their instruments.[50] In January 1947 Hodges and bandmates Carney and Brown, along with Billy Strayhorn (as arranger) received awards at a *DownBeat* concert in Chicago, with Duke Ellington as bandleader winning both for swing band *and* sweet band.[51] On December 29, 1948, the new issue of *DownBeat* announced ten awards for Ellingtonians, including Ellington, Hodges, Carney, Strayhorn, vocalist Al Hibbler, Lawrence Brown, Ben Webster, Jimmy Hamilton, and Sonny Greer.[52]

By February 1949 times were so bad for big bands that Ellington was forced to deny rumors that his orchestra was breaking up after a week-long engagement at the Million Dollar Theater in Los Angeles. He admitted to the *Capitol News* that he had an enormous payroll, however, saying, "Johnny Hodges gets $500 a week . . . whether the band plays or not,"[53] and the burden of maintaining twenty full-time musicians would soon turn the big bands into dinosaurs headed for extinction.

A year later, while *DownBeat* found it apt to describe its annual awards dinner in Chicago as a "Yearly Ducal Ceremony,"[54] for the first time in a decade Hodges did not place first on his instrument. Instead, the winner was Charlie Parker. The future had arrived.

12

Food and Drink

THERE WEREN'T MANY aspects of life that caused Johnny Hodges to drop his customary reserve, but food was one of them.

He was, according to several accounts, both a good cook himself and a lover of fine foods prepared by others; his reputation preceded him to the extent that chefs would prepare special dishes for him when he dined at their restaurants. He would often wait to see what others would order before making his selection. On a 1968 tour of Latin America, for example, Hodges is depicted by Stanley Dance in Mexico as "patrol[ling] the tables to decide which dish looks the most appetizing, muttering the while about nonexistent pork chops."[1] Later, in Argentina, he expressed enthusiasm for the local cuisine.[2] He was particular about his groceries, ordering ripe New England tomatoes in August by telephoning friends.[3] Although he learned to adjust to air travel when that mode of transit replaced the trains that carried the band in its earlier days, the one aspect of commercial aviation he never grew to tolerate was the food: "Ol' stroganoff again," he would grumble when a stewardess plopped that inevitable beef dish on his tray table.[4]

It is fair to say that he was just as much a gourmand as a gourmet, for he had a tall appetite for a short man. Early in his career a profile of the Ellington band that appeared in *Metronome* noted this paradox: Johnny Hodges, the anonymous author wrote, is "one of those small men who loves ... the wing of any chicken ... always has a box of food that's quickly devoured by the sea-gullic Ellingtonians ... spends his winnings on lamb chops and peas."[5] On a later occasion a waiter in Hollywood served him a smaller portion of beef than his companion received, and Hodges objected, saying, "Just because I'm smaller than he is, do you think I can't eat as much?"[6] A private man who avoided the press, he was persuaded by *Melody Maker*'s Maurice Burman to sit for an interview in exchange for a tray of sandwiches and a bottle of orangeade. After just six questions Hodges rose to go, taking the food with him as well as the drink, which he spilled when the exit door swung back on him, causing Russell Procope and Harry Carney to let loose with a raucous cheer in the manner of high school wags who loudly applaud when one of their fellow students trips and drops his tray.[7]

Food was a matter of such importance for Hodges that he used it as a metaphor for his music, by which he earned his daily bread. At a December 1938 recording date that produced the composition ultimately known as "Hodge Podge," Hodges asserted his rights in a work that Ellington had fashioned from a riff of his by saying, "Come out of my kitchen!"[8] Ellington backed down, and Hodges was credited as co-composer. Over the years, Hodges would use the phrase to warn off imitators of his style as well as poachers of his melodies, according to Ellington.[9]

As for liquor, an occupational hazard for one who made his living in places where alcohol was served, Hodges could take it or leave it alone. Until late in life he drank both Canadian whiskey (he favored Seagram's VO) and gin, and then, when his doctors recommended that he give up drinking, he switched to sauterne, a semi-sweet white wine.[10] He also drank beer, and on the 1968 tour of South America he enjoyed the local Rio Segundo brand so much that he wrote a song about it. Then—anticipating the craft beer movement that began a few years later—he joined in a conversation disparaging American beers by comparison to those made in Mexico, Brazil, and Argentina.[11]

Hodges "liked whiskey, but he was not its slave,"[12] according to Stanley Dance. On the other hand, when someone else was buying, Hodges would imbibe freely. A jazz enthusiast who encountered Hodges in a London pub in 1963 saw his "drinking allowance for the entire weekend" evaporate when he offered to buy Hodges a drink. The sax man ordered a double gin, which he proceeded to drink down quickly because he was on a break between shows at a nearby theater. When the fan got up to leave so that he wouldn't miss the second set, Hodges replied wearily, "I wouldn't worry about that. We're going to play the same shit we played in the first."[13]

Hodges's temperance may have been self-imposed, but it received reinforcement from Ellington, who would punish a musician who showed the effects of alcohol by calling a number that featured him. The bandleader would loudly praise the soloist, then launch into "yet another solo showcase for the not-too-steady soul. And sometimes a third solo in a row," according to Nat Hentoff, who said that Hodges was the victim of this form of torture on a May 1964 date in Chicago. "It was impossible for Hodges to play a poor solo," Hentoff said, "but it is intriguing to hear the mildly inebriated saxophonist doing just a little slipping and sliding, although he always recovers."[14] Just a year later, as the band practiced the music from Ellington's first Sacred Concert for an album, Hodges had either learned his lesson or outgrown the need to resort to alcohol to get through the tedium of rehearsal. Rex Stewart's corner of the studio "became very popular as various members stopped by, paper cups in hand, ready for a little taste" from a "bar" that consisted of one bottle each of vodka and bourbon. Stewart noted that "change was evident as the elder statesmen [Hodges, Cootie Williams and Harry Carney] did not join the youngsters."[15]

As for drugs, Stanley Dance writes that Hodges "was never a drug addict,"[16] which suggests—perhaps unintentionally—that Hodges sampled drugs but rejected them. Hodges had seen what heroin did to John Coltrane, whom he had to fire because of his habit, and Paul Gonsalves, who is seen nodding off on stage in one concert film,[17] and so he had first-hand experience to warn him of the dangers of the harder stuff. Other evidence supports the conclusion that Hodges was never a user at all. "There was a period," wrote Ellington's son Mercer, who became band manager in 1964,

> when the logical thing for people to do in show business was to smoke pot instead of drinking whiskey. It made sense for a number of reasons. You weren't hung over when the effect of the exhilaration wore off, and you were supposed to be able to think or keep yourself more balanced through the time of the high. So for a while everybody took to pot because they felt it was healthier, more constructive.... Eventually... they went back to whiskey. Whiskey lasted longer and was more sociable. You could drink it in public places, be seen doing it.... Pot was underground and chancy, and when you had begun to get prestige through your ability pot could harm your social acceptance.[18]

Yet when pot became fashionable among the young, Hodges was contemptuous. "These kids coming along now are really ridiculous!" he said once when the subject came up, according to Mercer Ellington.[19] And jazz scholar and critic Gary Giddins tells the story of students who offered Hodges a joint at a 1969 college concert in Iowa. "If looks could kill," Giddins recalled, "Johnny would have done for them with one glare."[20]

13

The Coming of Bird

IN THE OCTOBER 1, 1944, issue of *DownBeat* a reviewer gave readers his impression of singer Billy Eckstine's new band, which included several former members of the Earl Hines orchestra such as trumpeter Dizzy Gillespie and an alto saxophonist named Charlie Parker. "Driving force behind the reeds is Charlie Parker, destined to take his place *behind* Hodges as a stylist on alto sax" (author's emphasis).[1] It is difficult in retrospect to imagine that Johnny Hodges was once ranked ahead of Charlie Parker, now considered the greatest jazz practitioner of the alto of all time, but Hodges had won the *DownBeat* Readers Poll for alto saxophonists every year since 1940, and he would go on to win the poll five more times before the tastes of that magazine's readers caught up to Parker's new musical syntax and elevated him to first place.

Parker was known as "Yardbird" because of his fondness for chicken;[2] the fowl are referred to colloquially as "yardbirds" in areas where they are raised for food in poor people's yards. That moniker was shortened over time to "Bird," which proved more durable because it suggested the stratospheric heights of invention to which Parker flew, far beyond the previously known limits of his instrument. As Ralph Ellison wrote, "Parker was a most inventive melodist, in bird-watcher's terminology, a true songster."[3]

While still in his teens Parker moved from Kansas City, Kansas, to Kansas City, Missouri, where he found a place to live near Vine Street, a center of night life during the corrupt administration of Mayor Tom Pendergast. The nightclubs there never closed; entertainment was needed for the patrons, and an independent strain of regional jazz developed, a cross between music that made its way up two rivers from New Orleans and the sounds heard by radio from New York. It was a tough school for a young man to learn in; one night in 1936 when Parker joined a jam session and didn't perform to the exacting standards of the other musicians (including members of Count Basie's band), drummer Jo Jones sent a cymbal flying across the dance floor to register his low opinion of Parker's style.[4] Harder metal is formed in hotter crucibles, however, and Parker was determined to prove himself.

On Thanksgiving Day 1936, Parker traveled to the Lake of the Ozarks, a resort area southeast of Kansas City, for a gig. As the car he was traveling in neared Musser's Ozark Tavern, the site of the job, it hit a wet patch and skidded off the road, rolling over several times. Three of Parker's ribs were broken, and his spine was fractured. Parker used the period of idleness during his recovery to "woodshed" and improve his technique. He began to practice constantly, and when he returned to Kansas City the following autumn, "the difference was unbelievable," according to bassist Gene Ramey. " 'Here comes this guy,' the cats used to say. 'He's a drag.' They couldn't believe it, because six months before he had been like a cryin' saxophone player."[5]

Parker's transformation into a protean improviser wasn't complete until he moved to New York in 1939 and was exposed to musicians who were pushing jazz's harmonic boundaries. One was Tadd Dameron, the inventive pianist and arranger whom Parker may have first encountered when both were associated with Harlan Leonard and the Rockets, a Kansas City band.[6] According to Dameron's account, Parker was cleaning a club during the lean years when he couldn't find work as a musician, and he joined an after-hours jam session. Dameron said, "I could hear his message. . . . We were playing Lady Be Good and there's some changes I played in the middle where he just stopped playing and ran over and kissed me on the cheek. He said[,] 'That's what I've been hearing all my life, but nobody plays those changes.' "[7]

Another musician who influenced Bird's thinking was William "Biddy" Fleet, a journeyman guitarist whose career extended back to the time of Jelly Roll Morton.[8] Bird had tired of the standard chord changes of the swing era and was looking for new models. "I kept thinking there's bound to be something else," he said in a 1949 *DownBeat* interview. "I could hear it sometimes, but I couldn't play it." Fleet showed Parker new jazz progressions, and one night while playing "Cherokee" Parker realized he could achieve the effect he had been searching for by using the higher intervals of a chord as a melody and running those notes through changes. In Bird's words, he "came alive" with the realization, and bebop was born.[9]

The birth of one style in an art form generally means the death of another, but only after a long period of decline such as that which passed before Parker dethroned Hodges. Parker slowly came to the attention of other musicians, but "they couldn't figure what Bird was doing, because they had their minds set on Johnny Hodges, Benny Carter," according to Fleet. "These was [*sic*] the top alto men. . . . They were playing the *right* horn. They were playing right changes and doing a beautiful job at it. What Bird did, Bird played the right changes and, where they would go from one chord to another, Bird played that in-between. And *that* made his playing sound different."[10] Parker's innovations went beyond the harmonic to the rhythmic. As bassist Chubby Jackson said,

> When bop first came out it was very amazing to all of us. We were used to the milky alto saxophones of Benny Carter, Willie Smith, and Johnny Hodges and more melodic-type of passages. Then the staccato concept came through with Dizzy and Bird, and at first it was a little raucous. It was cooking, but it was so strange.[11]

The transition in fashion from mellifluous to manic in turn upset the prevailing conventions by which an altoist's tone was judged.

Hodges is said to have disapproved of Parker's style at first, as a member of the old guard in any trade might react to an innovative newcomer with a disruptive approach. Ben Webster, as devoted an acolyte of Hodges as anyone, took Parker into one of his groups over Hodges's protests. "Nobody wanted to let him play with us, not even Ellington," Webster reportedly said. "But I saw how talented he was right from the start."[12] On first hearing Parker, Webster was shocked by his facility at high speeds: "That was quite a thrill. The guy scared me to death," he said.[13] But Webster also sounded a cautionary note: "This kid will mess up a gang, a real big gang of saxophone players," he said. "He won't disturb me, because I'm only trying to play the little that I know how to play, but you watch! He will really destroy a lot of saxophone players!"[14]

Similarly, Hodges—like the tree standing by the water in the old spiritual— was unmoved by the new wind that blew in from Kansas City. He had great respect for Parker, but he refused to change in response to the bop revolution. "A lot of 'em tried to jump on the Charlie Parker bandwagon—but there was only one," Hodges said later. "I don't think you get any credit for trying to copy somebody's style." Instead, Hodges stuck with the tone and phrasing that were uniquely his. "I've just seemed to stay at one particular style for a good many years—and haven't changed," he said in 1964. "Other people probably went along with this style and came back. But I still stayed where I was. That's where I'm at. I'm still here. Too late for me to change now."[15]

Parker ultimately expressed regret that he had sacrificed tone and phrasing to speed. In an anecdote recounted by Michael Segell, Parker rented a studio near one occupied by Jimmy Abato, a saxophonist who had played with Claude Thornhill, among others. Abato gave lessons, and Parker would sometimes stop practicing when he heard Abato talk to a student about "intonation, the blend of colors in [the] sound, control." Abato's mantra was, "The sound of a saxophone is all about control." One day Abato heard a knock and opened the door to find Parker, asking if he could sit in on a lesson. After it was over, the two went to a bar where, according to Abato, Parker

> started to cry, tears running out of his eyes. He says, "You know, I must have hurt a lot of young saxophone players." I say, "What are you talking about, you're the god of this thing." He says, "No, I never liked the way I sounded, and I'm sure kids all over who listen to my recordings think this is the way the saxophone should sound." He liked what he was doing, but didn't like his sound, and he felt like he'd badly influenced a whole generation of saxophone players.[16]

Ralph Ellison described Parker's tone as "vibratoless" and thought that Bird and his imitators made a virtue out of necessity, that their thinner sounds—with timbres that were "flat or shrill"—reflected "amateurish ineffectuality," as though they were incapable of creating the full-bodied notes of Hodges and others who preceded them.[17] This judgment is too harsh; the beboppers *could* have created the sounds of earlier players, but they didn't want to. The damage to the existing order had been done, however, and a strange new beauty, as Mallarmé said of Degas, had been born.

The sound of Hodges' alto, unlike Parker's, had a broad appeal, according to Jimmy Heath, who emulated Hodges and Benny Carter before he heard Parker, then switched his allegiance. Hodges "had the kind of sound that was beyond the instrument," he said. "It sang. It was so personal and so beautiful that people just liked his sound and its special quality. The mass audience wouldn't appreciate Charlie Parker like they did Hodges," Heath claimed. In his view Hodges

> could have gone to any country town in the South and played the saxophone and people would have liked it better than what Parker was doing, which was very fast and modern. Hodges's sound is the sound of music. It was a beautiful, pleasant sound, no unnecessary tricks, no sophisticated chord sequences.[18]

Hodges would eventually grow tired of comparisons with Parker. On a 1964 date in Liverpool, England, he complained that nobody ever talked to him about anything except Charlie Parker and Sidney Bechet.[19]

The changing of the alto guard from Hodges to Parker represented a transition in jazz from a music in which intellect was subordinate to emotion, to one that reversed that order; whereas previously jazz was primarily a music to dance to or at least to move one's body rhythmically to, it now became a music to be listened to—thoughtfully. Although even the most ardent of Hodges's fans would rank him below Parker by some absolute standards—primarily, the two players' relative virtuosity and improvisational creativity—these are not the only dimensions of assessment. As Ezra Pound put it, "music begins to atrophy when it departs too far from the dance,"[20] and on this point Pound had a bebop counterpart: Dizzy Gillespie, who said, "Jazz should be danceable. That's the original idea, and even when it's too fast . . . it should always be rhythmic enough to make you wanna move. When you get away from that movement, you get away from the whole idea."[21]

The Ellington orchestra had played a major role in American social dance, as a reviewer noted in covering a 1942 date in Chicago: "Dance music, dance styles, dance bands have all risen through some form of exploitation of Duke's ideas. . . . Always a leader, the Duke *is* dance music, jazz, and swing. . . . His is a music of cultured restraint where dance music, per se, is concerned."[22] It was nonetheless the case that Ellington's band created jazz that was sufficiently sophisticated to cause audiences to sit rather than get up and dance. "Of all our band leaders he best succeeds in making jazz seem an end in itself and not merely an invitation to dance," wrote Howard Barnes in the *New York Herald Tribune* in 1930.[23] In January 1934, following a performance at the Palace Theater in Akron, Ohio, a reviewer wrote, "More than any of the colored shows that have been on local stages in recent weeks, Ellington's places the burden of entertainment upon music. And surprisingly he has turned his band away from the swift syncopations of the radio to a concert style that is as much more entertaining as it is radically different."[24] In July 1937 the Ellington orchestra moved a critic in attendance at a concert in New York to say that the band was "distinguished from all other Negro outfits in that it sells itself with music rather than roof-raising noise and clownish antics."[25]

There were at least two explanations for the Ellington orchestra's production of music to be listened to, rather than danced to. The first was Ellington's own artistic ambition, which was of the highest order; he continually sparred with critic John Hammond, who thought his more complex works represented an abandonment of the music of his people, and while his symphonic works may sometimes strike the ear as pastiches that don't constitute a coherent artistic whole, they were important forms of self-justification for him. The second was the complex nature of the Ellington book, which was composed, like a coral reef, of musical elements of varying intensity over time. The band's shows at the Cotton Club were part minstrelsy, part dance revue, and part hot dance music for patrons, but during the first set, in the early hours of a typical performance, the fare was low-volume *tafelmusik* (a German word meaning "table music"), comparable in an American vernacular to that composed by Telemann, to be listened to while dining; Ellington's Washington, DC, contractor-cum-manager Louis Thomas referred to it as "under-conversation music."[26] Hodges once explained this practice from his perspective in the reed section: "Like when we play dances or something. . . . Sometimes in places like small clubs we're supposed to play real soft for the first hour," he told an interviewer in 1964. "If I have to do that it doesn't bother me at all."[27] Ellington thus developed early on a repertoire of music that was not intended to be danced to, and he demanded a listener's level of attention until the end of his composing days.

The connection between jazz and dance may strike a current fan of either art form as curious, but it was once common. The enjoyment of jazz was not always the intellectual exercise it is today, when it is either performed before seated audiences or absorbed privately in a stationary state. For most of its history, jazz was the music that accompanied American social dance; Ellington's band played dances throughout his career, the last just two months before his death in May 1974,[28] and he incorporated dancers into his act from the earliest days at the Cotton Club to the Sacred Concerts near the end of his life, when he used Bunny Briggs to depict the theme of "David Danced Before the Lord With All His Might."[29] When Hodges went out on his own he played dances as well, as evidenced by a picture of his group, with Al Sears soloing, before a group of ecstatic dancing college students during Hodges's sabbatical from Ellington.[30] Many songs from the Ellington book that have come to be considered jazz classics—"Caravan," "Cotton Tail," "Harlem Air-Shaft," "Mood Indigo," and "Ko-Ko," to name just a few—were labeled foxtrots when issued on records, and thus were intended as music for dancing.[31]

Despite his symphonic aspirations, Ellington "loved the excitement of clubs and dance halls, and around this time, when jitterbugging to jazz rather than shaking to rock 'n' roll was what the young did, the frenzy at dances he played was often intense," according to Derek Jewell. Some fans objected to Ellington's danceable numbers, in contrast to critic John Hammond, who criticized Ellington when his music started to develop from popular dance rhythms into longer forms. Of those high-browed fans who didn't want their listening experience to be sullied by the innocent joy of dancing, Duke cracked, "If they'd been told it was a Balkan folk dance, they'd think it was wonderful." [32] In 1971, near the end of his life, Ellington was asked whether jazz was music for dancing. "To ask whether jazz is music for dancing is to introduce a category or classification I resist," said the man who resisted categories throughout his life, "but I would say that our music is intended to inspire or sustain dancing." [33] Ellington harmonized the two different ends to which his music, which he referred to as the "music of our race," was put, thus: "What we know as 'jazz' is something more than dance music. When we dance it is not mere diversion or social accomplishment. It expresses our personality, and right down in us our souls react to the elemental but eternal rhythm." [34]

The criticism of bebop by those who enjoyed dancing to swing music was that you couldn't dance to bop, to which. Gillespie rejoined, "I could dance my ass off to it. They could have, too, if they had tried." [35] Others disagreed; when Ralph Ellison was asked to describe the reaction of New Yorkers to bebop, he said it "was mixed because most people couldn't dance to bop. Few people were capable of dancing to it; it was more of a listener's music." [36] Gillespie, conscious of his obligations as an entertainer, would dance solo after a fashion when playing with his big band, but according to Ellison, when he played in a small-group setting with Parker the two "often were so engrossed with their experiments that they didn't provide enough music for the supportive rite of dancing." [37]

Another force that hastened jazz's transformation from dance music to a listener's genre was the federal "cabaret tax" imposed in 1944 on all receipts of "any venue that served food and drink and allowed dancing." Originally imposed at the rate of 30%, later reduced to 20%, the tax was initially thought to affect only upscale nightspots, but as interpreted by the federal taxing authority it was applied to "any room in any hotel, restaurant, hall or other public place where music or dancing privileges or any other entertainment, except instrumental or mechanical music alone," was provided along with food or beverages. [38] Thus, owners of bars, hotels, and restaurants had a financial incentive to prohibit dancing and to book only instrumental music.

And so the beboppers arrived on the scene. "The spotlight was on instrumentalists because of the prohibitive entertainment taxes," said drummer Max Roach, and the dancers headed for the exits. [39] The art form had changed—matured in one sense, lost its innocence in another—and an intellectual aesthetic replaced the emotional one. Unlike the music of its African roots, bebop didn't require communal participation beyond the nod of a head, the snap of a finger, or an occasional shout of appreciation, and it lost a large part of its audience as a result. Upon leaving Parker's quintet in 1951, trumpeter Red Rodney formed his own group, and his manager got on the phone to find him work. On a call to the owner of a Boston-area club, his manager started his spiel by saying, "I got this terrific bebop band for you . . ."

The line went dead.[40]

14

The Rabbit Strays

THE SUCCESS OF Hodges's small-group recordings brought him name recognition and made him stand out from the crowd of Ellingtonians, causing his value in the market for sidemen to rise. In 1942 jazz critic and producer John Hammond tried to persuade Hodges to join a racially integrated band he was assembling for the CBS television network under the direction of Raymond Scott.[1] Scott had started his career as a staff pianist for CBS in 1931 and was named music director in 1938.[2] According to drummer Stan Shaw, who played in one of his configurations, Scott's arrangement with CBS "was absolutely unique because at that time they hired conductors and then they assigned the musicians to go and play with them. Raymond Scott's deal was that they hired him and I don't know whether he had free rein to hire everybody in the orchestra or if he had to use a certain percentage of staff musicians, but he had the freedom to hire a lot of people. So he hired *a lot* of jazz musicians."[3] Among the distinguished players who worked under his direction was Ben Webster—but not Johnny Hodges.[4]

Hodges turned down Hammond's offer of $125 per week, about $1,800 in today's dollars,[5] a rejection that wasn't well-received. A persistent critic of Ellington over the length of their respective careers, Hammond wrote Hodges a sharply worded letter that was included in an article in *Orchestra World* by Leonard Feather headlined "Hodges Refuses Scott Offer; He's Accused of Sabotage!"[6] A recurring theme in Hammond's unfavorable view of Ellington's music was that the composer had "purposely kept himself from any contact with the troubles of his people" and that consequently his music lacked "the slightest semblance of guts."[7] Duke was becoming, in Hammond's view, a black musician for white audiences, affecting a musical sophistication that was a rejection of his racial heritage.[8] Hodges responded by saying, "Duke Ellington and his orchestra have done more for the advancement and dignity of the colored musician than Hammond and Scott will ever do."⁹ The tone of the statement is uncharacteristically high-flown for Hodges, leading one to suspect that it came from the pen of a publicist and not the lips of the alto, who might have produced a saltier reply.

After the incident, Hammond began to lump Hodges in with Ellington as a target of his brickbats. Hammond had persistently sniped at Ellington in an effort to persuade him to make his orchestra conform to his ideal of what a jazz band should be, but he had previously exempted Hodges from his fire. That changed with Hammond's broadside "Is the Duke Deserting Jazz?" in the May 1943 issue of *Jazz,* in which Hammond gave Hodges a mixed review for his play at the first Carnegie Hall concert, saying that Hodges was his "favorite of all alto men" but that he "turned on the schmaltz in 'Day Dreams' [*sic*], with the result that the audience loved it and would gladly have had an encore."¹⁰

Hodges's decision to turn down the position with CBS was one of several occasions on which he would decide to stay with Ellington, opting for life on the road instead of a more comfortable position. In June 1948, when Ellington went to Europe to recover from surgery and took only trumpeter-violinist Ray Nance and vocalist Kay Davis with him because of the restrictions imposed by the British musicians' union, the rest of the band was at loose ends and small combo jazz broke out, as if by spontaneous combustion. Hodges and fellow Ellingtonian Russell Procope sat in with organist Wild Bill Davis one night at a bar in Atlantic City while on vacation, receiving an enthusiastic response from an audience that included the owner of New York's Apollo Bar, who encouraged Hodges to put together a "little band" to play in his club.

Hodges assembled a group that included Billy Strayhorn (piano), Tyree Glenn (trombone), Jimmy Hamilton (clarinet), Sonny Greer (drums), Al Hibbler (vocals), and later Junior Raglan (bass), and in Hodges's words they put "125th Street on the map again."¹¹ The engagement lasted three weeks, and upon Ellington's return from Europe he "got right off the boat and came to the Apollo Bar to find out what was going on, and whether we were going to continue with this little band," Hodges said. "But we were loyal, and we broke the band up, and came back."¹² The reunion on August 10, 1948, has been described as a "welcome home party" for Ellington thrown by Hodges and his group, which makes it sound as if absence had made the hearts of those left at home grow fonder of their boss.¹³

Ellington managed to keep his orchestra together during the forties when other big bands failed, in part because he could subsidize his operation with royalties from his many compositions.¹⁴ Small groups, on the other hand, were thriving; their overhead was lower, and they typically played a bouncier style of jazz that lent itself to livelier dancing. A leading practitioner of this more energetic mode was rhythm and blues alto man Louis Jordan and his tight combo, the Tympani Five.[15] The new style anticipated rock 'n' roll and appealed to younger listeners and dancers to whom Ellington's outfit, which had been around for two decades, represented their parents' music. Hodges had begun to grumble about leaving as the big band era declined. "For a couple of years before he finally left, Johnny told Duke he was going to go," recalled his wife, Cue. "Duke said, 'What do you want to do? Make your own records? You can do that with me.'"[16] And he did make his own records, including an album made from three April 1950 sessions in Paris that included expatriate tenor Don Byas, recorded while the Ellington band was touring Europe.[17] But that apparently wasn't enough for Hodges.

Hodges considered his time as a small-group bandleader at the Apollo Bar a success, and with that experience still fresh in his mind, he became more receptive to overtures to leave Ellington. "That was just a little preview," Hodges recalled in 1964, "and it turned out all right. So we decided to try it again."[18] Sonny Greer was an early co-conspirator: "Now and then Johnny and I would talk about the summer of '48 when we had such a ball playing at the Apollo Café. We were talking about it one night on the road, when he told me he was going to leave the band and go with Norman Granz, and asked me if I wanted to come."[19] Granz, described by jazz critic Whitney Balliett as a "lean, fast-talking, sandy-haired man . . . with bullying eyebrows," was a tireless producer of jazz records and performances who, in Balliett's words, "is generally regarded as the first person who has ever been able to successfully mass-produce jazz."[20] Since Hodges was dissatisfied with his lot as a subordinate star in another's man constellation, Granz encountered no resistance when he made his pitch: "I didn't have to persuade Johnny," he said. "All he wanted was the financial and organizational support to permit him to pull the plug with Duke."[21]

After the fact, Hodges said that Ellington had tried to persuade him to take over the orchestra along with Billy Strayhorn during the band's 1950 tour of Europe because "he had some picture work to do over there" but that Hodges had declined because he "didn't want to do it then."[22] This claim has some surface plausibility because Ellington had made a short film for Universal-International in 1950[23] and had toured Europe with personnel that differed slightly from his regular lineup.[24] Hodges would give as additional justification for his decision to leave that "there was a rumor that [Ellington] was gonna retire and he was going back to Europe for this picture and stay over there for about a year," but no additional support has been found for that assertion.[25]

Hodges had quit the Ellington outfit before, according to lyricist Don George, who collaborated with Ellington, but these breaks must have been too brief to be detected by the jazz press, and George does not identify them.[26] A saxophonist named Eddie Logan, now lost to history, is said to have substituted for Hodges on Ellington tours of New England; perhaps Hodges took time off to visit family or childhood friends when he was near Boston.[27] In January or February 1951 (accounts differ),[28] Hodges took the leader's leap of faith and made a very public break with Ellington along with a two other defectors from the orchestra, drummer Sonny Greer and trombonist Lawrence Brown. They were joined by Ellington alumni Al Sears on tenor and Joe Benjamin on bass, along with pianist Leroy Lovett and trumpeter Nelson Williams (who was soon replaced by Emmett Berry).[29] "I decided to do it, see," Hodges said, "with the influence of a couple of guys who urged me on to do this so I tried it."[30] Within a month the group played a "break-in" engagement at the Newark Holiday Inn (with Lloyd Trotman replacing Benjamin on bass), and shortly thereafter on March 9, 1951, they had their first formal gig at the Blue Note in Chicago, complete with new uniforms.[31] The group featured a rotating cast of characters during its lifespan; in one of his rare interviews Hodges fondly recalled picking out music for a lineup that included Brown on trombone, Berry on trumpet, Harold Francis on piano, Arthur Clark on tenor, Allan Walker on drums, and Barney Richmond on bass.[32]

After the fact, Granz was candid about the role he played in Hodges's departure. "Sure I pulled Johnny and the others out of the band," he told Derek Jewell. "I'd used him on jam sessions, and from time to time after the war I'd presented Duke's band in concerts."[33] The reason Granz gave for aiding and abetting the getaway was that he felt Hodges had been "kept down" by Ellington,[34] and he wanted to record him as a featured artist "outside of the Ellington context." Hodges had received more solo opportunities than any other musician in the band, but Ellington needed to balance competing egos by giving other musicians a fair share of time in the spotlight. Ralph Ellison suspected that the motives of promoters such as Granz weren't purely aesthetic, saying, "The big bands were broken up by agents who convinced sidemen that they would make more money by going on the road as members or leaders of small combos."[35] Granz had a financial interest in luring Hodges away from Ellington: he signed him to tour and record for his record labels. Ellington—who could be magnanimous when a musician asked for time off or freedom to play or record with others—reacted with uncharacteristic bitterness. Granz recalled, Ellington "didn't call me directly, [but] he let it be known that he thought I was making a terrible mistake—Johnny wasn't good enough to make it under his own name. This came from Duke, who had been producing Johnny as a small-band solo act for many years."[36]

There had been tension between Hodges and Ellington in the past, but it had generally been kept in check. On one occasion Hodges made a casual remark that Ellington considered a slur on his beloved mother, Daisy. According to arranger Jimmy Jones, Ellington "picked Johnny up off the ground and held him there—Johnny was a whole lot shorter of course—with his feet dangling off the ground and told him, 'Don't you ever say anything like that again.'"[37] Ellington's reaction was entirely in character with the reverence he expressed for his mother by other means, and on other occasions: when fêted at a seventieth birthday party at the White House by President Richard M. Nixon, he acknowledged the honor by saying, "There is no place I would rather be tonight, except in my mother's arms"; he never forgave John Hammond for panning his *Reminiscing in Tempo*, a mournful piece he wrote as a musical expression of his grief over his mother's death; and he broke with his long-time manager Irving Mills when he discovered that Mills falsely claimed to have spent $5,000 to buy his mother "the most expensive casket made" but instead had chosen a model that cost only $3,500.[38] Ellington may also have used the provocation of the allegedly insensitive remark to put Hodges in his place; Hodges was known for his dry wit, and he usually used it to good effect, defusing tension among band members with a well-timed quip. That he used his humor in an offensive manner on a subject as sensitive as another man's mother reveals the depths of resentment he must have felt toward his employer; as Freud pointed out, sometimes humor is used indirectly to express hostility toward superiors that social norms forbid us from expressing directly.[39]

Hodges had on another occasion expressed a sharply disparaging assessment of Ellington's claim to jazz preeminence to cornetist Ruby Braff. "Duke and Johnny Hodges had long periods when they didn't speak to each other," Braff said, continuing,

> At one time they lived in the same apartment block. I was waiting with Johnny Hodges outside the building for a cab one time when Duke came down, also looking for a cab. They didn't speak but Johnny said to me loudly[,] "What do you think about a guy who has to have a whole band to say what he wants to say? What do you think about a guy like Louis Armstrong, who can speak for himself all on his own and make the whole world listen?[40]

Familiarity breeds contempt, of course, but the animosity implicit in these remarks betrays a deeper antipathy than one would expect merely from constant exposure. Hodges sounded as if he felt, at least on this occasion, that Ellington's success was undeserved. At other times he was complimentary of the bandleader's piano playing, work ethic, and creativity, but he was also—at least during this period of his life—bitter; he began to feel that he was capable of leading his own group and making the money a front man earned, and perhaps reaping the other benefits that accrue to men who are successful entertainers. Ellington had not one but several girls in every town. "Duke would check into two, three or four hotels, hand out keys to different ladies, then later on, pick out the hotel room he wanted to go to," according to Don George.[41] Ellington had both a wife, Edna, from whom he was permanently separated, and two long-term live-in mistresses, Mildred Dixon and Beatrice "Evie" Ellis, who indulged his philandering ways; he used these apparently conventional relationships as foils to keep women he dallied with from getting too close to him. Hodges, on the other hand, married two women who traveled with him when they could, as did the wives of only a few other Ellingtonians, such as Tyree Glenn. "The wives," according to Helen Oakley, "were a separate unit,"[42] but Hodges's wives kept him on a short leash. It may have been galling for Hodges, whose solos inspired romantic thoughts in the minds of so many women, to see Ellington reap the fruit of the seeds he'd sown.

Cue Hodges revealed that her husband was aware of the damage he'd done by departing, although he denied any spiteful intent: "Johnny knew Duke was hurt. That wasn't what he wanted. He wanted something good for himself. He didn't want something bad for Duke."[43] Publicly, Hodges cited artistic reasons for the departure. "We didn't like the tone poems too much. The boys like to stick to the old stuff,"[44] he said diplomatically at the time, but after he returned, when one might expect hard feelings to have softened, he was blunter; on a tour of England, Scotland, and Wales in 1958,[45] when asked by Maurice Burman of *Melody Maker* what he thought of Ellington's "programme," he responded, "I wouldn't say. What he likes and what I like are two different things."[46] The repertoire of Johnny Hodges and His Orchestra (or in a smaller configuration, the Johnny Hodges Septet) was, accordingly, made up largely of familiar tunes from the Ellington catalog, jazz standards, and a few originals.[47] Over the course of his career Hodges had been put off by music that was unduly complex, preferring simplicity as the proper setting for his style. "He would make this sound pretty," Billy Strayhorn said of musical ideas he would develop for Hodges. "When you get into it, when you write it, there may be some awkward technical aspect that he will point out to you as concerning his performance. You don't want *that*. . . . If he says, 'This is awkward here. This is an awkward position of notes,' then you say, 'Is it truly? Is it impossible?' If he keeps trying it, and it is impossible, you say 'Well, all right, I'll change it.'"[48]

Hodges's distaste for Ellington's high-brow aspirations was in part a matter of personal musical disposition, since he was a font of blues riffs and a student of the New Orleans school whose headmaster Sidney Bechet considered an ability to sigh-read music to be unnecessary, even an encumbrance for a jazz musician. But it was also a function of the fact that Hodges, although he had taken more instruction than he would claim (perhaps preferring to be thought of as a primitive), was not a quick study. During the 1960s Tony Bennett's music director, John Bunce, began to use the Ellington band to rehearse his arrangements. At one such session Hodges put down his horn halfway through the first number and walked out of the room, forcing the band to take a five-minute break. Russell Procope told Bunce not to take it personally—Hodges was merely angry at himself because he couldn't read his parts. After Procope played the music for Hodges he picked it up quickly, as usual.[49]

Trombonist Lawrence Brown echoed, in slightly different terms, Hodges's musical rationale for wanting to leave:

> When I left in 1951, it was because I was tired of the sameness of the big band. It's the worst thing in the world if you get in a big band and have to play the same old mess night after night, show after show, especially if you're doing theatres. Pretty soon, you know, you just can't play anything. Things were at their peak when I quit so far as my money was concerned, but the flexibility of the small band, the opportunity to spread out, make it interesting to the musician. And Johnny Hodges had a terrific little band.[50]

Tenor Al Sears gave a more mercenary reason for the Ellington personnel's decision to leave their apparently comfortable and secure gig. The orchestra had just made a West Coast swing on which some musicians had failed to show up for dates. As a form of discipline and in response to the prevailing business climate for big bands, Ellington decreed that he was going to cut wages when the band got back to New York.[51] Money had long been a source of friction between Ellington and Hodges. Even after Hodges rejoined Ellington and the latter's son Mercer became the band's manager, Hodges demanded that he be paid in cash on a daily basis, forcing Mercer to carry large wads of bills with him. "I don't trust myself or anyone else," Hodges said. "When I was pickin' cotton I used to get paid at the end of every day. I want to owe nothin' to anyone and have nothin' owed to me either."[52] One assumes that Hodges's image of himself as a boyhood field hand is fictitious, there being no cotton fields in either Cambridge or Boston, but it reveals his self-pitying view of his financial situation compared to Ellington's.

Sears, whose full name was the punnish "Albert Omega," served as manager of Hodges's group from its beginnings at the request of Cue Hodges and Helen Procope, Russell's wife.[53] Sears was three years younger than Hodges and had replaced him on alto in Chick Webb's band when Hodges joined Duke Ellington in 1928.[54] During his five-year tenure with the Ellington orchestra (for which Hodges had recommended him), Sears functioned as Ellington's personal manager, inspiring the leader to adopt the phrase "You take care of it, Searsy!" as the universal solvent to operational problems, major and minor.[55] Sears handled the business side of Hodges's group with energy and dispatch, procuring dates that the diffident and taciturn Hodges probably could not have obtained on his own. When he left the group in 1952 Sears had lined up eight months' worth of bookings, so the group was in good shape despite his departure, at least for a while.[56]

Sears was also the source of the group's greatest popular success; he was featured on "Castle Rock," a rhythm and blues number on which Hodges didn't solo. In the words of Stanley Dance, the piece appealed to audiences who "were then shrinking from the complexities of the new jazz and finding some comfort in R&B."[57] In 1951, the year Ike Turner's early rock 'n' roll record "Rocket 88" was released (and four years before Bill Haley and the Comets released their seminal hit "Rock Around the Clock"), Sears gave a copy of "Castle Rock" to disc jockey Alan Freed, an early promoter of rock 'n' roll.[58] With its steady beat, early date of provenance, and links to Freed, "Castle Rock" may thus be entitled to a small share of the credit—or blame, depending on one's view—for the birth of the music that would displace jazz in Americans' hearts and wallets. Sears didn't let pop acclaim inflate his assessment of the relative merits of his talents compared to those of Hodges, however. "Johnny would play something really beautiful," Sears said, "and then I'd get up, stomp my foot and break the house up."[59] When Sears left, Hodges replaced him with Arthur "Babe" Clarke and Ernie Scott for live performances and used Flip Phillips and Ben Webster for studio dates when Granz wanted an upgrade at tenor.[60] Then sometime in late 1953 or early 1954—accounts differ—Hodges hired a young tenor who had first been recorded while a member of the Melody Masters, the U.S. Navy's swing band at Pearl Harbor, Hawaii.[61] The new man was John Coltrane.

It is hard to believe, a half century after Johnny Hodges and John Coltrane died, that Hodges was Coltrane's first model,[62] but it was so. Then he and Benny Golson "went to see Dizzy Gillespie perform with Charlie Parker; from that point he emulated Parker."[63] Hodges's shimmering tone was the central element of his style; Coltrane's had less luster to it, despite the efforts he supposedly made to imitate the older player's sound. The object of a Coltrane fan's adoration is the tenor player's fecund musical imagination, not his tone. Hodges, on the other hand, was more of an inspired primitive, to use a term that Whitney Balliett applied to Ellington's players with a few exceptions (including Hodges) in describing their landmark 1940 performance at the Crystal Ballroom in Fargo, North Dakota.[64] Tone and phrasing were paramount to Hodges, but not to Coltrane.

The lack of resemblance between the tones the two men achieved on their respective instruments was not for lack of trying on Coltrane's part. When he was starting out, Coltrane tried to achieve legato phrasing but could not. He felt, in the words of his biographer, J. C. Thomas, "strangely about the pressure in his mouth, the grip like a wrench clasped around a pipe that his mouth must make on the mouthpiece to keep the sounds coming out beautiful and true."[65] Coltrane's inability to replicate Hodges's tone may have been the result of the younger man's poor dental health. Dental trouble has plagued jazz horn players since the time of Joseph "King" Oliver, one of the genre's founding fathers. Oliver had been hired for a recording session with Hodges in 1928 but hadn't played much, according to Hodges, because he "was having his teeth fixed at the time."[66] Coltrane had a sweet tooth all his life, sucking constantly on Butter Rum Life Savers even in his thirties,[67] and developed numerous cavities. He came to fear the drill so much that it sometimes took two or more assistants to hold him in the chair on his infrequent trips to the dentist. As a result, the hard work involved in forming the correct embouchure to produce a sound like Hodges's may have been painful and difficult for Coltrane.[68] In the early 1960s Coltrane had his teeth removed and a new set of bridgework installed,[69] but by then his complex style had been formed, and it resembled that of Hodges not at all. Whitney Balliett, a somewhat grudging admirer of Coltrane, described his tone as "harsh, flat, querulous, . . . at times almost vindictive," and "bleaker than need be,"[70] words never used when describing Hodges.

Coltrane's application for inclusion in Leonard Feather's *Encyclopedia of Jazz* states that he played with Hodges for part of 1953 through 1954,[71] but his tenure was briefer than that handwritten entry makes it sound. Coltrane is not listed among the sidemen on any of Hodges's dates in November or December 1953, and after confirmed appearances (and two recording sessions) with Hodges that began on January 18, 1954, and ended on July 2 of that year—less than six months later—he left the band.[72] Perhaps Coltrane exaggerated his tenure with Hodges owing to chagrin at having failed to live up to his idol's standards, for he had been fired.[73]

Coltrane became a heroin user shortly before joining Hodges sometime in mid-1952 after he left the orchestra of Earl Bostic.[74] Hodges's attitude as a leader was positively Ellingtonian: What you did was your business, as long as you didn't mess up the music.[75] Coltrane began to nod out on the bandstand when he wasn't playing, sometimes drawing timely nudges from other members of the band while Hodges faced the audience to solo. "It was obvious that [Coltrane] was using drugs, and when this got to be a habit, Hodges talked to him and asked him to watch it," said the group's bassist, John Williams. "John agreed with him, realizing that Johnny was right. But the next night, or the night after that, it would happen all over again, just as before." When Coltrane's heroin habit began to adversely affect his playing and the group as a whole, he was let go.[76]

There are only a handful of recordings on which Coltrane plays with Hodges. One, made on July 2, 1954, at Radio Recorders in Los Angeles with Johnny Hodges and His Orchestra, produced the numbers "Burgundy Walk," "On the Sunny Side of the Street," and "Sweet as Bear Meat." Coltrane solos on none of them—his playing is limited to ensembles.[77] Earlier in that month or possibly in late June of that year, a session at an unknown location resulted in "Thru for the Night,"[78] "Castle Rock," "In a Mellotone," "I've Got a Mind to Ramble Blues," "Don't Cry Baby Blues," "Burgundy Walk," and "Don't Blame Me." Coltrane solos on the first three; the last-named number finds him starting out in a style that fits in comfortably with the easy swing feel set by a group that included Ellington alums Shorty Baker on trumpet and Lawrence Brown on trombone,[79] but by the end of the tune one hears Coltrane trying out the sort of less lyrical lines that would come to characterize his playing in a modal style. On "Don't Blame Me" Coltrane is the only soloist.[80] The first six numbers are continuous, with no audible splices, and from the crowd noise in the background one concludes that they were recorded at a dance or a club; Coltrane can be heard warming up between "In a Mellotone" and "I've Got a Mind to Ramble Blues."[81] Finally, there was a session on August 5, 1954, again at Radio Recorders. Accounts differ as to whether Coltrane performed on this date; liner notes to two albums indicate that he can be heard on "Used to Be Duke" and a ballad medley, but the log from the recording session indicates that he was not.[82]

Coltrane would look back on his time with Hodges without bitterness about his dismissal. "He still kills me!" Coltrane said years later.[83] "We played honest music in this band. I really enjoyed that job. I liked every tune in the book. Nothing was superficial. It all had meaning and it all swung. And the confidence with which Rabbit plays! I wish I could play with the confidence he does."[84] In a 1961 interview Coltrane would call Hodges "the world's greatest saxophone player."[85] In a 1964 interview Hodges said that he and Coltrane had intended to record an album together, but that nothing came of the plan.[86]

It was no doubt hard for Hodges to fire Coltrane, whom he was personally fond of[87] and whose talent he admired. In 1962, eight years after he and Hodges parted company, Coltrane recorded an album with Ellington that included the Ellington standard "In a Sentimental Mood." When Hodges heard Coltrane's treatment of the number, he said, "As long as I've known this song, I think Coltrane gave the most beautiful interpretation I've ever heard."[88] His opinion was a knowledgeable one; the song had been one of his featured numbers for more than three decades. As for the music that Coltrane composed himself, Hodges was less enthusiastic. Asked by British jazz writer Max Jones in 1964 whether he liked Coltrane's music, Hodges bluntly replied, "I don't, but my son does."[89]

Because Coltrane's career has been thoroughly documented, one can get from his schedule a sense of the hectic routine that drove Hodges back to Ellington. From January 18 through July 2, 1954, Coltrane played dates with either of the Hodges band's configurations in East St. Louis, Illinois; Chicago; Washington, DC; Pittsburgh; an unknown city in Ohio; Baltimore; Philadelphia; Chattanooga, Tennessee; Montgomery, Alabama; Atlanta; Philadelphia; Buffalo; Detroit; Los Angeles; Portland; Seattle; then Los Angeles again. All told, during this period the group played approximately seventy-eight performances at seventeen separate stops in 166 days. The longest time spent at one location during this stretch was an engagement at the Royal Room in Los Angeles that possibly lasted for three weeks.[90]

A road trip such as this, with several tacks back and forth across the continent, might have been manageable if tiring for a band with the staff and experience of the Ellington orchestra, but it must have been overwhelming for Hodges, especially after the departure of Al Sears. The band remained a musical success after Sears left, but Hodges found that the burdens of leadership without the former's organizational skills were not for him. Somewhat to his

credit, Hodges lacked the capacity for showmanship and the willingness to inflate and project one's personality that are required of the front man for a musical group. A review in *Variety* following a July 4, 1954, gig at the Black Hawk
in San Francisco paints a picture of Hodges as uncomfortable in his role:

> A strong hypo[dermic] to this crew would be a little effort on the part
> of the leader to act as emcee of his own program. He does not even an-
> nounce the numbers and the band merely plays, soloists and ensemble,
> with no thought to visual presentation. This may be okay for the dyed-
> in-the-wool Hodges fan, but it is a bit hard on the average customer
> who doesn't dig jazz the most.[91]

Hodges would plead guilty to this charge when asked. "I've never been
the emotional sort and it's too late for me to change now," he told the British
jazz writer Maurice Burman. "I've never jumped around. I don't think a good
showman is necessarily a good player."[92]

In early 1955, when jazz broadcaster Willis Conover asked Hodges, "Do
you ever get eyes to go back to Ellington?" he said, "No, I haven't mentioned
that, I mean, a lot of people ask me the same thing. They have had different
write-ups in magazines about it, you know. So they—most of the people think
that we're mad at each other for something, but was nothing like that, 'cause
we talked about this thing years ago. In fact I tried it in 1948 when he went to
Europe." When asked whether he'd been happy leading a group of his own,
he confessed that the experience had been up and down, saying, "I can't say
it's easy. I wouldn't say it's easy. I can say now that I know the responsibilities
that Duke has, which I didn't know before. . . . I only have six—six headaches,"
meaning the number of musicians he had to worry about. "I don't have the
headaches he has."[93]

And so Hodges broke up the band. "Too many headaches," he would
later say of the hassles of everyday management—the contracts, travel and
monetary arrangements, the hiring and firing of personnel.[94] The burden of
business minutiae and the unwanted glare of the spotlight ultimately became
intolerable to Hodges when they began to undermine his music. "I had to
scuffle and when you scuffle you can't play what you like," he said. "When you
are famous and popular"—like his former boss Ellington—"you can."[95] Duke
"had people to worry for him," he told Henry Whiston,

> but if you have your own band you have to rush, get the tickets, get the
> money, go to the union and pay the tax. Then you have seven pieces

and you're supposed to start at nine o'clock and it's five minutes to nine and there's only five there, so you start worryin'—where's the other two? And here they come, two minutes to go, and then you got to worry about where you're goin' to work the next week—so it was too much for me. Once you get set like Duke is, you don't have to worry, 'cause you pay someone to worry for you.[96]

Despite Hodges's self-criticism, he and his groups were favorably received. A 1954 story in a Los Angeles newspaper said that Hodges' group "drew more calls" for a "recent coast to coast Telethon than any other star, including those of movies."[97] The *Baltimore Afro-American* reported that of the four acts featured at a March 22, 1954, concert—the others being Billy Eckstine, Ruth Brown, and The Clovers—"Johnny Hodges has probably been in the limelight the longest. . . . Hodges' orchestra is composed of outstanding side-men soloists who learned their P's and Q's as members of the nation's leading jazz bands. And although the Hodges band is extremely young, it has won top praise from the critics.[98]

That last assertion was a bit of an overstatement. A March 1954 review by Stanley Dance in *DownBeat* gave *Johnny's Blues (Parts I and II)* only two stars of a possible five. Dance found the music "pretty pedestrian from knowing jazzmen like these," although he said that "Rabbit . . . blows well enough on part two." But the overall feel, he concluded, was "one of disinterested routine . . . this could well have been left unreleased."[99]

After he dissolved the group Hodges began to play on the *Ted Steele Show*, a half-hour afternoon program on the DuMont Television Network, along with drummer Cozy Cole and trumpeter Jonah Jones.[100] Steele was a bandleader, vocalist, songwriter, emcee, and newscaster in the early days of television,[101] making a six-figure annual income from his various entertainment and media roles that, adjusted for inflation, would translate to a seven-figure sum today. While he and his band are not remembered for their contributions to jazz today, his taste in musicians was unexceptionable. In addition to Hodges, Steele's show featured Louis Armstrong, Jack Teagarden, Barney Bigard, and Earl Hines, among others,[102] so it was no embarrassment for an Ellington alumnus at loose ends to appear with him. On the other hand, Steele was a leader of the rearguard opposition to bebop, banning it on the Los Angeles radio station where he worked on the grounds that it "tends to make degenerates out of our young listeners."[103]

The show ran only for a half hour on the air, but according to Hodges, in the studio the musicians played "from three 'til five, five days a week. That was nice," he recalled a decade later. "I used to come on at four and I got so that I used to pick out the numbers to play. I wanted to play one fast number and one slow number." Nice work if you can get it, but Hodges ultimately found Steele's music a little too sweet for his tastes.

> It got to the point where I got some real elderly fans, those sewing circle people, you know. These women that was at home doing the sewin', and washin' and things like that, and these people that had club meetings. So, at four o'clock every day, I had to play some kind of a slow pretty number for these people in New Jersey.[104]

He decided to return to the Ellington fold but was too humbled to ask for his job back himself. Instead, he asked Cue to do it. "His wife called up," Ellington recalled, "and asked if I wanted an alto player. I said[,] 'Oh yeah!'"[105] Because she had been a supporter of her husband's decision to go out on his own in the first place, the apparent contradiction between her encouragement for both his departure and his return may be understood by reference to that most fundamental household consideration: money. "As a middle-aged man with growing children," noted Stanley Dance, Hodges "appreciated the increased financial security."[106] Cue may have had her eye on the prize of a bandleader's big salary at the outset, but when the venture turned out to be less lucrative than expected, she herded her husband back to his musical home.

Hodges's return to the man who'd first brought him fame and to whose musical legacy he would contribute so much was an admission of defeat and of his subordinate status in the grand scheme of jazz, but he took on the demeanor of dutiful if proud employee, as evidenced by this exchange in the studio during the recording of "Chelsea Bridge" for the album *Ella Fitzgerald Sings the Duke Ellington Song Book*. The band is walking through the opening bars, with Fitzgerald tagging along vocally behind, when Ellington calls out, "Hold it a minute. Hey, Rabbit," looking for help from his old off-the-cuff composing partner, whom Helen Oakley said "was an absolute song factory."[107]

"Yes sir?" Hodges dutifully answers.

"Uh, Rabbit," Ellington continues, "gimme something at the end of that first eight, will you?"

"What eight?" Hodges fires back at his boss in a rather brusque tone, asking him to be more specific. Ellington then makes clear that he means the end of the first statement of the opening passage, and the band plays on.

And so grew an Ellington tune as before, now that the Rabbit was back in his hutch.

15

The Rabbit Returns

JOHNNY HODGES RETURNED to the Ellington fold in August 1955.[1] He was "playing as well as ever; but his reappearance caused some bad blood between the band's Old Guard (who regrouped around The Rabbit)," according to jazz writer Raymond Horricks,[2] and newer members of the band, who had begun to infuse the orchestra's music with more modern sounds than those produced by the veterans. Charlie Parker, who had displaced Hodges atop polls and in the hearts and minds of jazz fans and critics, had died on March 12 of that year, but Hodges's status in the jazz world when he ended his self-imposed exile from Ellington was accurately summed up by critic Whitney Balliett of the *New Yorker* as "an out-of-fashion leader of a small semi-rock-and-roll-group."[3]

In Balliett's view, Hodges had been hit by a "double whammy."[4] "He suffered, along with his colleagues, from the rise of bebop, but he also suffered because Parker, the leader of that movement, played the same instrument." The problem was analyzed by Balliett thus: "Jazz thrives both artistically and socially on rebellion," he wrote, and its "audiences, more unskilled than not, often train their ears only on what they are told is worthy by the jazz press, which tends to confuse newness with progress and progress with quality."[5]

At the time of Hodges's return the Ellington organization was at a low point in its history. Beginning in June it provided music for Elliott Murphy's Aquacade, a water-themed variety show at the site of the 1939 World's Fair in Flushing Meadows, New York. The program included ice skaters, "dancing" water fountains, comedians, and other entertainers; the orchestra was thus reduced to the level of a stage band, playing not as a featured attraction but as filler. Norman Granz used the occasion of Hodges's return to turn out more product under the saxman's name for his record labels; Hodges was back in the reflected light of the larger Ellington celestial body, and the publicity surrounding the healing of the two prominent figures' rift represented a marketing opportunity. First, Granz took Hodges and five other Ellingtonians into studios in New York to make the album *Creamy* on September 8, 1955, then in January 1956 he assembled seven Ellington employees plus Hodges to record eight numbers, including two by Hodges ("You Got It Coming" and "Duke's Jam"), two by Hodges and Strayhorn ("Hi'ya" and "Texas Blues"), and Strayhorn's "Snibor." The results were released as *Ellingtonia '56*.

When the Ellington orchestra returned to New York after a long tour in January 1956, jazz critic Nat Hentoff, reviewing a performance for *DownBeat*, wrote, "Mr. Hodges, one of the monumental figures in jazz on his instrument, plays with the suave, liquid legato of yore but more strength has been added. When he really feels like blowing, as in 'All of Me,' 'I've Got it Bad' and the fortunately revived 'Jeep's Blues,' the Rabbit is the biggest you ever heard." Hentoff struck a defensive note with regard to the band as a whole, reflecting the downgrading it had suffered in ratings by critics and fans, who ranked them a distant fourth in the 1955 *DownBeat* Reader's Poll Big Band category, with Count Basie's band first:

> The Basie band rocks the blues more dynamically than Duke's, although the Duke's men also play the blues feelingly; and the Basie band as a unit swings harder. But the Basie band can't play ballads at all well, while Duke's can. Nor does the Basie book or conception encompass as varied a range of moods, colors and thematic content as Duke's.[6]

Hentoff's colleagues at the magazine felt the orchestra's best days were behind it; in April 1956 one review called *Ellington Showcase,* a collection of ten numbers recorded from 1953 to 1955, "not the highest quality Duke by any means,"[7] and a month later another warned fans to "get the originals before you add" *Historically Speaking: The Duke,* a reworking of past hits, to their collections.[8] It was this artistic funk that followed the orchestra as it slouched toward the American Jazz Festival in Newport, Rhode Island, notwithstanding the bright spots provided by the return of Hodges and Billy Strayhorn, who, Hentoff noted, was "devoting more time to refurbishing and adding to the band's book."[9] At the urging of Ellington's publicist, Joe Morgen, *Time* magazine had agreed to write a profile of Ellington, and the subject was nervous that the article would focus on the past rather than the present and the future: "I think it would be better for you—well, for me too, of course, if we don't get, uh, too historic," Ellington said to the magazine's music editor during the interview.[10]

The story of Ellington's phoenix-like rise from the premature ashes of his career at Newport has been told many times before: on a bill that featured Teddy Wilson, Anita O'Day, and cool jazz artists Jimmy Guiffre, Chico Hamilton, and Bud Shank, the Ellington orchestra was consigned to a split shift, like the junior waiter at an upscale restaurant, opening the day's performances with a short introductory set *and* closing them out. At one point during the break, after waiting three hours to go back on, Ellington complained to George Wein, the festival's producer, of the vaudeville-like treatment he was getting, saying, "What are we—the animal act, the acrobats?"[11] Four members of the band had missed the brief first set but appeared for the second, which would feature a joint work by Ellington and Strayhorn, *The Newport Jazz Festival Suite*, commissioned by Wein. Ellington spoke to his men between sets like a football coach giving his team a halftime pep talk, telling them that once they got through the suite they'd "relax and have a real good time" playing *Diminuendo and Crescendo in Blue*, a work he composed in 1937 and which he'd been revising since, inserting a succession of slow movements between the diminuendo and the crescendo parts. He had more recently—as tapes from 1951 and 1953 reveal—hit upon a simpler solution; have tenor Paul Gonsalves improvise in a blues mode with just the rhythm section.[12]

Gonsalves was an erratic employee; his fondness for drink and drugs is apparent from film of the band in which he leans at a nearly horizontal angle, catching a nap when not gainfully employed by ensemble playing or solos. When Ellington called *Diminuendo and Crescendo* Gonsalves pretended not to know which number the bandleader meant, and Ellington, not taking any chances, made himself clear: "It's the one where we play the blues and change keys," Ellington replied. "I bring you on, and you blow until I take you off, and we change the keys."[13] After an uninspiring opening to the set that included the new suite, the crowd was restive. Ellington "had to change the energy," in the assessment of trumpeter Clark Terry, "but he knew how to come out of it,"[14] and he made good on his promise to loosen things up, hitting the keyboard aggressively with the opening vamp of *Diminuendo and Crescendo*. Gonsalves followed with a succession of rocking choruses that would not have sounded out of place coming from a member of the bar-walking school of tenor sax.

The crowd responded with enthusiasm to Gonsalves's abandon and was soon in a frenzy of the sort that was common at performances of rock 'n' roll music but which was unheard-of at a jazz concert, with the possible exception of the reception that greeted Benny Goodman's band at the Palomar Ballroom in Los Angeles in August 1935. From his seat on the bandstand

Johnny Hodges looked on impassively at first—he had, after all, heard Gonsalves perform his solo several times before—but he eventually warmed up when he saw what was happening: "Even the super-placid Johnny Hodges," wrote producer George Avakian, "who will probably not raise a half-masted eyelid come millennium-time, smiled and beat time back" at Jo Jones, who, out of sight of the audience, urged the band on using a rolled-up newspaper that he rapped against the stage like a drumstick. Hodges probably made the same mixed assessment of the solo that one listening to it sixty years later is inclined to hand down; judged for its content alone it was nothing special, but as the tinder that ignited an unprecedented fire under the audience, it was remarkable.

Wein, concerned that he had a tsunami on his hands, motioned for Ellington to end the set, but the bandleader wasn't about to wipe out deliberately while riding a wave that could revive his career. He called on Hodges, first with "I Got It Bad and That Ain't Good," which would normally have calmed the seas a bit. Perhaps out of tune as a result of his long layoff while Gonsalves soloed, Hodges played two of the sourest notes of his career on the opening verses, coming in below the pitch with his trademark scooping ascensions, but missing the mark each time. By the third verse he had righted the ship of his sax and sailed on, and the crowd, in a forgiving mood, gave him a rousing hand. He then launched into a moaning "Jeep's Blues," the mellow song that had made his name as a blues wailer in 1938, but it had the opposite of its intended effect as the audience remained boisterous. After several more numbers Ellington finally called out "We *do* love you madly," with added emphasis to his signature sign-off to make clear that the night would regretfully have to come to a close.

There followed a wholesale reassessment of Ellington's career; his band was, in the words of *Time* magazine, "once again the most exciting thing in the business," and he himself "had emerged from a long period of quiescence ... bursting with ideas and inspiration."[15] Ellington put the transformation in quasi-religious terms. "I was born in 1956 at the Newport Festival,"[16] he would say from then on, and there was more than figurative truth in this statement; through the boost in popularity he received from that one summer night, he would gain more freedom to write the sophisticated works that germinated in his imagination. After the explosive performance, Columbia Records offered Ellington a three-year contract that was lucrative by any measure but particularly so for a big band at the beginning of the rock 'n' roll era. None of his records would ever sell as many copies as the concert album made from the 1956 Newport festival, but Ellington's revenues would be sufficient for Columbia to renew his contract for an additional three years when it expired.[17]

There were several new and longer works in the pipeline that would satisfy both Ellington's restless musical imagination and his desire for royalties and that called for enhancement by the horn of Hodges. *Such Sweet Thunder*, a suite of twelve short takes inspired by characters or scenes from Shakespeare's plays, was composed for the 1956 Stratford (Ontario) Music Festival and first performed on April 28, 1957. The relation between the music by Ellington and Strayhorn and the Bard's texts is, to borrow a skeptical simile from Thelonious Monk, like that of dancing to architecture; the title of the first section, which is also the name of the work as a whole, is taken from a line in *A Midsummer Night's Dream* that describes thunder as a "musical . . . discord, such sweet thunder,"[18] but Ellington is quoted in the liner notes as saying that the piece was inspired by *Othello*. Hodges provides the horn counterpart to the voices of Juliet Capulet in "Star-Crossed Lovers" and is teamed with trombonist John Sanders in "Up and Down, Up and Down (I Will Lead Them Up and Down)," one of a succession of instrument pairings in the manner used by Puck in *A Midsummer Night's Dream,* who brings unexpected couples together through his magic. Hodges also has a languorous solo meant to evoke the romantic mood aboard a barge floating down the Nile carrying Antony and Cleopatra on "Half the Fun."

The next artistic work in line under Ellington's new contract was *A Drum Is a Woman*, a mythic tale of the origins of jazz. The piece had been conceived in 1941 when Ellington was working with director Orson Welles, who planned to use it in a film. Like many of Welles's grand projects the movie was never completed, and Ellington's vision for the work might not have been realized but for a commission by the CBS television network. The work was recorded in September 1956 by Columbia Records, a CBS affiliate, then broadcast on May 8, 1957, with dancers and four singers, one a soprano from the New York City Opera. Everyone involved in the production was African American, a milestone comparable in the world of television to shows that featured black hosts Hazel Scott in 1950, Billy Daniels in 1952, and Nat "King" Cole in 1954, but with a significant difference; it was an ambitious work that demonstrated Ellington's sincere commitment to the highest artistic standards for his race and himself and not simply a popular variety show. Looking back over his career in 1966 Ellington would name *A Drum Is a Woman* as his most satisfying longer work, although the critical reception was mixed. Hodges's contribution includes a typically lush solo accompanied by a harpist.

Riding the surging tide in Ellington's popularity that followed the triumph of Newport, Hodges went back into the studio, recording two albums on Verve, first *Duke's in Bed* on September 1, 1956, then *The Big Sound*, recorded in two sessions in June 1957. For *Duke's in Bed*, Hodges and eight other Ellingtonians were marketed under the name "The Ellington All-Stars Without Duke." The cover of the album is a partial shot of a bed with a woman's shoes on the floor alongside a casually tossed-off red garment, an allusion to the bandleader's reputation as a Lothario. The title comes from a tune that, jazz critic Bill Simon wrote, "Ellington himself sent over . . . explaining why he wasn't there in person;"[19] it is an up-tempo dramatic number that Ben Webster would record in 1965,[20] and the tone of the piece is one of irritation at having been roused from post-coital slumber.

Hodges was the featured artist on the 1957 album *The Big Sound: Johnny Hodges and the Ellington Men,* with Billy Strayhorn playing piano as well as arranging, along with fourteen other Ellington men. There are five numbers by Hodges and two collaborations by him and Mercer Ellington ("Viscount" and "Bouquet of Roses"), along with Strayhorn's "Johnny Come Lately," first recorded by the Ellington orchestra in 1942 (and sometimes referred to as "Stomp"). Hodges is in fine form, fanning the flames of "Johnny Come Lately," which, like "Take the A Train," echoes the hectic pace of urban life. Clark Terry, thirteen years Hodges's junior, pronounced himself impressed with the way his bandmate could "still sound good after all these years" (Hodges was forty-nine when recording began in June 1957). "He can slur so that no one note sticks out," Terry said, and there was his "tone of course, and the fact that he can play as soft as anybody and as loud as a trumpet if he wants. He has about the warmest sound of anyone."[21]

In 1958 Hodges would reunite with Ben Webster on a succession of albums, beginning in April with *Blues-a-Plenty*, then join Mercer Ellington on *Stepping Into Swing Society* in July. The fall of 1958 saw Hodges teamed up with Roy Eldridge and a familiar cast of characters from the Ellington band—Ray Nance, Lawrence Brown, Jimmy Hamilton, Ben Webster, Billy Strayhorn, Jimmy Woode, and Sam Woodyard—to record *Not So Dukish* for Verve on September 10. Along with the title track, perhaps intended to convey the message that with the addition of Eldridge it was not just another Ellington sideman session, Hodges assessed the success of his return from years of scuffling as a bandleader with "Jeep Bounced Back."

Ellington and Hodges were paired in sessions for Verve in August 1958 and February 1959 that produced two of the most popular albums of their work together, a somewhat anomalous result since the majority of the musicians playing on the two dates were Basie alumni (Jo Jones on drums and Harry Edison on trumpet) and sidemen hired for the occasion: on bass either Sam Jones, who most recently had played with Dizzy Gillespie and Thelonious Monk, or Al Hall, best known for his work with Erroll Garner; and Les Spann on guitar and flute. Other Ellingtonians heard on some of the 1958 numbers were Lawrence Brown, trombone; Ben Webster, tenor; Billy Strayhorn, piano; and Wendell Marshall, bass.

The music from the project was released in 1959 as *Back to Back: Duke Ellington and Johnny Hodges Play the Blues*, and in 1960 as *Side by Side: Duke Ellington and Johnny Hodges Plus Others*. Critics applauded *Back to Back* for allocating more time to Ellington's work on the keyboard, which he preferred to subordinate to the sound of the full band; "a record for those who have felt they didn't get a chance to hear enough Ellington piano," the *DownBeat* reviewer wrote.[22] Ellington was known to say his real instrument was his band, not the piano, and his solos on *Back to Back* reveal the mind of a composer on something of a busman's holiday; rather than fire off arpeggios to impress the listener with his virtuosity, his right hand tends to sketch themes suitable for framing by ensembles.

Since his return to Ellington several critics had remarked that Hodges had never sounded better, and on *Back to Back* and *Side by Side* several stars came into alignment to produce a masterpiece of combo jazz: First, Hodges is back with Ellington, whose playing behind him represented a respite from the rock-oriented numbers that had been his combo's biggest successes during the years the two men spent apart. Second, the 1959 album is dedicated to the horn-based blues of the W. C. Handy–New Orleans axis, the sounds from which Hodges drew his first breath as a saxophonist. Hodges turns the decorous "Wabash Blues," a hit for white bandleader Isham Jones in 1921, into a paragon of African American music, his opening riff a tone parallel to the "woman wailing for her demon-lover" in Coleridge's *Kubla Khan*.[23] These two albums have "been in print somewhere in the world from the day they were first issued,"[24] evidence of the classical stature they have achieved.

In November 1958 Hodges recorded twelve George Gershwin tunes with the Stuttgart Light Orchestra conducted by Wolfram Rohrig, released on Verve as *Johnny Hodges and His Strings Play the Prettiest Gershwin*.[25] The album represented the first time Hodges recorded with strings. Although he was not classically trained, his virtuoso talent was recognized by others who were, and he could hold his own among them despite his catch-as-catch-can musical education; he would perform Ellington's *Night Creature* with the Detroit Symphony in March 1963[26] and would record *Sandy's Gone* for Verve in September of that year with the Claus Ogerman Orchestra.[27] Ogerman was an arranger and composer who worked, from the 1970s on, almost exclusively in the European classical tradition, including pieces for the American Ballet Theater and *Symbiosis* for jazz pianist Bill Evans and orchestra.

In 1959 Ellington was invited by Otto Preminger to write the score for *Anatomy of a Murder*, a quantum leap up from his earlier work for short films. The film was a big-budget Hollywood project based on a best-selling crime novel with Oscar-winning actor Jimmy Stewart in the lead role and a respected director in Preminger. The addition of Ellington (who also played a bit part as a roadhouse pianist) as composer of the score was based both on merit and on the publicity the involvement of the top jazz bandleader would generate for the movie, which was nominated for the Academy Award for Best Picture. Hodges's alto is heard in Ellington's "Flirtibird"—with its "irresistibly salacious tremor"—as a leitmotif when actress Lee Remick appears on screen,[28] and he is featured extensively on the ballad "Haupé.[29] Ellington's music earned Grammy Awards for best soundtrack album and best background score but failed to receive an Academy Award nomination.

In April 1959 and September 1960 Hodges recorded the music that would be issued as *The Smooth One*. It was scheduled for release in May 1961, but, in the words of Stanley Dance, "no finished copies appear to have escaped the warehouse" until 1979.[30] Hodges is the composer of fifteen of the nineteen compositions, all written in the Ellington style. The first session produced a series of riff-based tunes whose titles—"First Klass (C'Mon Home)," "Second Klass," "Straight Back," "Steerage," and "Third Klass"—play on the different classes of accommodations on ocean liners. It was an experience that Hodges knew well, having first traveled by sea to Southampton, England, aboard the S.S. *Olympic* on June 2, 1933, with the Ellington orchestra for a tour that included stops in France, returning from Cherbourg to New York aboard the *Majestic* on August 8.[31] These numbers may have been intended as a unified composition, but they strike the ear as simply a series of unrelated blues, not a work of high artistic ambition, which Hodges was more than willing to leave to Ellington and Strayhorn. That this is the case becomes apparent when one considers the comment Hodges made as he unpacked the box of charts that Tom Whaley, Ellington's long-time copyist, brought to the session: "Too much music," he muttered. "The best record sessions are those where you go [i.e., play] for yourself."

On one of the obligatory rabbit-themed numbers ("The Hare"), Hodges served as arranger-on-the-fly; he "decided he would like a riff behind his second chorus, so he twisted between musicians, chairs, and microphones to whisper in the appropriate ears. Back in position a split second before his solo was to begin, feet planted wide apart, left toe and right heel marking the time, he was swinging at once, tone and phraseology combining in exquisitely volatile flight."[32] In an interview with Stanley Dance at this session, Hodges provided an insight into one of his conventions for naming compositions, namely, the vernacular speech of his fellow workers in the demi-monde of the night life. Asked where the title "The Peaches Are Better Down the Road" came from, for example, he replied, "It's the kind of saying I hear people use. Like if you ask the waiters in these clubs how they're feeling and they have real tired feet they'll say, 'The peaches are better down the road.'"[33] Hodges had an ear that transmuted the vernacular—in whatever form he encountered it, melodic or spoken—into his music.

Over the years a number of Hodges recording sessions would be lost or shelved: parts of two sessions in January and February 1961, and a June 1960 session with Ben Webster and Jimmy Rowles on piano have never surfaced. Hodges would refer to the last-named session with regret: "The best record sessions are those where you go for yourself," he said, repeating the rule he had cited at the *Smooth One* sessions. "The one I made out on the Coast with Booty [Wood], Lawrence [Brown], and Ben [Webster]—we had no music."[34] A November 1960 recording date with Ben Webster in San Francisco went unissued for decades, perhaps because Norman Granz had so much Hodges inventory he didn't get around to it. It is now available along with a January 1961 set. Six of the tunes from the 1960 session were saved only because they were taped by Ben Webster on a do-it-yourself basis.[35]

Over time, Hodges began to tire of the nomad's life even as part of the Ellington band, whose organizational infrastructure and financial support surpassed what he had commanded as leader of his own group. A January date on a 1963 tour of England found the band playing in frigid conditions in a Liverpool theater. Hodges examined his alto and jokingly asked for some antifreeze, an uncharacteristic complaint from a player who was said to be able to pick up any horn and be in tune immediately. After he'd played three numbers he was about to sit down when Ellington called on him to take another bow, and Hodges was heard to say, "Lay off it[,] Dukie. Every time I bend down I can feel the ice cracking off the back of my pants."[36]

As a respite from the road that the Ellington band traveled, Hodges would sometimes play freelance gigs in his old home town of Boston. In 1957 he joined the trio of saxophonist Jimmy Tyler at Connolly's Stardust Room on Tremont Street,[37] and in 1964 he hooked up with Ellington trombonist Lawrence Brown and a rhythm section for a couple of weeks. The money for short-term excursions of this sort wasn't great, but they appealed to Hodges as occasions to try out his ideas every now and then. "I've only one ambition now," he said. "I'd like to settle down at home and take time to compose— really work on writing some tunes. I may just do that," he said—but he didn't live long enough.[38]

On a subsequent tour of England in 1966, the band stayed at the Palm Court in Liverpool, and Hodges and the other band members were in a bad mood due to poor service and mediocre lounge music ("That is one crazy double," Hodges said of a musician who played both clarinet and cello). After a gin and water had been procured for him, he began to complain about the itinerant musician's lot. "I guess I could make a living just doing albums and the occasional tour with someone like Wild Bill Davis," he said, referring to the jazz organist. "It takes about three days to make an album, and pays a couple of hundred dollars and royalties," Hodges mused. "If I worked on records for other leaders as well, I could do quite nicely."[39]

Rock 'n' roll played by young musicians had begun to supplant the jazz-inflected rock that Hodges's group played; young people wanted their music to be sung and played by musicians closer to their age whom they could emulate or relate to romantically. In 1962 *Billboard* reported that sales of jazz records had increased over the course of the previous three years and that some jazz singles and albums had even become pop hits.[40] On February 9, 1964, however, the Beatles appeared on the *Ed Sullivan Show*, a nationally televised variety program, and jazz's market share would begin a slow decline that has continued to the point where jazz is now tied with European-style classical music as the least-popular genre, a doleful confirmation that jazz is, as its devotees have long maintained, America's classical music. "Suddenly you couldn't visit friends who had adolescent children without having to listen to them bang on guitars and little electric pianos," complained Ralph Ellison, and "yet for all its tastelessness, at a time when Johnny Hodges was hardly making a living, such noise became the source of great wealth and facile celebrity."[41]

Outside the Ellington Constellation: The 1950s and 1960s

DURING THE SUMMER and early fall of 1957 a group of Ellingtonians led by Clark Terry on trumpet got together for two sessions in New York that were packaged under the title *Duke With a Difference*.[1] Although the songs selected were considered Ellington warhorses, they were given fresh arrangements by Terry and by Mercer Ellington, and the album lived up to its name. Joining Terry from the Ellington organization were Johnny Hodges, Paul Gonsalves on tenor, Tyree Glenn on vibes, Jimmy Woode on bass, Sam Woodyard on drums, Quentin Jackson and Britt Woodman on trombones, and Billy Strayhorn playing piano on two numbers. Luther Henderson, a classmate of Mercer Ellington's growing up in the Sugar Hill neighborhood of Harlem who orchestrated Duke Ellington's symphonic works (thereby acquiring the reputation of being Ellington's "classical arm"), plays celeste on one track.[2]

On November 14, 1957, Hodges—using the pseudonym "The Rabbit"— was lumped together with Terry, Harry Carney, Willie Cook, Gonsalves, and Woodman as an "Ellingtonian sideman" on *Taylor Made Jazz: The Music of Billy Taylor*. Taylor, a pianist (not the former Ellington bassist), went on to become a broadcaster, educator, and advocate for jazz as well as a musician. All of the songs on *Taylor Made Jazz* were composed by Taylor; Hodges is singled out for his "exquisite performance" in "Theodora" in liner notes that perceptively describe his solo as "lean of line yet directly moving."[3]

On November 17, 1959, Hodges joined baritone sax player Gerry Mulligan for one of a series of collaborations between Mulligan and other leading jazz artists produced by Norman Granz. Mulligan had previously made an artistically successful album with Ben Webster, and he looked forward to working with Hodges, whom he had admired since he started out playing alto as a teenager. Hodges was on record as an admirer of Mulligan as well; in a 1955 interview he said that, hearing Mulligan stretch out in a jam session at Birdland, he was "surprised" at his talent, having previously heard him only in three-minute snatches on records.[4] Mulligan and the personnel on the album besides Hodges—Buddy Clark on bass, Claude Williamson on piano, and Mel Lewis on drums—were a generation younger than Hodges, having all been born in the second half of the 1920s; the album thus represented an opportunity for Hodges to awaken like Rip Van Winkle in a modern setting he'd missed out on while working for three decades in the Ellington mode, and he responded with renewed vigor. Hodges and Mulligan each contributed three originals; Mulligan's include two that allude to Hodges's most commonly used nickname: "Bunny," which despite its title lopes along at an un-rabbit-like speed, and "18 Carrots for Rabbit," a faster number on which the two swap short solos. Hodges's contributions include two gently swinging pieces and "Shady Side," which Nat Hentoff accurately characterizes as "infectiously autumnal" in his liner notes.[5]

In March 1961, while Ellington was in France to complete the sound-track for the movie *Paris Blues*, Hodges toured Europe for two weeks under the auspices of Norman Granz along with six other Ellingtonians including Al Williams replacing Ellington on piano, Lawrence Brown on trombone, Harry Carney on baritone sax, Sam Woodyard on drums, Aaron Bell on bass, and Ray Nance on trumpet, violin, and vocals. One of their concerts was made into an album released on the Pablo label titled *Johnny Hodges at the Sportpalast, Berlin*.[6]

In August 1962 Hodges, tenor Coleman Hawkins, and trumpeter Roy Eldridge got together for a date at the Village Gate that was a musical old timers' game of sorts; Hawkins was fifty-seven, Hodges fifty-five, and Eldridge fifty-one, all senior citizens when judged by the short lifespan normally allotted to jazzmen owing to the rigors of their profession. The occasion was a booking with Hawkins as headliner that Hodges and Eldridge had been invited to sit in on. Although the tempos are slower and the notes fewer than might have been the case in the trio's salad days, all three are in fine form, even displaying a few new tricks for relatively old dogs; Hawkins sounds as if he's listened to Coltrane, and Eldridge hits the high notes that were his calling card. Hodges is as sultry as ever.[7]

Then, in December 1965, Hodges recorded an album that gave ammunition to those who had criticized his playing over the years as saccharine.

Lawrence Welk, the television bandleader who got his start playing not with black jazz musicians but with bland white bands such as The Hotsy Totsy Boys,[8] had long admired Hodges's playing. One day while driving, according to Welk, he was so struck by the beauty of a Hodges solo on the radio that he decided to ask him to cut an album. Hodges agreed and flew to Hollywood to record twelve songs with an orchestra that included strings, each arranged by a different man, among them Benny Carter. Welk's affection for Hodges was genuine, and when he expressed it to the jazzman upon his arrival Hodges opened up in a manner uncharacteristic for him. "I'm very happy to be here," he said with a smile instead of the bored expression he usually wore, glad to be greeted as the star and not just a planet in the Ellington solar system.[9] The music in some cases strikes the ear as "easy listening," but it contains enough substance to hold a jazz fan's interest. Ellington himself had expressed admiration for Welk's music in a 1963 interview with a Canadian disc jockey, saying, "I like Welk,"[10] a declaration that reads as if it exceeds the bounds of mere professional courtesy.

Hodges had previously recorded albums with strings—most recently *Eleventh Hour* with Oliver Nelson as conductor and arranger—but Welk was a white square, while Nelson was a black jazz soloist on alto, tenor, and soprano sax before he became more widely known for his talents as composer and arranger, and so the jazz purist's complaint about strings wasn't held against him. Hodges's playing on the Welk album retains an unsentimental core throughout the album, and the criticism that has been leveled against him for his decision to play with the kitschy Welk was, ultimately, misplaced. On this record and the Gershwin album with strings that he made in 1958 with the Stuttgart Light Orchestra[11] that Stanley Dance called "misguided,"[12] his tone, "though rich and sensuous, retains its masculine strength, the phrasing being disciplined by a strongly musical mind,"[13] in the words of music critic G. E. Lambert. One need only compare a latter-day sentimentalist on the soprano sax such as Kenny G to Hodges to detect the difference between emotion used in the service of melody and emotional technique used as superficial decoration, like gingerbread trim on a Victorian house. Hodges was occasionally charged with descending into schmaltz by critics from John Hammond[14] to Nat Hentoff, who said that Hodges was sometimes guilty of an "excessive ripeness" that made his work "resemble the mooning of an over-age courtesan,"[15] but if the standard to be used over the course of a long career is a preponderance of the evidence, Hodges beats the rap.

What kept Hodges's style in check? First, his own self-respect and the model of his first inspiration, Sidney Bechet. Bechet, like a musical

Walt Whitman, contained multitudes; he was "a man of catholic musical tastes . . . who could improvise on all sorts of themes," but there wasn't a sentimental bone in his body. Even as he neared the end of his career and decided to cash in on the Dixieland revival of traditional jazz, Bechet's playing remained "intensely dramatic and passionate,"[16] and the same can be said of Hodges. Second, Hodges was a member of an elite fraternity—the EKEs, or Edward Kennedy Ellingtons. Although band members had to put up with a good deal of cornball showmanship from Ray Nance and the various dancers who from time to time were added to stage shows, they were a brotherhood of mature musicians who scrapped for solo time and held themselves to high standards. They were true artists in the hot jazz mode, and as a matter of pride they would have laughed at a colleague who corrupted their communal pursuit of beauty with excessive emotion or hackneyed technique.

The jazz album with strings has historically been a form of social climbing by jazz musicians, an attempt by purveyors of a parvenu music to achieve respectability that would be unnecessary if jazz had developed in respectable circumstances. Nonetheless, jazz figures as important as Charlie Parker and Clifford Brown had recorded albums with strings; both have remained in print since they were first issued, and neither man viewed his work as a concession to popular tastes. Parker was a musical omnivore with a genuine interest in classical music. In a 1948 Leonard Feather "Blindfold Test" Parker said he liked "all of Stravinsky—and Prokoviev, Hindemith, Ravel, Debussy."[17] In a 1954 radio interview, when asked to name his next musical venture, Parker said he was going to Europe to study with Edgard Varèse at the French composer's invitation.[18] One night in the 1940s, when Igor Stravinsky came to a club where he was playing, Parker inserted a theme from *The Firebird* into a solo, to Stravinsky's delight. Parker was sincere in his ambitions and once became irritated when he turned around while conducting a band to find Dizzy Gillespie mocking him in pantomime. For Parker, playing with strings was a validation, not a degeneration.

But Parker died in 1955, and Brown in 1956, and their approach to jazz, which wore its erudition lightly, died with them. Anger as a valid emotional theme in jazz first became fashionable in the late 1950s, when Charles Mingus released *Mingus Ah Um*, an album that included "Fables of Faubus," a protest song about Democratic governor Orval E. Faubus of Arkansas, who opposed racial integration of that state's public schools. The album with strings came to be viewed as a sellout, although the format has been revived in recent years by, among others, trumpeters Wynton Marsalis, Roy Hargrove, and Jeremy Pelt. Historically speaking, there is thus no reason to write off Hodges as a traitor to jazz merely because of this one album; if Welk's name were removed and a blindfold test of the sort administered by Leonard Feather given, it is likely that an objective listener would find it no less agreeable than similar albums by other jazz artists of the era.

There were economic reasons for Hodges's foray into what one might diplomatically call light classical jazz. He had a daughter in college when the 1960s began and a son of college age when the album came out. He may have been the highest-paid musician in the Ellington orchestra, but his sometimes precarious health and the years he had spent on the road must have made a well-paid recording gig with a popular bandleader seem attractive. Welk extended a standing offer to Hodges to join his band,[19] and the proposition had its appeal. "Those guys have a nice job, mainly studio work, and three months off a year when you can do what you want," Hodges said. "I could make my albums and maybe do a few club jobs and things." He ultimately declined the offer, though, saying "I don't know, I've been with Duke a long time now."[20]

There is an adage invoked by musicians who walk both sides of the street that divides popular music from that which aspires to art: "You do the gig you need to do, so you can do the gig you want to do." Hodges may have played with sweet musicians such as Welk on occasion, but he always returned to a steady diet of hotter sounds when he'd had his fill.

17

The Quality of Song

THE SONGLIKE QUALITY of Johnny Hodges's playing, in both his bluesy and his romantic modes, has been commented on frequently enough to merit closer consideration. He was admired by jazz singers including Bing Crosby, who said to Leonard Feather, "Holy Toledo! That must be the best saxophone solo ever played!" after hearing Hodges take his turn on "I Got It Bad (and That Ain't Good)." Tony Bennett by metaphor equated his style with song: "The best singer in the world—what else?" he said when asked what he thought of Hodges.[1] "Nobody sings on the alto saxophone like Johnny Hodges," wrote Stanley Dance. "He sings all kinds of songs. He sings slow and sad songs, and he sings pretty and perky songs. His lyric gift is such that whatever he sings has beauty, grace and warmth."[2] Dance speculated that Hodges's ability to "sing" so effectively on his horn was one reason why the Ellington orchestra was frequently "able to operate without a vocalist for a long period."[3]

Jazz musicians made the connection as well. Earl Hines compared Hodges to Ella Fitzgerald. "Ella's a *natural!*" he said. "And when she started scatting, she wasn't just imitating somebody's horn. Musicians came around to pick up on her ideas, on what she was doing. She was to singing what Johnny Hodges was to saxophone."[4] Fitzgerald and Hodges were paired twice, the first time in 1957 on *Ella Sings the Duke Ellington Song Book,* then in 1965 on *Ella at Duke's Place.* In both cases the music consisted exclusively of compositions by Ellington and Strayhorn or pieces associated with Ellington's orchestra, and both were produced by Norman Granz, who managed Fitzgerald for many years. Ellington had admired Fitzgerald's voice since she first came to jazz prominence as a member of Chick Webb's band in 1937, but his recordings with her arose less from bilateral agreement than from a three-party armistice. Granz had been the instigator of Hodges's departure from the Ellington band in 1951. According to Granz, the two didn't speak for a year afterward, and when they subsequently worked together, their relationship was strained. "Duke liked life to go smoothly," he said. "If anything disturbed his equanimity, then that was a great drag to him. He was incredibly *égoiste* in the French sense. It disturbed him equally if the room service didn't work somewhere, or if Johnny Hodges quit the band. Both upset his life, and he hated it. So he was really piqued when I took Johnny away."[5]

When Hodges returned to Ellington in 1955, Granz negotiated a deal that allowed Hodges to record with Ellington if the latter's band would cut an album for Granz—two, if Fitzgerald were involved.[6] As a result of this détente, the sessions for the first album were "a panic scene," in Fitzgerald's words, "with Duke almost making up the arrangements as we went along." Fitzgerald was caught in the middle and, understandably upset, wanted to cancel the project. "She wanted to walk out," Granz said, and Strayhorn "spent a lot of time holding Ella's hand and saying, 'There, there, it's going to be okay.'"[7]

The album has had a long life despite its troubled birth: Both Hodges and Fitzgerald were too professional to let studio tensions get in their way. While fellow romantic Ben Webster on tenor gets a larger share of the album's spotlight, Hodges is heard to brief but pleasing effect on "I'm Just a Lucky So-and-So," "I Got It Bad (and That Ain't Good)," and "The E and D Blues (E for Ella, D for Duke)," a rocking number on which Fitzgerald and Hodges trade two-bar riffs.

On *Ella at Duke's Place*, the second installment of Granz's ransom, Hodges is frequently the principal instrumental element behind Fitzgerald (although on the album cover he is identified as the trombone player), taking extended solos on "Passion Flower," written by Strayhorn and Ellington with Hodges in mind, as its "long notes and lugubrious harmonic contours seem to cry out for" Hodges's trademark glissando. "Imagine My Frustration" is a rock-flavored number that, performed in an instrumental version, earned Hodges what Leonard Feather described as the biggest ovation of his career at the 1965 Monterey Jazz Festival.[8]

In 1956 Hodges was part of a session with singer Rosemary Clooney and the Ellington orchestra that represented a milestone in the use of the long-playing album as a vehicle for jazz. Executives at Columbia didn't believe that the 33⅓ rpm LP was the appropriate format for jazz,[9] but jazz enthusiasts working at the label were freed from prior limits by the promotion of Mitch Miller following the success of his choral version of "The Yellow Rose of Texas." Producers George Avakian, head of the division, and Irving Townsend, who would go on to produce the best-selling jazz album of all time, Miles Davis's *Kind of Blue*, wanted to make a splash with Ellington's first recording, and they decided to include a singer, the first such collaboration in Ellington's career.

Their choice for his partner, Rosemary Clooney, seemed odd despite her commercial appeal. She was one of the label's most popular artists, but she was best known for a string of ethnic-tinged pop hits under Miller's direction, most notably "Come On-a My House." She possessed a swing sensibility, however, having started out with a big band, and she had the sort of clear, refined voice that Ellington favored. Duke liked his horns to growl, but not his female singers (except for Adelaide Hall in the early years). Hodges had recently returned to the Ellington band, as had Strayhorn, and the latter was put in charge of the project because of his facility in working with singers. There was one practical impediment: Clooney was having a difficult fourth pregnancy, and on doctor's orders was confined to her home in Los Angeles. The band recorded the instrumental tracks first, and Clooney's vocals were overdubbed in her home, a novel solution at the time. The resulting album, *Blue Rose*, was an artistic but not a commercial success because it "fell between the jazz and pop audiences."[10]

A similar but less noteworthy collaboration was put together by Townsend for Columbia in 1960 when he added Hodges and tenor Ben Webster as sidemen on an album by singer Jo Stafford, *Jo + Jazz.*[11] The session represented a stretch for Stafford who, like Clooney, was not known as a jazz singer. Although she emerged as a soloist with Tommy Dorsey singing the jazz standard "Embraceable You," she was better known for her best-selling treatments of popular tunes. Hodges solos on Ellington's "Just Squeeze Me" and "Day Dream." Another recording worthy of mention in this vein is *Joya Sings Duke,*[12] a 1965 session with Joya Sherrill, who sang with Ellington from 1944 to 1948 and wrote the words to *Take the A Train.*[13] Hodges's solo on "Prelude to a Kiss" drew critical praise.

Then there is the oft-cited comment by Charlie Parker, who compared Hodges to Lily Pons, a coloratura soprano of the day, on listening to "Passion Flower" during a 1948 Leonard Feather blindfold test. "That was Duke," Bird said, "featuring Johnny Lily Pons Hodges!" Some who are familiar only with the reference to Lily Pons have suggested that Parker was being facetious, but read in full context it is clear that Parker's admiration is sincere. "I always took my hat off to Johnny Hodges 'cause he can *sing* with the horn; oh, he's a beautiful person," Parker said. "That record deserves all the stars you can muster,"[14] he added, referring to Feather's ranking system.

By way of comparison, the musicians whose efforts Parker ranked *beneath* those of Hodges on the exam were Dizzy Gillespie, Charlie Barnet, a Dixieland group, alto Sonny Stitt with Bud Powell on piano and Kenny Dorham on trumpet, the Benny Goodman Sextet, Stan Kenton, and his old boss Jay McShann, playing with Parker himself. ("How do I sound to myself?" Parker said in response to Feather. "Nowhere—I should say not!") The only music besides Hodges's that Parker said to give "all the stars you've got" was Stravinsky's *The Song of the Nightingale*.

Stanley Dance noted that it

> made good sense to get Hodges on a vocal date, but it could also cause problems. He could complement a singer admirably with his exquisite tone and his flair for melody, but he could also virtually "outsing" any singer on his alto. He never intentionally tried to upstage a singer, but he sometimes did so unconsciously simply by expressing himself on his horn.[15]

When he was paired with an inferior vocalist, such as Chubby Kemp on a 1950 small-group session, the contrast was jarring. Singers who knew Hodges only by ear before they met him held him in awe. Delores Parker Morgan, who had sung with Fletcher Henderson and Earl Hines before she joined Ellington in 1947, recalled her first encounter with Hodges thus: "I was singing, and Johnny Hodges came and stood beside me. I looked and said 'My God, I'm standing next to Johnny Hodges!' "[16]

When he broke away from Ellington, Hodges was frequently paired with vocalist Al Hibbler by producer Norman Granz. In 1952 Hibbler recorded six sides with the Johnny Hodges Orchestra; in all cases, Hodges and the other instrumentalists take a back seat to Hibbler. Hodges and Hibbler were a compatible duo, with the latter's orotund phrasing (described by Ellington as "tonal pantomime")[17] matched by the former's expressive tone.

Whether Hodges influenced jazz vocal styles is a matter of conjecture, but great leaps across musical synapses aren't required to make the connection. Ivie Anderson, Ellington's regular vocalist from 1931 to 1942, "mirrored Hodges's habit of scooping up to his longer notes from a quarter of a tone or so below their actual pitch"[18] and imitated his style in phrasing lyrics. In 1942, when he was in his late twenties, Frank Sinatra opened for the Ellington orchestra at a Hartford theater four years before the singer released his first solo album, so he had early exposure to Hodges's style.[19] While he would cite trombonist Tommy Dorsey as his main instrumental influence,[20] Sinatra acknowledged his debt to Hodges among other black instrumentalists in a 1958 interview.[21] Sinatra also performed on the same bill as Hodges at the 1946

Metronome All-Stars session,[22] and he reportedly became a great admirer of Hodges's style, as evidenced by his reaction a quarter century later while recording *Francis A. & Edward K.*, a joint effort with the Ellington orchestra.

By then, the peak of the Blanton-Webster era had receded into the distance. According to arranger Billy May, the excellence of those days "was completely gone, they had started to go to pot although they still had that distinctive sound." Things were so bad that May added several studio musicians who would follow the charts and act as bell cows to lead the somewhat tired Ellington veterans. "You never saw such completely disconnected people in your life," said trombonist Milt Bernhart, who was in attendance. "There was Johnny Hodges and Paul Gonsalves, and they were thinking about what they were going to have for dinner that night—everything else but this."[23]

Despite his usual outward appearance of boredom and distraction, Hodges, ever the professional, produced two memorable solos on the album, the first on "Yellow Days," the second on "Indian Summer," the track that is cited most often as the album's masterpiece, according to Sinatra biographer Will Friedwald. Nelson Riddle, Sinatra's long-time arranger, said it was "the only chart he wished he had written." Hodges plays "one of the most sensual solos of his life," which Bernhart remembered as "the only thing really good that happened" at the session—"quintessential Johnny Hodges." Sinatra, the epitome of cool in his time, made it a practice not to gush over the playing of musicians who backed him; he wouldn't "offer more than one or two complimentary words" unless a soloist was really exceptional. But Hodges's solo moved him when he heard it played back. "My God!" he said. "That's unbelievable, John."[24] Hodges said nothing, according to eyewitness accounts, as was his custom.

Hodges influenced the music that May wrapped around Sinatra's vocals as well. May was responsible for the "slurping" saxophones one hears on Sinatra tracks from the fifties, modeled on the style of Hodges (and to a lesser extent Willie Smith, Jimmie Lunceford's alto). "I thought it would be interesting to have the whole section do it," May said.[25] The effect May created was like a chorus of Johnny Hodges clones behind the singer, a lush wall of sound.

Sinatra's enduring achievement was to spike "pop-song tenderness with blueslike invective,"[26] in the words of Friedwald, and this technique enabled him to elevate Tin Pan Alley tunes to American art songs; they fall "somewhere in the middle" between "conscious, sublime, personal art, and simple folk songs," as Hans Castorp says in Thomas Mann's *The Magic Mountain*.[27] Sinatra learned "not to be afraid of schmaltz. It's okay when it's honest," opines Friedwald, "especially when, as with jazz's greatest sentimentalist,

Johnny Hodges, it's leavened by a touch of the blues."[28] That assessment, though largely accurate, gives too little credit to Hodges, who was a romantic or a sensualist, but not a sentimentalist.

The British writer R. H. Blyth, who popularized Japanese verse forms such as haiku among English readers, developed a handy definition of "sentimentality" that achieved wide currency when it was paraphrased by Seymour Glass in J. D. Salinger's novella *Raise High the Roof Beam, Carpenters*: We "are being sentimental," Salinger wrote, "when we give to a thing more tenderness than God gives to it."[29] Hodges, like Billie Holliday, performed sentimental love tunes but never burdened them with more emotion than their slight frames could bear. He never held a note longer than necessary to achieve an effect, nor wailed in an excessive manner to express sorrow, nor put on the trappings of woe when he played the blues. By comparison to rock guitarists who grimace in agony when they merely bend a note, Hodges was a dispassionate artist at his easel who expressed deeply felt emotions through the use of tone and colors, not flashy effects. He stopped short of the lachrymose, leaving dancers and listeners (especially women) not weeping but dreaming of romance. Spectacle, as Aristotle pointed out in his *Poetics*, is the least artistic element of tragic art, a classification that is properly applied to African American blues of the type played by Hodges, with its capacity to produce a cathartic effect by inspiring feelings of sadness, then releasing the tensions thus created.[30] Hodges's art endures because he kept his tenderness in reserve—never laying it on too thick—and used technique to express emotions without maudlin flourishes.

18

Lagomorphology

WE ARE LEFT with the question, after all the recordings and one-night stands have been accounted for, who was Johnny Hodges? A picture emerges from Hodges's words and actions, along with scraps of information contributed by different observers that, like the various versions of the samurai's death in Kurosawa's *Rashomon*, sometimes conflict with each other. If students of Bird (Charlie Parker) were ornithologists, we may need to figuratively pursue lagomorphology (the study of rabbits) in order to understand Johnny Hodges.

He played several brands of saxophone, including Conn 6M and Buescher 400 model altos and a Buescher straight soprano sax.[1] At the end of his career he also played a Vito brand alto manufactured by Leblanc.[2] He preferred a white Brilhardt mouthpiece, model 5.[3]

Hodges may be seen rarely and heard more often in movies of the Ellington band, including dramatic films such as *Black and Tan*, in which he is shown playing a clarinet; *Murder at the Vanities; Belle of the Nineties; Symphony in Black; Cabin in the Sky;* and *Reveille With Beverly.*[4] His most extended appearance on screen is a scene in *Check and Double Check*, a comedy in which black characters are portrayed by white actors in burnt-cork makeup to simulate black skin, most notably Freeman Gosden and Charles Correll, the stars of the radio comedy *Amos 'n' Andy.*[5] Hodges appears with the orchestra for a period of approximately four minutes and plays a soprano sax solo on "Old Man Blues," an Ellington composition, switching from alto in mid-tune to do so. Hodges's taciturn demeanor does him credit as other members of the band engage in somewhat exaggerated showmanship, mugging and gesturing, while he presents his usual placid countenance to the camera. Despite its now-embarrassing depiction of black manners and language through white actors, *Check and Double Check* is historically significant. It includes "the first credited appearance of a black orchestra in an otherwise all-white Hollywood film," and Ellington's music is used for more than mere background.[6]

Hodges appeared on television with the Ellington orchestra on local and national programs including the *Today Show*, the *Ella Fitzgerald Show*, and the *Timex All-Star Jazz Show*s of 1957 (when he played the "Ballet of the Flying Saucers") and 1959.[7] He appeared in "soundies," precursors of the music videos of today, such as "A Bundle of Blues," "Record Making with Duke Ellington and His Orchestra," and "Symphony in Black,"[8] as well as newsreel footage. He can be heard and seen in documentaries of the band, including a 1965 concert in Copenhagen;[9] *Memories of the Duke*, a film of an Ellington concert in Mexico; and *On the Road With Duke Ellington*.[10] At the lowest level of artistry—commercial—there are films in which the music of Ellington and Hodges serves as decorative background in pitches for products such as cigarettes and airlines.[11]

Hodges had a pet monkey that he cared enough about to grow concerned when a 1961 recording session for the *Paris Blues* soundtrack ran late. He asked Stanley Dance whether he would "go out for him before the shops shut" to get grapes for the monkey.[12] Dance was Ellington's Boswell, ready and willing to do whatever was required for the great man in order to gain access to his life and music, so much so that trumpeter Buck Clayton once said, "Every time that Duke wanted a pee, Stanley was there to unzip his fly."[13] This crack casts Dance as a sycophant, but we are in his debt for most of the first-hand accounts of the reticent Hodges that survive. On this occasion and perhaps others, Stanley got the monkey his grapes.

Hodges was a fan of the New York Yankees,[14] a betrayal of his hometown teams (the Red Sox and the Braves), but one that was understandable given that he moved to Manhattan just as the Yankees began a long period of dominance, winning nineteen World Series during his residence, while neither Boston team had won a World Series since the Red Sox in 1918.

Hodges was a member of the Freemasons, the fraternal organization that dates to the fourteenth century and prohibits discussions of politics and religion among members at their gatherings.[15] If, like many other older jazz musicians, he declined to take a public stand during the civil rights upheaval of the 1960s, he was nonetheless sensitive to the turmoil of those years and to the occasional need for acts of personal grace to bridge the prevailing mood of racial polarization. Bill Berry, a white trumpeter who played for Ellington, said that during

> the height of all the Civil Rights business . . . we used to play black theatres in Chicago and New York and the mood was not too friendly

towards white people. At the Regal Theatre in Chicago, the black guys in the band were afraid to go there it was so rough. The first day we were there, as always, you had a nine or ten o'clock rehearsal and then Johnny took me . . . around three or four restaurant bars in the vicinity of the theatre and introduced me to the bartender or the owner. I didn't realize it at the time but that was so I could go in these places all that week we were there, I don't think anybody else white would have gone, and if anybody gave me a hard time, the bartender would say, "Wait a minute, he's all right." And that was all Johnny.[16]

Hodges grew tired of life on the road, but he accommodated himself to the routine. When the band traveled by bus, he took the most coveted seat, the first one on the right-hand side, to which he felt entitled as the band's top soloist.[17] When the band traveled internationally Ellington said he "used to marvel at the effortless way our veterans like Harry Carney, Johnny Hodges, and Russell Procope made the transitions" from one far-flung outpost to the next. "They are among the world's most experienced travelers," Duke said; "they don't ruffle easily."[18] Hodges was said to be a bargain hunter when he traveled internationally, only buying things abroad that cost less than similar items would cost at home.[19]

Upon arriving in a new locale Hodges was the first to explore the territory and discover where the nearest cobbler, dry cleaner, and other providers of essential services were located. "He was a great investigator," said Mercer Ellington.[20] He also, according to Mercer, became a "suitcase freak. He only carried one at a time, but sooner or later he'd buy another one."[21] Hodges developed a strategy to deal with cramps on long-distance flights—"kicking off his shoes and elevating his feet on the back of the seat in front of him"—that wasn't available to taller members of the organization. "Sitting in one position so long is bad for the circulation," he said.[22] Still, five years before he died his response when asked about the band's demanding schedule was an exhausted "I wish we could sit down for a while."[23]

He smoked cigars (primarily in his youth) and cigarettes as he grew older, but he gave up the habit late in life on his doctor's orders.[24]

He was a gambler, particularly at "tonk," a form of gin rummy.[25] He claimed to have great success at games of chance such as Keno, the numbers, and lotteries, but as someone who insisted on being paid in cash and who carried around what Harry Carney called a "Mexican bankroll"—a large bill wrapped around a bundle of singles—it is possible that he exaggerated his winnings; gambling, like fishing and sex, is a subject about which men have been known to make inflated claims.[26]

He was, according to his long-time bandmate Sonny Greer, "very even-mannered,"[27] but he had his feuds. He would sometimes go without speaking to Barney Bigard "for months, then suddenly they would be on good terms again,"[28] and during 1958 he refused to ride with Cootie Williams when picked up in London by a British jazz writer. "You take who you like, young man," Hodges said, "but I don't run with Cootie."[29] His relationship with Ellington was occasionally strained, as Ben Webster would recall: "There might be a shout between them, but half of Johnny's heart was Duke's heart and half of Duke's heart was Johnny's heart."[30] Ellington's nephew Michael James said that "they were like brothers" in that there was frequently friction between the two, but they nonetheless defended and looked out for each other. When a club owner canceled a Boston booking after learning that Ellington was overseas and thus would not be part of the group, for example, some band members complained that Ellington had known what would happen in advance. "No, he didn't," Hodges snapped. "He doesn't lie."[31]

He had an aloof bearing that others interpreted as bored or distracted. When he soloed he would display no emotion, although "his eyes were constantly on the move." When asked the inevitable reporter's question as to what went through his mind while he soloed, he said, "I never think about what I'm playing." Although this answer may strike the reader as zenlike, his approach was, as always, practical and not mystical. "Remember," he added, "there's a lot of things I've been playing for years and I couldn't change them if I wanted to."[32] When asked what he was looking at while off on a flight of melodic fancy, he said, "I count the number of empty seats, then I count all the entrance doors in the theater."[33]

Another reading of his placid man-who-has-seen-it-all mien is that he was "cool two decades before it became fashionable," as suggested by Stanley Dance.[34] Lester Young, the man who is generally credited with the first use of the word *cool* as a term of approbation,[35] was a contemporary of Hodges, having been born in 1909. The tones the two men produced on their horns were vastly different, but Young's style on the tenor sax was similar to that of Hodges' on alto, especially on slow numbers, on which he projected a world-weary air comparable to that which Hodges affected in 1942 on Mercer Ellington's "Things Ain't What They Used to Be." Perhaps it was a case of two men simultaneously contracting early cases of the coming zeitgeist, "*cool*" now being used by many people whom Young and Hodges would undoubtedly consider to be unhip. In the narrower sense of *cool* as a musical style, Hodges and Young filled a space that hot soloists in the Coleman Hawkins mode, ebullient practitioners such as Louis Armstrong, and lyric players such as Benny Goodman left open for their more muted and blasé approach.

Hodges was, at the same time, a disciplinarian among the Ellingtonians and a bad boy with a sense of entitlement; an antinomian, he believed in rules but thought they shouldn't apply to him, and considered himself saved by the divine grace of his tone from adherence to the Laws of the Band. Later in his career he and clarinetist Jimmy Hamilton would battle to see who would be the last man to take his seat at the start of a show. "There was an old belief that the man who rushed to take his seat first was the one most afraid of losing his job," said Ellington's son Mercer. "So they *all* developed a reluctance to get onstage."[36] At the 1960 Monterey Jazz Festival, Hodges didn't take the stage until after the rest of the band had played "Perdido."[37]

Michael James said that musicians from other bands he encountered in bars would ask him, "Who's *running* that band? . . . I went to see Duke and Johnny Hodges got up and went to the bar to get a drink."[38] At the same time Hodges played the role of classroom monitor, whipping newer members into shape. He would address all and sundry as "young man,"[39] to most ears a salutation likely to be followed by a lecture, and would reprimand junior musicians who showed signs of intoxication with the words "How come you can be so evil and play so angelic?"[40] Once, to put an overly ambitious neophyte in his place, he cracked, "I've been playing this for 30 years, man, and I don't need that kind of help," and he would often function as self-appointed conductor, waving his hand behind his chair to direct the play of an errant bandmember.[41]

He seemed to be a reluctant soloist. According to Harry Carney, at first he wouldn't stand up to solo; later, when the band began to use amplification, he would approach a microphone hesitantly, although he eventually perfected the placement of his body and the bell of his horn to use electronic enhancement effectively.[42] An overwrought characterization of Hodges in a 1944 *New Yorker* article said that he "advances toward the front of the stage threateningly and . . . holds his instrument as if it were a machine-gun with which he was about to spray the crowd,"[43] but his bandmate Shorty Baker interpreted his demeanor in a less sensational light, saying, "Nobody knows what Johnny Hodges feels inside when he walks out to the mike. He may look as though he is on his last walk to the gallows, but he appreciates the applause and he thanks the audience with a million-dollars-worth of melody!"[44] The air of gravity that came over him when it was his turn to solo was a reflection of the fact that he was a craftsman, not a showman. "It's hard work. Very hard. Still hard, and always will be hard—see? Everybody thinks it's something easy after you've been playing twenty or thirty years. But it's *always* hard."[45] Apparently minor details such as the placement of his feet when he set himself to solo were the product of professional premeditation. His colleague Cootie Williams explained: "[S]o many young musicians don't even know how to stand properly."[46] Hodges knew how, placing his feet at approximately a 45° angle.

He was, at the same time, the dourest personality in the Ellington band and the one who could be depended on to deflate rising tensions with his droll sense of humor. "[N]o matter how tense the environment," said Julian Priester, a trombonist who was with Ellington for a brief period in 1969, "he injected such humor into the atmosphere that tension subsided right away."[47] His bandmate Al Sears said, "We sat beside each other for seven or eight years. We laughed about things. But it was always a chuckle. He didn't smile too much."[48] There is also evidence of his comic touch in his fondness for curious expressions that he picked up in his travels and appropriated as song titles. For instance, "Can a Moose Crochet?" comes from a saying used as an "emphatic negative" he had heard on a road trip to the West.[49]

Once he entered the romantic realm from which he drew inspiration for his solos his imperturbability became impregnable. Nat Hentoff recalled a date in Boston in the late 1940s at which Hodges was taking a solo when the dancers stopped and vacated a wide space on the floor for two knife-wielding combatants. "The other Ellington musicians leaned forward, still playing but clearly fearful" of bloodshed, while "Hodges, looking on impassively, did not in the least break the romantic mood he was setting." The two angry men were ultimately dragged off while Hodges played on, not missing a note. The "other musicians relaxed," Hentoff noted, "but Hodges didn't have to."[50]

As for his view of his place in the grand scheme of things, in a 1964 interview given when he was on the home stretch of his long career, he recalled one international tour the band made where nearly "everywhere we went revolution broke out, or we just missed an incident. Guys were walking the streets with machine guns. But I'll tell you this," he reflected. Music "has a whole lot to it. It can soothe a lot of pain, and it'll get closer to people than money can. . . . [Y]ou can go to the most prejudiced state and they will accept the music you play. . . . Yes, music's a hell of a weapon."[51]

19

The Blues

THE BLUES IS both a musical idiom and an inheritance. You can learn the conventions of the blues—the twelve-bar standard length, the chord progressions, the flatted thirds and sevenths—and still not strike a listener as playing the blues when you try to. The man who first grafted the shoot of the blues onto the larger stalk of American popular music, W. C. Handy, put it thus:

> To one not born in the environment and lacking a folklore memory, it is difficult to express in musical notation all that Negro music implies. Herein lies an enigma as deep as the secret of the blues. . . . It is my contention that all real work in typical Negro music can come only from one to the manner born. It's his mother tongue. The art of writing blues or spirituals can be assumed but cannot be delegated outside of the blood.[1]

Johnny Hodges was born and raised in the Boston area—not fertile ground for African American music—and mastered the blues through assiduous devotion to the recordings of Louis Armstrong and Sidney Bechet, two jazz practitioners from New Orleans who played frequently, but not exclusively, in a blues style. Hodges thus falls into Handy's category of one who assumed the blues even if the circumstances of his childhood meant he wasn't born to them—except by virtue of his genes. Helen Oakley, who persuaded Duke Ellington to feature Hodges playing the blues in small-group settings, said that "the 'blues' as interpreted by Johnny Hodges might serve as a symbol of the eternal and all-powerful cry" of his African race. "It has something more to it than merely swing, it has in it something of religion, something not to be caught in words, something of the supernatural. Underlying everything, there is the strain of melancholy, of elusiveness, of the indefinable."[2]

A linguistic link connected Hodges to the sounds he heard on recordings made by musicians far to the south. Stanley Crouch suggested that Ben Webster, an acolyte of Hodges, "appropriated the entire vocabulary of Negro vocal and instrumental timbres into his saxophone" and expanded its powers by "capturing the timbres of Negro speech, song, instrumental techniques and the percussive rhythms of Negro dance."[3] Hodges was certainly surrounded by black speech in his home and in Boston's South End and may have harkened to the sounds of Bechet as a displaced person latches on to one whom he hears speak in his native accent. However Hodges arrived at his final destination—through musical mimicry, a common tongue out of Africa shared with the New Orleans masters, or racial DNA—-a bluesman he became.

Although the blues cannot be, in Handy's high-flown phrase, "delegated outside of the blood," not all African American musicians can or even want to play the blues. Dizzy Gillespie claimed to be an example of the latter group, saying that though blues was the music of his people, "I'm not what you call a 'blues' player. I'd love to, I feel it, but I'm not. . . . Mine ain't the real blues with toe jam between your toes, come in and bend a note around the corner." Gillespie valued the blues more highly when he heard others who possessed the gift he thought he lacked such as Hodges, of whom he said, "Johnny Hodges is a blues player, quiet as it's kept, from Boston, Massachusetts. He could moan a while. Moaning—all that goes with the blues."[4]

But the blues as played by Hodges and the music commonly described as the blues today are so different as to be almost two different genres. The popular understanding of the term *blues* as this book is written consists of species that don't represent the entire genus. The music that is sold as the blues today is of two types: first, urban, electrified blues, and second, acoustic country blues, both dominated by the guitar. The blues of the Louisiana jazzmen that Hodges imbibed has largely been forgotten or is now misplaced in the cornball catch-all category "Dixieland." In the words of Ralph Ellison, by "the twentieth century the blues divided and became, on the one hand, a professionalized form of entertainment, while remaining, on the other, a form of folklore,"[5] with jazz and horn-based blues treated as the former, and guitar-based blues considered as the latter, even as that style has become ever more mannered. Jazz scholar Sidney Finkelstein found in the blues that Hodges played a further dimension, saying, "[T]he folk-song character of many of Ellington's blues is of a sweeter type than those of the Mississippi blues singers or the Louisiana jazzmen, suggesting that they have their origins in the mountain ballads which have been the source of other jazz standards such as

'Careless Love Blues' or 'How Long Blues.' "[6] If a promoter of a blues festival were to book a band playing blues in the style of Johnny Hodges today, the audience would greet the music with consternation, even catcalls—"That's not the blues!"—and demands for refunds. The blues of today comes in a limited number of shades, using fewer than all twelve notes in the musical scale, whereas the blues as played by Hodges is multi-hued and performed by ensembles that include a number of wind instruments. How to explain this apparent case of mistaken identity?

Handy, the man generally given credit for converting the blues from a rudimentary folk art into one memorialized by notation and performed before audiences far removed from the communities from which it sprang, took the music of itinerant minstrel shows that he had heard (and played) and transformed it into a popular and commercial mode of African American culture.[7] Handy formalized unwritten blues—"the song of a Negro plowman"[8] he heard in the spring, for example—and turned them into compositions that spread first via sheet music and then by gramophone discs, which became the dominant musical technology in 1910. Handy self-published his first blues composition, "Memphis Blues," in 1912, and two years later it was released on record.[9] Johnny Hodges was born in 1907, and so he caught the first wave of the blues surging across America at flood tide.

The result, after a fitful start, was a national sensation. A man whom Handy identified only as "Z," one of two white men who persuaded him to sell the copyright to "Memphis Blues," told him he was convinced the song would sell several hundred thousand copies, calling Handy "the greatest ragtime writer of the day."[10] New lyrics were added and, Z wrote to Handy twenty years later, "a brown-skin gal . . . put the new song over" with her performances at a New York cabaret."[11] "Almost instantly the word *blues* replaced the word *rag* in hit songs, soon to be replaced in turn by *jazz*," according to Gary Giddins,[12] and the connection between the two was not just sequential but also lineal. "Blues Is Jazz and Jazz Is Blues," noted the *Chicago Daily Tribune* in an early written use of the term *jazz* to refer to a musical style derived from the blues. "What are the blues?" an interrogator asks in the newspaper story. "Jazz!" proclaims a young female piano player. The blues "aren't new," she says. "They are just reborn into popularity," and their "trade name" is jazz.[13] It is this dialect of the blues that one hears in the notes of jazz musicians, not the latter-day blues we have come to know primarily through the work of white guitarists imitating black forebears. In Handy's view, his codification of the blues "set a new fashion in American popular music and contributed to the rise of jazz, or if you prefer, swing."[14]

This is not to suggest that Handy is solely responsible for the influence of the blues on jazz. Gunther Schuller wrote that "blues and early jazz met mostly in the vaudeville-minstrel shows and carnivals around the turn of the century.[15] King Oliver, Louis Armstrong's inspiration and mentor, is believed to have been born as early as 1881 or as late as 1885 and was playing professionally by the time he was fifteen (as computed from the latter year);[16] his compositions include "West End Blues" and "Canal Street Blues." Sidney Bechet, whose birth year is a matter of some speculation but was probably 1897,[17] was a noted soloist in the blues style.[18] Bechet and Oliver grew up in New Orleans and never learned (and in fact refused to learn) to read music, so the blues entered jazz via unwritten sources as well as through sheet music.

Although some early jazz songs fail to satisfy a strict definition of the blues because they depart from the standard twelve-bar format ("Jazz Me Blues" comes to mind), such tunes are typically played with accents that the ears of an earlier generation would recognize as "blue." The revival of the more primitive styles of blues in the middle of the twentieth century was in part a reaction against these jazz-inflected blues, which had become overly refined in big band arrangements and were accordingly rejected by revivalists who wanted to trace the river of the music to its headwaters in their quest for the earlier unwritten blues that had inspired Handy. He described it as the "twelve-bar, three-line form . . . with its three-chord basic harmonic structure . . . used by Negro roustabouts, honky-tonk piano players, wanderers and others of their underprivileged but undaunted class from Missouri to the Gulf."[19]

That the horn-dominated variety of blues played by Louis Armstrong and Sidney Bechet is just as legitimate and authentic as the guitar-based music we think of as the blues today can be demonstrated by a sampling of the music listened to by patrons of small taverns known as "juke joints" in the Mississippi Delta in 1941. A Library of Congress researcher visited five such establishments in Clarksdale, Mississippi, that year and made a list of the records he found in their jukeboxes. There were ten by Count Basie's band; eight by alto sax man Louis Jordan; six by Jimmie Lunceford's band; two by Johnny Hodges ("Good Queen Bess" and "That's the Blues, Old Man"), although none by the larger Ellington orchestra; two by Billie Holiday; two by Jay McShann; and three by Louis Armstrong. All of these artists can be accurately classified as practitioners of blues in a jazz style or jazz in a blues style. The two categories form apparently different surfaces on a musical Möbius strip, and it is generally impossible to say where one category leaves off and the other begins when the blues is played in this mode, which is certainly not the style of blues popular today.

By contrast, the number of records in the more primitive style (without horns or in rare cases with a single trumpet or saxophone) found in the Mississippi juke joints was significantly smaller. The most popular artist was Big Bill Broonzy with three records; next were Sonny Boy Williamson, Roosevelt Sykes, Memphis Slim, and Peetie Wheatstraw with two apiece. Musicians in this latter class were even outnumbered by white swing bands such as those of Artie Shaw and Woody Herman.[20] The patrons of such rural entertainment spots apparently preferred to listen to horn-complemented jazz when they went out on the town and put their money where their tastes lay, perhaps because their lives of hard labor and isolation in the county made them yearn for urban sophistication. This speculation is supported by Ralph Ellison, who said that the music commentary that he and others in Oklahoma read in northern black papers "brought the excitement of the big cities to the provinces."[21] The self-conscious primitivism of so many white musicians who claim to play the blues in our time thus appears as something put on, a *nostalgie de la boue* (yearning for the mud), as the French say, like "distressed" jeans made to appear worn when newly sold. In their misguided pursuit of an idyllic Eden that black residents of the rural South sought to escape, their faux bumpkinism recalls Antisthenes, the Greek philosopher who, to show his wisdom and humility, wore an old robe that Socrates saw through, literally and figuratively, saying, "Your vanity shows through the holes in your clothes."[22]

Handy's orchestra was, according to him, "the first . . . in the land" to include a saxophone (a tenor), and thus the instrument began to acquire a repertoire in the blues. These are the blues that Johnny Hodges played and composed and which he rang changes on so prolifically throughout his life.[23] "He has a million of 'em," Duke Ellington once remarked with amused admiration after Hodges supplied a riff for an improvised blues at a recording session.[24] Jazz historian and critic Albert Murray said that Hodges "functioned in effect as Ellington's instrumental extension of Bessie Smith,"[25] and James P. Johnson echoed this sentiment, saying, "Old Duke's main blues singer was always old Johnny Hodges on that alto, even when he had Herb Jeffries."[26] Hodges's departure from the Ellington orchestra in the early fifties was fueled in part by his fondness for the "the old stuff" and his distaste for the more modern effects that his boss sometimes experimented with. In an incident recounted by jazz critic Dan Morgenstern, Ellington once called for an arrangement by Teo Macero, "an ambitious composer with modernist leanings." The "ensemble began to struggle through it, producing odd and un-Ellingtonian sounds. Hodges stopped playing, held up his part for all in the band to see, and slowly and deliberately tore the music paper in half."[27] Ellington never called the piece again.

When he returned to the Ellington fold, Hodges found an outlet for his love of the blues and its simplicity by playing with organist "Wild Bill" Davis. The two had first paired up in the summer of 1948 when Ellington was overseas. He left the rest of his orchestra behind in the United States and, as Hodges told it, "While we were laying off, Russell Procope and I came to Atlantic City with our wives for a little vacation." He continued,

> One night, we decided to go to [Gracie's Little] Belmont to hear Wild Bill [Davis]. He invited us to a jam session, so we took our horns and we jammed and jammed, until seven or eight in the morning. Our jamming drew most of the people over from the Club Harlem, and a couple of clubowners from New York heard us.[28]

Davis played the Hammond organ, and that night in Atlantic City may properly be cited as the birth date of the organ-sax combo format, which survives to this day, undergoing a recent revival as part of the "acid jazz" movement. Davis was a pianist and arranger with Louis Jordan from 1945 to 1948 but began to specialize on the Hammond organ in 1949. His switch resulted in the prototype for the organ combo; beginning in 1951 he toured with a trio that included guitar and drums, and his music found wide acceptance among rhythm and blues fans.[29] Before that time the organ was rarely used in jazz, Fats Waller and Count Basie being notable exceptions.[30]

Davis cited Ellington as an influence in his writing and arranging. The two met in 1945, when Davis played an engagement with Louis Jordan in New York.

> We were there three months, on the same bill as Duke Ellington. That was where I got to know him. I did a couple of arrangements for him and one of them was "Love You Madly." Arranging was my true love, but it meant sitting up and writing all night long. On the organ, I could do the same thing almost instantly, and my main approach to that instrument was from the standpoint of arranging for a band. With the Hammond organ and Leslie [revolving] speakers, I could get closest to the sound of a full band, which was what I was trying to duplicate."[31]

Davis was thus able with a small group to give Hodges a large ensemble backing, the orchestral support that the Ellington orchestra provided him, and the jeweler's cotton on which the gems of his solos rested. With the addition of Hodges on sax, the organ combo overcame the stigma of the skating rink, the setting where Davis had first played the instrument in Chicago, and sax-organ combos grew in popularity. The format was economical, allowing clubs to pay a handful of musicians rather than a big band; the two instruments produced a sound that could be either powerful or intimate and so could be calibrated to fill venues both large and small.

The first recording that featured Hodges and Davis was *Blue Hodge*, released in 1961. Davis recalled the session and his impression of Hodges thus:

> I don't suppose there is anybody in the business who can do more with a melody than Johnny Hodges. Although I'd known and admired him for a long time, I'd never had the pleasure of working with him before we made that *Blue Hodge* album for Verve. You find out so much more about a musician when you work with him and I soon realized this was one time when melody wasn't going to be neglected, so I decided to do all I could to enhance what he was doing. I believe that you've got to tell a story in any kind of music, too. It should have a beginning, continuity, climax, and an ending.[32]

It was Hodges's first experience recording with an organist, and he was pleased with the results. "Turned out real good," he said. "[T]hat Wild Bill Davis can play!"[33]

There followed two albums in 1963: *Sandy's Gone*, which has Hodges and Davis playing pop music in a big band setting, and *Mess of Blues*, a small combo recording. Hodges contributes two riff blues to the latter, "A&R Blues" and "Little John, Little John" (perhaps a reference to his son), and Davis adds one of his compositions ("Stolen Sweets"), consistent with Hodges's policy of including at least one Davis original on their albums. "I try to accommodate a guest who is on the date, like Wild Bill Davis, by using one or two" of his songs, he told British jazz writer Max Jones.[34] The prize of the session is the jazz standard "I Cried for You," the song on which Hodges backed Billie Holiday in 1936. When Hodges finished his treatment of the melody there was nothing but silence and appreciative glances at what he had wrought, according to Stanley Dance, who was in attendance.[35]

In 1964 Davis appeared on the Hodges album *Blue Rabbit*, and in 1965 Davis and Hodges were busy collaborating on *Joe's Blues*, *Wings and Things*, *Blue Pyramid*, and *Con Soul and Sax*. On *Blue Pyramid* Hodges's son formed part of a rotating team of three drummers. The selections include two compositions on which Hodges shares credit, "At Dawn," with long-time Ellington copyist Tom Whaley, and "Rabbit Out of the Hat," a collaboration with Mercer Ellington. There are also two works written solely by Hodges, "Hash Brown" and "Blues for Madeleine," the latter a tribute to French jazz critic Madeleine Gautier, who (with co-author Hugues Panassié) rated Hodges "with Benny Carter the best [alto] in jazz" in their Dictionary of Jazz.[36]

The Hodges-Davis collaboration ended with the release of the live album *In Atlantic City* in 1966. This effort represented a return to the beginning for Hodges and Davis because it was recorded at Grace's Little Belmont, the club where the two had first played together in 1948. On this occasion Hodges was in town to play with the Ellington orchestra, but he found the time and energy to join Davis as well. Hodges was fifty-nine, but he had recently taken steps to improve his health; he'd given up smoking six years earlier, and he hadn't had a drink for three and a half months. He looked, according to Ellington chronicler Stanley Dance, "surprisingly fit."[37] Though it was a live club date, the musicians treated the occasion as a studio session, playing multiple takes until Hodges was satisfied.

At the time there was a lively jazz scene in Atlantic City, and the organ-sax combo had developed to a point where, in Hodges's words, the saxophonists went around "like gunfighters trying to cut each other down," while younger musicians were intrigued by an alignment that featured Lawrence Brown on trombone rather than a tenor. "You can tell by the way they look that Lawrence got to 'em,"[38] Hodges said.

Hodges's next organ combo album, *Rippin' & Runnin'*, was recorded with Willie Gardner on organ, not Davis. Gardner appeared on other albums but has gone unnoticed by jazz encyclopedists.[39] The session was put together by Verve A&R (artists and repertoire) man Esmond Edwards, who sought to put Hodges in a "contemporary setting, with young, imaginative jazzmen in the rhythm section." It was "very different from the Hines/Hodges kind of setting," Edwards said, "but it seemed to work very well for Johnny. He opened up in a manner that's relatively rare for him."[40] Hodges's wife Cue contributed one number, "Cue Time," a comfortable blues of the sort that her husband favored, which fit him like a sweater she'd picked out knowing his size. "Rio Segundo," a Hodges composition with a Latin flavor, is the song that he promised a brewer he would dedicate to a beer he'd sampled on the Ellington orchestra's tour of South America in 1968. "Jeep Bounces Back," another Hodges number, recalls his earlier popular variations on the theme of that nickname of his.

Hodges would reunite with Davis on April 27, 1970, four years after their live session in Atlantic City. On that day, they went into the National Recording Studios in New York to record five numbers for the last album Hodges would make with Duke Ellington. It would be Hodges's musical return to New Orleans, the city whose native sons Armstrong and Bechet had first inspired him a half century earlier.[41]

20

The Out Chorus

IN MARCH 1970 Johnny Hodges traveled to New York from an Ellington date at the Royal York Hotel in Toronto to record the last album released under his name as a featured artist, *3 Shades of Blue: Johnny Hodges with Leon Thomas and Oliver Nelson*.[1] The musicians in the sessions represented, on one hand, several members of the jazz establishment: Al Grey (trombone), Frank Wess (tenor), Earl Hines and Hank Jones (piano), Ron Carter (bass), Grady Tate (drums), and Hodges. On the other, there were younger musicians, twenty-four-year-old Randy Brecker on trumpet and singer Leon Thomas, in knitted African *kufi* hat, both of whom seemed, from their smiles on the album cover, happy to work with Hodges, the old master with his conked hair and look of well-fed seniority.

The arranger was Oliver Nelson, who had worked with Hodges on the 1962 album *The Eleventh Hour*, an attempt to exploit the latter's reputation as the most romantic saxophone in the business.[2] The set list was a mixture of Ellington numbers, familiar and obscure, with compositions by Nelson and Thomas, a member of the Count Basie Orchestra in the early-to-mid 1960s who had begun to sing in a manner that improbably combined yodeling with scat-singing. He is perhaps best known for *The Creator Has a Master Plan*, a 1969 avant-garde hit (if that's not an oxymoron) with Pharoah Sanders.[3] The arrangements by Oliver—a quarter century younger than Hodges—were energetic, and Hodges rose to the challenge on the upbeat tempos, while settling into his familiar groove on bluesier selections. One can imagine Hodges rolling his eyes at the experimental efforts by Thomas (three decades his junior) to break new ground; jazz critic Nat Hentoff is diplomatic in the liner notes, drolly observing that the singer "is going his own way into the farther possibilities of vocalizing the new jazz."[4]

After those sessions Hodges rejoined the Ellington band as it finished the Toronto gig, then hit the road to play fourteen one-nighters in approximately a month across Canada and the western United States.[5] At the end of this trek the full Ellington complement settled in New Orleans for a five-day engagement at Al Hirt's night club, then two days of performances at the New Orleans Jazz & Heritage Festival.[6] George Wein had commissioned an Ellington suite for the festival, and the band began to rehearse the piece in a manner Ellington sometimes used to develop new works on the fly: he inserted parts of the composition into the band's playlist in the final days before the festival, making for some dissatisfied customers. One man's persistent requests for "Sophisticated Lady" went unsatisfied, and after the band played a movement of the suite instead, the disgruntled patron stood up, unsteady on his feet, and said with slurred enunciation, "I don't believe you even know *how* to play 'Sophisticated Lady.'"[7]

On April 25, 1970, the band performed a partial version of *New Orleans Suite* at the festival, where it was well received. Wein was moved; "It gave me a chill," he said. "That was Duke at his greatest."[8] The performance included only five movements; four others—including a star turn for Hodges on soprano sax, "Portrait of Sidney Bechet"—were still being written, and Ellington began in earnest to complete them. Three decades had passed since Hodges had last played the soprano, his first musical love, on a recording date; the tune was "That's the Blues Old Man," a number he composed.[9] Hodges had stopped playing soprano, according to Rex Stewart, when he had asked Duke for extra pay to play a second instrument. Hodges was within his rights to do so, as the by-laws of Local 802 provided that (with few exceptions) a musician who played two instruments was entitled to double pay. As Stewart put it, "Request denied, and that golden tone exited from Ellington's band forever."[10]

Hodges kept the soprano sax that Bechet had given him long before, but he used it so little he would say he was "about ready to make a lamp out of it."[11] Every now and then he would idly suggest that he was going to take up the instrument again, but he would always renege. Harry Carney interpreted this demurral to mean that "Johnny wouldn't have any trouble *playing* it, but ... he isn't going to play it in public unless he can play up to the level he sets himself."[12] Ellington had been thinking about how he might "persuade [Hodges] to get his soprano out once more" for the Bechet portrait;[13] he asked his son Mercer to talk to Hodges to see if he would relent, and Hodges replied, "It will cost him." When Mercer relayed Hodges's response to his father, Duke said, "Pay him what he wants."[14]

Hodges had not been in good health. He came down with swollen glands on the band's September 1968 tour of South America, missing several performances, and in April 1969 he suffered a heart seizure and had to leave the band for two months.[15] A British jazz writer, interviewing Hodges during a European tour in November of that year, noted that he had opted out of ensemble playing and confined himself to solos. He began to skip dates that didn't appeal to him, such as a sacred music concert scheduled for December in Detroit, just one night after flying back from England. "The band's playing at a church next Monday," Hodges said, "but I ain't going."[16]

He had been a lucky all his life, and his good fortune had carried over to the natural shocks the flesh is heir to. According to Mercer Ellington, he had three times happened "to be near the best possible hospital" when he had heart attacks; in the case of the April 1969 incident, he was stricken on a flight following a three-night stand at the Atkinson Hotel in Indianapolis while sitting next to an oxygen tank. There was a doctor on board, and he was rushed to a hospital as soon as the plane landed.[17] Norris Turney and Gregory Herbert substituted for him on alto for a period of almost two months.[18]

On May 11, 1970, however, his luck ran out. At the end of a long stretch of touring, both domestic and international,[19] his strength may have been at an ebb. At his dentist's office in Manhattan, he got up from the chair to go to the bathroom partway through a procedure, took a few steps—and collapsed.[20] He did not recover, and was pronounced dead at Harlem Hospital at 4:30 P.M. that day. "I sent him to the dentist," his widow said, "and the Lord brought him back."[21]

His Certificate of Death gave his name simply (and incorrectly) as "John Hodges." The cause of death listed was hypertensive cardiovascular disease—elevated blood pressure resulting in heart failure—due to cardiac hypertrophy, a thickening of the heart muscle that decreases the size of the chambers of the heart. That organ, which we consider the seat of the emotions, had toughened on the outside just as Hodges himself had maintained his steely exterior throughout his career, while a warm core burned within it—and him. He had poured his heart into song for four decades with Ellington, and it had finally given out.

Funeral arrangements were made by Russell Procope, Hodges's colleague in the reed section. Ellington avoided funerals, as he did any intimation of mortality, but he attended Hodges's ceremony and comforted Hodges' mother, the "Good Queen Bess" referred to in his genial song, who kissed her son for the last time as he lay in his casket. "He was a good son to me," she said to Stanley Dance, who reported that she "then turned away, upright, composed, dry-eyed."[22] The death of her only son must have affected her more deeply than she revealed at the time; she survived him by only a few months. "She got sick and lost the desire to live," her granddaughter Lorna Hodges Mafata said.[23]

The ceremony was arranged by Procope at the Harlem Masonic Temple of which both men were members, thereby avoiding affected religious sentiment that Hodges would have scoffed at.[24] Ellington eulogized Hodges thus:

> Never the world's most highly animated showman or greatest stage personality, but a tone so beautiful it sometimes brought tears to the eyes—this was Johnny Hodges. This is Johnny Hodges.
>
> Because of this great loss, our band will never sound the same.
>
> Johnny Hodges and his unique tonal personality have gone to join the ever so few inimitables—those whose sounds stand unimitated, to say the least—Art Tatum, Sydney [sic] Bechet, Django Reinhardt, Billy Strayhorn.
>
> Johnny Hodges sometimes sounded beautiful, sometimes romantic, and sometimes people spoke of his tone as being sensuous. I've heard women say his tone was so compelling.
>
> He played numbers like "Jeep's Blues," "Things Ain't What They Used To Be," "I Let A Song Go Out Of My Heart," "All Of Me," "On The Sunny Side Of The Street," Billy Strayhorn's "Passion Flower," and "Day Dream" and many more.
>
> With the exception of a year or so, almost his entire career was with us. Many came and left, sometimes to return. So far as our wonderful listening audience was concerned, there was a great feeling of expectancy when they looked up and saw Johnny Hodges sitting in the middle of the saxophone section, in the front row.
>
> I am glad and thankful that I had the privilege of presenting Johnny Hodges for forty years, night after night. I imagine I have been much envied, but thanks to God. . . .
>
> May God bless this beautiful giant in his own identity. God Bless Johnny Hodges.[25]

Ellington's prediction that his band would never sound the same was more than post-mortem flattery; when Hodges died "virtually all of the recent pieces associated with him were eliminated from the then repertory of the band," according to jazz scholar Gunther Schuller, because his loss "was such for Ellington that he could not bear to have anyone else play them—even if there had been someone in the band who *could* play them."[26] Norris Turney, who took over as first-chair alto, wrote a tribute to him—"Checkered Hat," after an article of headgear that Hodges favored—and that was that.[27]

Hodges was buried in Flushing Cemetery in the borough of Queens, New York, next to the plot that would later hold his wife Cue, who died in 1993, and his son, who died in 1984. The *New York Times* seemed to go out of its way to get the facts of his life wrong in its obituary the next day. It repeated the oft-committed error that his birth year was 1906, didn't include "Cornelius" in his name, and gave his wife's name as "Ethel," not "Edith." As for references in the broader stream of American culture beyond the narrow channels of jazz, this writer has found only two: First, in the Raymond Carver short story "Vitamins," the narrator says a black musician named Benny "liked to talk about Johnny Hodges, how he'd played sax back-up for Johnny. He'd say things like, 'When Johnny and me had this gig in Mason City.' "[28] Second, in a 1996 episode of the CBS comedy *Public Morals*, a cop speaks wistfully about Hodges, a bit of dialogue that a television critic described as out-of-character "cerebralspeak," a measure of the depths of obscurity to which the man who was once one of the most famous saxophonists in the world had fallen.[29]

Hodges's death had a deep impact on Ellington, who carried his eulogy around with him until he died, or, rather, had his factotum Stanley Dance keep a copy in a briefcase to read when Ellington was in a morose or reflective mood.[30] On a 1971 tour of Europe Ellington stood up from the piano bench at a concert in England to announce a tribute to Hodges. After conducting the band through the first few bars, he stopped the music in dissatisfaction— a breach of decorum unthinkable for Ellington—and called out "Stop, stop! I think we can do better than that. Kindly start again, gentlemen." This was during a down period in the band's history, and though the "rest of the concert was slipshod too. . . . Duke let it go. He wouldn't have it for Hodges, though," according to Ellington's longtime friend Renee Diamond.[31] The bond between Ellington and Hodges was sealed for the last time when, at Ellington's funeral four years later, Hodges's alto sax was heard from beyond the grave in a tape of "Heaven" and "Almighty God" from Ellington's *Second Sacred Concert* that was played at the ceremony.[32] "This created a very beautiful mood," wrote Stanley Dance, "but Johnny's chorus was simply too much in the circumstances, and the tears really rolled." Count Basie, sitting "in the front row opposite the family . . . wept unashamedly."[33]

In a comment following her husband's death, Hodges's widow made it clear that, in her view, her late husband was a great artist in his own right, and not just an appendage of the Ellington corpus: "Writers talk about Johnny like he was another instrument that Ellington played. But he was his own man all the way—with or without Duke. When he made music, he made the music he wanted to, the way *he* wanted to."[34] Hodges himself had said, "What he gets me to play is my own idea—nobody else's. Nobody tells me how to play anything. He says 'You play this' and I play it my way. That's all. That's the way it's been—and that's the way *he's* been over the years."[35] This is supposedly a paradox, given that Hodges was a member of an orchestra, but Ellington on numerous occasions put a particular solo or passage entirely within the discretion of his employees, particularly Hodges and Billy Strayhorn, his two principal composing collaborators.[36] "They'd been so important to him," Norman Granz said. "He'd wave his hands and say to Strays at the piano or to Hodges, 'Do a little thing in here,' and they'd do it, help him out." And, Granz noted, the relationship was reciprocal: "It wasn't only that Duke wrote for Hodges. Sometimes *Hodges* played something with *Duke* in mind."[37]

A Vito brand saxophone that Hodges used late in his career ended up in the hands of Frank Wess, who is best known for his work with Count Basie's band and who had played on Hodges's last album. The horn is ornately engraved; Hodges's name appears on the body, the bell of the horn, and the mouthpiece. Each key bears decorative figures, and atop the octave key is a snake's head, a symbol of good luck from the game of craps, with diamond chips for eyes that may have brought a smile to the face of the lifelong gambler. On the body is engraved the image of a wasp, which in some African traditions is a symbol of control over life's circumstances.[38]

In the end, Hodges didn't do too badly for himself. He lived longer than the average male, black or white, born in the first decade of the twentieth century by thirty years in the former case and fifteen in the latter.[39] His estate was valued at $86,000, which in 2017 would have equaled more than $546,000, a sum few jazz musicians then or now could hope to accumulate in a lifetime. This figure would not include property he held jointly with his wife or life insurance payable to his survivors, of which he reportedly "carried a good deal."[40] One source describes a $25,000 policy, which would be worth about $158,000 today.[41] He would have done better if, early in his career, he hadn't sold the rights to his songs on a piecework basis, as many other musicians have done to their regret, but in his case he sold them to Ellington, so it is not clear that he lost much in the transaction. On one hand, Ellington was Hodges's employer and thus had a colorable claim to the riffs that Hodges produced so prodigiously during rehearsals; under copyright law an employer can assert ownership in an employee's output as "works made for hire," compositions deemed to have been created by an employer if written by an individual within the scope of his employment. That this was Ellington's view—at least as a starting point in negotiations—is apparent from remarks he made about a joint work in which Hodges had no interest, "Mood Indigo." Mitchell Parish had written the lyrics to the song but received no royalties from it because, as Ellington said, "he was signed with the company, so they just bought him outright, and he was on a regular stipend, on a salary."[42] Ellington understood that it was in his financial interest to stand on his rights in this regard, and he did so to the maximum extent possible without losing an employee as valued as Hodges.

On the other hand, Ellington provided a ready market for the riffs produced by Hodges, sparing him the time and trouble of working them into finished products and shopping them to other bands. Hodges was free to keep his marketable musical thoughts to himself rather than sharing them within Duke's earshot (although it is difficult to imagine how Hodges could have been more reserved than he was). He didn't, and he was rewarded by his salary, which was usually the highest among Ellington's musicians.[43] In addition, there were the sums Ellington paid to buy rights to Hodges's contributions and the share of composers' credit he gave him. According to trumpeter Freddie Jenkins, Ellington would share credit with a musician if the riff "didn't require too much work to fit the band." If, on the other hand, the bandleader had to "take it home, arrange it up, add what needs to be added to it and it comes up a number," he would take full credit.[44]

Hodges would frequently grumble about the arrangement,[45] but even the most ardent of his fans must admit that Ellington fashioned scraps of melody into saleable goods in a way that made him more than a mere compiler of musical inventory. By this capacity for aggregation of sounds he heard around him, he produced the revenue that kept the band together and the musicians—including Hodges—well paid. And then there were the burdens that Duke bore as leader. Hodges discovered during his time as front man of a combo that he was not well suited to handle the managerial and promotional side of the music business, but he had developed a case of "bandleader fever" or "leaderitis," as Rex Stewart called it, terms musicians use to describe the ailment that infects a delusional peer who believes the additional money made by the man whose name is on the music stands isn't commensurate with the work required to manage a group.

According to Ellington, Hodges influenced a number of musicians in his lifetime,[46] and this assertion is more than mere puffing about a key employee; sources cite Hilton Jefferson, Johnny Bothwell, Willie Smith,

Russell Procope, Toots Mondello, Woody Herman, and even Benny Carter as having imitated or been influenced by his style.[47] On one occasion when Ellington heard a recording by Herman of "I Got It Bad and That Ain't Good" on a radio show, he asked the host, "Are you sure that's not Johnny?"[48] Hodges's influence was confirmed by jazz critic and novelist Albert Murray in a fictional reverie describing the effect Hodges had on those who heard him from afar, as Sidney Bechet's records had in turn impressed Hodges.

Anytime a band pulled into town early enough before the engagement it was always the same story no matter where it was:

"Man, here that bad Mr. Johnny Hodges. Man, here the Rabbit, in person all the way from the Cotton Club in the Heart of Harlem. Hey Johnny, you know that thing you did called Squaty [sic] Roo? Man I played that record and some cats around here started to give up blowing. Then they borrowed my record and like to wore it out. You got them working, Johnny."[49]

While Charlie Parker's imitators would admit to their thefts, however, Hodges's would plead not guilty. According to a story told by Phil Woods, fellow altoist Gene Quill was coming off the stand at Birdland when a member of the audience accused him of being nothing more than an imitator of Parker. Quill offered the man his alto and snapped "Here—*you* imitate Charlie Parker!"[50] Conversely, when Tab Smith, who played alto for Lucky Millinder and Count Basie, was told he had a tone like Hodges's he indignantly replied, "What do you mean, I sound like Johnny? I'm Tab Smith, and that's who I sound like."[51] Perhaps the technical immensity of the task of copying Parker made those who stole from him proud of their grand larceny, while merely purloining Hodges's tone was considered an embarrassing misdemeanor on the level of shoplifting.

Woods was primarily a Parker devotee, so much so that he married Chan Parker, the woman by whom Parker had two children,[52] but late in life he returned to the music of Hodges. "I love going back before bebop now," he said. "Johnny Hodges was the first alto player I saw live when I was young when Duke's band came to town."[53] Woods's revived appreciation resulted in what appears to be the only tribute album dedicated to Hodges, "Flowers for Hodges," which includes four Ellington-Strayhorn numbers associated with Hodges, plus a vocal tribute by Woods with lyrics (in part) as follows:

When I hear someone play
Alto sax the wrong way
I am tempted to say
Remember, Johnny Hodges
The Rabbit—my first habit.
When they ask when I heard
The first music of Bird
I must give them the word
I worship Johnny Hodges
The Rabbit—he's still my habit.[54]

Woods said that although Parker was the music of his youth, "the years have sweetened my pleasure of listening to Johnny Hodges."[55]

Bob Wilber, born twenty years after Hodges, was said by Whitney Balliett to have played "an unimpeachable Johnny Hodges"[56] at the 1980 Newport Jazz Festival, and there was a reason for the resemblance: Wilber, like Hodges, was an admirer and student of Sidney Bechet; in 1945, when he was just sixteen, he sought an introduction to Bechet, then became his student and later lived with him. Another admirer was Jimmy Heath, who candidly admitted, "Before I had heard Parker, I wanted to play like Johnny Hodges and Benny Carter.... With Bird, technique was overwhelming, but with Hodges it was the sound that was captivating."[57] It is fair to say, however, that today Hodges has no school such as those who follow in the broad and powerful wakes of Parker, the first saxophonist as deity, and Coltrane, the second coming. "No one has a tone like that," pianist Jess Stacy said of Hodges. "He took it to the grave with him."[58]

Echoes of Hodges's blues style can be heard in Parker's "Cool Blues" and "Funky Blues," a number he recorded with Hodges and Benny Carter in a June 1952 studio jam session put together by Norman Granz. "As advanced as Charlie Parker played," wrote J. J. Johnson, the bop trombonist, "he never lost sight of tradition and 'grass roots' in jazz. I suspect he enjoyed playing with Hodges" on that date.[59] Parker's rubato phrasing on ballads such as "Embraceable You" recalls the scooping that Hodges perfected, beginning a phrase below the implied starting point, then rising and taking off, like a water bird breaching the surface of a lake. Sonny Stitt was a Boston native often accused of being nothing more than a carbon copy of Parker, but before he turned to bop he "played like Johnny Hodges when he was drinking, and like Benny Carter when he wasn't," according to Ellington trumpeter Willie

Cook.[60] "The alto players I knew were Bird, Johnny Hodges, Willie Smith, and Benny Carter," Stitt said. "That's where I got my foundations. They never showed you nothin' but they left something there for you."[61] Lee Konitz, like many altos of his generation, listened to Hodges and Benny Carter when he was starting out, then to Parker, whom he found to be "too strong" an influence. "[T]o learn a Charlie Parker solo," he said, "can change your life."[62] The measure of the respective influence of Hodges and Parker may be taken by the fact that in 1976, six years after the former's death, the Schwann catalog listed only five albums by Hodges still in print, as opposed to approximately forty by Parker.[63]

Hodges's legacy was carried forward more directly by tenors such as Ben Webster and Don Byas. "He showed me the way to play my horn," Webster said after Hodges died. "That's what I tried to do—play Johnny on tenor."[64] Hodges "brought out the tenderness in Ben," Al Sears said. "Johnny rubbed the edges off him."[65] That Hodges could serve as a model for tenors was attested to by no less an authority than Coleman Hawkins, the father of the jazz tenor. When they played together at the Village Gate in 1962, Hodges stepped aside after finishing a solo and looked at Hawkins to follow, but Hawkins nodded to pianist Tommy Flanagan to "take a chorus in between, quipping[,] 'Ain't no sense in no tenor following no tenor!' "[66]

With no immediate heir in Hodges's line, the kingdom of the alto was divided in two, like King Lear's Britain, with a polar zone—the cool jazz peerage of Paul Desmond (who said he wanted to sound like a dry martini), Art Pepper, and others like them—and the torrid equatorial kingdom allotted to firebrand Ornette Coleman—whose intense music Desmond said was "like living in a house where everything's painted red"[67]—and his followers. The band of temperate climate occupied by the music of Hodges had shrunk. The essence of his style—his individual tone—was inimitable, but echoes of Hodges's technique could be heard in the playing of Julian "Cannonball" Adderley, who even at his most boppish recalled Hodges's warmth, and who had a similar feeling for the blues (witness his hit "Mercy, Mercy, Mercy").

The two played together in the Ellington band for a time in the mid-1950s, shortly after Hodges's attempt to lead his own group ended. Adderley, still in his twenties, was given the second alto chair normally occupied by Russell Procope, who played baritone while Harry Carney took time off owing to a family illness. As Ellington was accused of doing to Benny Carter, he put the younger man at a disadvantage vis-à-vis his longtime star. After Hodges soloed on one of his featured numbers, Ellington would announce, "And now, also on alto saxophone, a young man who can really play the blues, Cannonball Adderley!" Ellington would then "throw me some blues changes," Adderley said, "and . . . spend the whole time talking with people at the front tables. I know he didn't have anything against me, so I didn't think of it as anti-Adderley, but it sure was very pro-Hodges."[68]

Hodges had named Adderley as one of the "younger guys" whom he liked when the question was put to him in 1960.[69] The feeling was mutual, as Adderley preferred Hodges's style to that of the succeeding generation of altoists, particularly the avant-garde who lived in the house where everything was painted red and who, in Adderley's opinion, cared little about tone and less about melody. In a 1961 interview Adderley criticized Makanda Ken McIntyre, a Boston native who had a style that resembled Ornette Coleman's. "Not everybody who comes along can automatically be great, when we had to pay dues for so many years," Adderley said. "Why should a guy such as Ken McIntyre come in with no experience, no dues-paying. . . and transcend a Johnny Hodges in acceptability?" McIntyre belonged to a later generation of jazzmen for whom the music had to be serious, even grim, in order to be acceptable, a view that Hodges surely did not share. "We kind of made fun of [McIntyre]," said saxophonist Sam Rivers, who moved to Boston in 1947. "People would see him coming and they'd leave the stand, didn't want to be there when 'rigor mortis' sat in. That's what we called him."[70] Adderley may not have been the voluptuary that Hodges was, but like Hodges he never dropped his tone in hot pursuit of a musical idea.

William "Sonny" Criss, a contemporary of Adderley's on alto, was another who combined a warm, romantic touch on ballads with a feeling for the blues like that of Hodges, but this writer has been unable to find any comment by Criss citing Hodges as an influence. Criss worked with Parker in Howard McGee's band in 1946,[71] and Whitney Balliett referred to him as a "Charlie Parker offshoot" after hearing him at the 1968 Newport Jazz Festival.[72] It may be that the gene Hodges carried is a recessive one and that it will skip several generations before it again manifests itself. Among living practitioners of the alto, Darius Jones, Steve Wilson, Mike Hashim, and Grace Kelly have all cited Hodges as an influence.

So is Hodges's style "the exhausted practice of a moribund convention" or the vital "expression of a long tradition," as Cynthia Ozick asked concerning Edith Wharton, a literary artist who fell out of fashion, then experienced a posthumous revival?[73] Baritone sax man Gerry Mulligan, who recorded an album with Hodges in 1959, delivered a persuasive defense of Hodges against the charge that he had been rendered obsolete by subsequent developments in jazz:

> [T]he compulsion to say something "new" every day is a significantly immature way of looking at life. The constant drive to force musicians and other artists to constantly invent something "new" is one of the banes of the creative life; and this particular kind of pressure, incidentally, also reveals something of our whole culture. In any case, if there are people who cannot hear how thoroughly mature and individual Hodges is, I'm sorry for them.[74]

As Telemachus says to his mother Penelope in *The Odyssey*, "It's always the latest song, the one that echoes last in the listener's ears, that people praise the most," and the long-standing recognition of this bias in favor of the new ought to prompt a re-evaluation of Hodges.[75]

Benny Green, an English saxophonist who was also a jazz critic, put Hodges's apparently antediluvian attitude in perspective:

> People whose interest in jazz begins with Charlie Parker never fail to fascinate me. They remind me of the man who, determined to finish 'War and Peace' once and for all, started at the account of the Battle of Borodino. . . . There were modernists before Parker and Gillespie. Modernism after all is not a style but an attitude, and in the pre-Parker generation, the most adventurous spirits were already playing a highly sophisticated kind of jazz. Of all those prewar giants, Johnny Hodges has perhaps shown the profoundest artistic wisdom, for he has never made any attempt to move with the times. He has never felt inclined to assimilate the harmonic devices of a younger generation.[76]

Substitute "Coltrane and Miles Davis" for "Parker and Gillespie" in the foregoing and the same analysis applies today.

Green argued that it is "not the artist's duty to keep abreast of the times" but rather "to preserve the homogeneity of his own style." Jazz, in his view, evolves, but its "individuals do not, in the sense that once a musician has acquired the nuances of his own generation, they are his for the rest of his life, whether he wants them or not. Had Hodges tried to assimilate the chromatic thought of Charlie Parker, jazz would have lost a great lyric player and gained just another imitator."[77]

The impact of subsequent revolutions in jazz taste was so great that Hodges's polished sound would become the object of not-so-gentle musical mockery in 1966 by tenor Archie Shepp at the Newport Jazz Festival, where his quintet parodied Ellington's "Prelude to a Kiss,"[78] and thirteen years later at the 1979 edition of that festival, where the World Saxophone Quartet "indulged in funny Stepin Fetchit stage business and heavy parodying of such as Duke Ellington and Guy Lombardo."[79] Suffice it to say that these parodists are unlikely to displace Hodges in the alto saxophone pantheon and that any musician who would lump Duke Ellington with Guy Lombardo for laughs should probably abandon both music and comedy.

Hodges was of the generation of jazz musicians whose emotional palettes contained many colors, not just black, white, and gray, and listening to them today is "a reminder of what jazz was like before the cool boys ripped out its heart," as Albert McCarthy said in a review of the *Ellington at Newport* album.[80] William Thomas McKinley, a composer and jazz pianist from whom this writer took a course in jazz in the early 1970s, used to say that in his view (which prevailed at the time among serious jazz musicians), there were only two emotions worthy of expression in jazz: rage and introspection. What about love, or more precisely, the animal spirits that are awakened when a man is attracted to a woman, and thinks of a melody to woo and maybe win her with? What about the blues? That cathartic musical experience enables one to emerge from depression by singing or playing about it without self-pity, in much the same way that Aristotle in *The Poetics* said that tragedy purges us of pity and fear. Mere introspection is incapable of producing the same salutary effect, although that is perhaps the point in the view of musicians and fans who prefer wandering in a maze to finding their way out.

What about the feeling of joy—experienced, for example, when the sun hits one's face on the sunny side of the street, a sentiment expressed so ably by Hodges with his noteworthy solo in the old chestnut that takes its name from that phrase? Innocent pleasure seemed to disappear as a proper emotional subject of jazz shortly before Hodges died, as did a great deal of lyricism. Despite the gloomy zeitgeist that the postwar generation that succeeded his may have inhabited, life goes on, and should be sung by the artists among us. Johnny Hodges was dour on the outside but had a heart that beat with sensuality, and he never abandoned his respect for the jazzman's craft even in his most tender moments. He had an ear for the blues but an eye on the "out chorus"—he wasn't interested in just blowing to be heard when his turn to solo came.

In his essay "Tradition and the Individual Talent" T. S. Eliot observed that we praise an artist for "those aspects of his work in which he least resembles anyone else," but the most original parts may be those in which his ancestors "assert their immortality most vigorously."[81] If Johnny Hodges's like is not found among us today, it is because he was that rarest of things—a true original, in a grand tradition.

Epilogue

A FINAL IMAGE of Johnny Hodges: He is in a hotel room in Toronto, on the road, along with a reporter and Otto Hardwick.

It is night, but Hodges has drawn the curtains to block out the glare of the city. He removes the lights from the room's lamps and replaces them with colored bulbs—yellow, red and blue. He sprinkles them with *eau de cologne* so that when they are lit—after they sizzle a bit—they give off a scent. The room is thus bathed in subdued light and the smell of perfume.

"They're Rabbit's love lamps," Hardwick says to the reporter. "He brings his own *ambience* with him." Hodges lies on the bed and closes his eyes, and the other two depart.

The sax man appears content; withdrawn into a world of his own, away from the hassles of travel and one-night stands, from whence he will return when he awakes to again take the slow walk to the microphone to solo, to create the sounds only he can make.

Acknowledgments

THE AUTHOR THANKS the following for their assistance or access to their collections:

Boston Musicians Association/Oral History Project
Boston Public Library
City of Boston, Massachusetts
City of Cambridge, Massachusetts
City of New York, Vital Records Department
Commonwealth of Massachusetts State Archives
DownBeat Magazine
The Duke Ellington Society, New York and Washington, DC, chapters
Hot Club of France
Jazz at Lincoln Center
Jazz Hot
Johnson Publishing Company, LLC (*Jet Magazine*)
Loudon County, Virginia
New England Historic Genealogical Society
New York Public Library
Rutgers University, Institute of Jazz Studies
The Smithsonian Institution, National Museum of American History
Tamiment Library and Robert F. Wagner Labor Archives, New York University
Tufts University, Digital Collections and Archives
Yale University, Oral History of American Music Archives

Notes

Abbreviations are listed by author name in the bibliography.

PROLOGUE

1. *See, e.g.*, Storyville Records, "Johnny Hodges Biography," http://www.storyvilerecords.com/artists/johnny-hodges.
2. Paul Bowles, "Duke Ellington in Recital for Russian War Relief," *New York Herald-Tribune* (January 25, 1943).
3. "Introducing Duke Ellington," *Fortune*, August 1933, p. 95.
4. Vail I, p. 187.
5. Steve Voce, "Duke Ellington: A Cold From Little Eddie," *Jazz Journal* (March 1963).
6. *Ella at Duke's Place*, Verve V/V6 4070, 1965.
7. Richard Loyd, liner notes to *Lionel Hampton All-Star Sessions, vol. 1*, Jazztory JTD 102407, p. 3, 2005.
8. Dance, Sportpalast (emphasis in original).
9. Stewart, Boy Meets Horn, p. 209.

CHAPTER I

1. Birth certificate of Cornelius Hodges, filed August 7, 1907, with the Cambridge, Massachusetts, Office of the City Clerk. The *H* in his father's name apparently stands for "Henry"; *see* U.S. Social Security Application for John Cornelius Hodge dated December 12, 1936 (U.S. Social Security Administration, Washington, DC).
2. For examples of Hodges's signature that clearly show an *s* as the last letter in his surname, *see* the program from a July 22, 1947, Ellington concert in San Francisco that appears in Vail II, p. 319, and payroll records in the Duke Ellington Collection, Archives Center, National Museum of American History, Washington, DC. While there are other autographs in which Hodges appears to drop the *s*, it seems that he does so in the manner of one who elides the end of his last name when signing in

haste. Hodges also signed his name occasionally in block letters; *see* Hodges's note "GET SUIT OUT CLEAN" on the lead sheet for "Ghost of a Chance" in the Duke Ellington Collection.

3. Marriages Registered in the City of Boston for the Year eighteen hundred and ninety-six, vol. 462, p. 217. Massachusetts State Archives, Boston.

4. State of Virginia, 1880 Census, Pittsylvania County, Danville Enumeration District 182, sheet 16, line 41.

5. Dance, Mosaic, p. 1.

6. Book Directories and Diaries & Directories of the Associated Musicians of Greater New York, Local 802 of the American Federation of Musicians, Tamiment Library and Robert F. Wagner Labor Archives, New York University, New York, NY.

7. State of Virginia, 1880 Census, Pittsylvania County, Danville Enumeration District 182, sheet 16, line 41.

8. Household of John H. Hodge, 1900 US Federal Census, Washington, DC, roll 162, page 18A, Enumeration District 0104. FHL Microfilm 1240162.

9. Massachusetts Vital Records, vol. 467, p. 150; vol. 487, p. 140; and vol. 521, p. 333, respectively.

10. United States Social Security Administration, www.socialsecurity.gov/OACT/babynames/decades/names1880s.html (the name Cornelius was given to 911 male babies in 1,177,193 born during the years 1880–1889).

11. William Faulkner, *The Hamlet*, p. 266. New York: Random House, 1964. The author, whose full name is Cornelius John Chapman, speaks from personal experience.

12. Herman Melville, "Bartleby, the Scrivener: A Story of Wall-Street," in *Great Short Works of Herman Melville*, p. 41. New York: Perennial Library, 1969.

13. Dance, Giants, p. 13. It is impossible at this date to verify Hodges's claim to habitual truancy for the years after 1917 as Massachusetts school records—if they survive—are sealed from public view for one hundred years. Inquiries to the Boston Public School Department on this point have been unavailing.

14. Dance, Mosaic, p. 2.

15. William Shakespeare, *King Henry the Fourth, Part One,* 1.2, *The Pelican Shakespeare,* p. 10, n. 77. New York: Penguin Books, 2000. Moorditch was an open sewer that drained Moorfields, an area outside the walls of London in the fifteenth century.

16. Ted Panken, "In Conversation With Johnny Griffin," http://www.jazz.com/features-and-interviews/2008/7/28/in-conversation-with-johnny-griffin.

17. Ulanov, Ellington, p. 75.

18. Ulanov, History, p. 179.

19. Stewart, Boy Meets Horn, p. 209. Steven Lasker offers an additional basis for this nickname, namely, concupiscence: "According to hearsay (the details were vague), in his youth he enjoyed so many different passion flowers." Lasker, Small Groups, p. 13.

20. Stewart, Jazz Masters, p. 130.

21. *Duke Ellington: Memories of Duke*, produced and directed by Gary Keys. Music Video Distributors, DJ-855, 2002.

22. Feather, Encyclopedia, p. 389, says that Procope joined Ellington in 1945. According to the same source, Procope himself remembered the year as 1946.

23. Lasker, Small Groups, p. 13; https://en.wikipedia.org/wiki/Bantam_BRC-40.

24. Jack Towers, "Duke and Bill Fondly Remember Their Good Friend Toby," Duke Ellington Society Newsletter, Chapter 90 (Washington, DC), 5/5 (May 1997), p. 2. *See also* Teachout, p. 86.

25. Stewart, Jazz Masters, p. 97.

26. Stanley Dance, liner notes to *Things Ain't What They Used to Be: Johnny Hodges/ Rex Stewart*. RCA Vintage LPV-533.

27. David Dicaire, *Jazz Musicians of the Early Years, to 1945*, p. 199. Jefferson, NC: McFarland, 2003.

28. Edward Shorter, *A History of Women's Bodies*, p. 128. New Brunswick, NJ: Transaction, 1991.

29. Lytton Strachey, *Eminent Victorians*, p. 138. New York: G. P. Putnam's Sons, 1918.

30. Stewart, Boy Meets Horn, p. 209.

31. Dance, Sportpalast.

32. Philip W. Payne, "Memo to the Subscriber," *Giants of Jazz: Johnny Hodges*. Alexandria, VA: Time-Life Records, 1981, n.p. It is of course possible that Hodges was pulling people's legs on this point.

33. Stewart, Boy Meets Horn, p. 209.

34. *Loving v. Virginia*, 388 U.S. 1 (1967).

35. Cambridge, Mass. Directory 1920, p. 631; Cambridge, Mass. Directory 1921–1922, p. 629. Bountiful, UT: American Genealogical Lending Library.

36. Whiston. The distance is actually between five and six blocks. In his 1966 interview of Hodges the British jazz writer transcribed the names of the streets as "Hammer" and "Connaught," but the Boston city directory for the years in question confirms that Hodges and Carney lived on Hammond and Cunard Streets, respectively. The Boston Directory for the Year Commencing July 1, 1925, Sampson & Murdock Company, 1925. Dance incorrectly transcribes the name of Shawmut Avenue as both "Charlotte" (Dance, Giants, p. 6) and "Shumant" (Dance, Ellington, p. 95).

37. The Boston Directory for the Year Commencing July 1, 1925.

38. Albert Benedict Wolfe, *The Lodging House Problem in Boston*, p. 75. Cambridge: Harvard University Press, 1913.

39. J. Anthony Lukas, *Common Ground: A Turbulent Decade in the Lives of Three American Families*, p. 165. New York: Vintage, 1985.

40. Wolfe, *Lodging House Problem*, p. 91.

41. Lukas, *Common Ground*, p. 166.

42. Paul Mariani, *Lost Puritan: A Life of Robert Lowell*. New York: Norton, 1994. The lines quoted are from a draft of "Man and Wife" and do not appear in published versions of the poem. Houghton Library, Harvard University, Cambridge, MA.

43. Dance, Giants, p. 7.

44. Maurice Burman, "Harry Carney Talks to Maurice Burman: All I Want Is to Stay With Duke," *Melody Maker* (October 11, 1958), p. 2.

45. School Documents, Boston Public Schools, 1894, pp. 350, 354. London: Forgotten Books.

46. Chapter 240 of the Acts of 1852, "An Act Concerning the Attendance of Children at School."

47. Dance, Giants, p. 7.

CHAPTER 2

1. Dance, Giants, p. 6.

2. "Saxophonist Johnny Hodges Leaves $86,000 Estate to His Widow and Children," *Jet* (December 28, 1972), p. 65.

3. Dance, Ellington, p. 95.

4. Dance, Giants, p. 6.

5. Henry Louis Gates Jr. and Evelyn Brooks Higginbotham, *Harlem Renaissance Lives from the African American National Biography*, p. 264. New York: Oxford University Press, 2009.

6. Smith, p. 153.

7. Dance, Ellington, p. 95; Dance, Mosaic, p. 1; Dance, Smooth One.

8. Dance, Ellington, p. 95. The name of the former is spelled "Hardwicke" in some sources; *see, e.g.*, Feather, Encyclopedia, p. 244. This book uses the spelling "Hardwick" except where quoting from a printed work that uses the alternative spelling.

9. Stewart, Boy Meets Horn, p. 208.

10. Hargrove, p. 40.

11. Lawrence, p. 90.

12. Chilton, Who's Who, p. 255.

13. Ian Carr, Digby Fairweather, and Brian Priestly, *The Rough Guide to Jazz*, p. 366. London: Rough Guides, 2004; Uncredited liner notes to *Johnny Hodges: Hop, Skip and Jump*, Past Perfect/Silver Line, 2002.

14. Dance, Giants, p. 6.

15. Vacca, p. 88.

16. <u>Pittsburgh Courier</u>, August 11, 1923.

17. Hargrove, p. 40. Hargrove records her name as "Clarissa."

18. Whiston. The detail that the bag was made from a sleeve of his mother's coat is found in Dance, Giants, p. 7.

19. There are various accounts of this first encounter between Hodges and Bechet, including Dance, Mosaic, p. 2; Dance, Ellington, p. 95; Whiston; and Nat Hentoff's interview of Hodges, quoted in his liner notes to *The Big Sound: Johnny Hodges and the Ellington Men*, Verve MG V-8271, 1957.

20. Dance, Giants, pp. 6, 7.

21. Ward and Burns, p. 106.

22. Whiston.

23. Dance, Ellington, p. 95.

24. Williams, Tradition, p. 71.

25. Burnett James, "Johnny Hodges—Two Tributes," *Jazz Journal* (July 1970).

26. Tomkins.

27. Maurice Burman, "Harry Carney Talks to Maurice Burman: All I Want Is to Stay With Duke," *Melody Maker* (October 11, 1958), p. 2.

28. Segell, p. 22.

29. Segell, pp. 39, 13.

30. Handy, p. 99.

31. Dance, Giants, p. 4.

32. Segell, pp. 13, 39, 89, 283.

33. Dance, Giants, p. 16; Segell, p. 40.

34. "Saxophonist Johnny Hodges Leaves $86,000 Estate to His Widow and Children," *Jet*, December 28, 1972, p. 65.

35. Hargrove, p. 39.

36. The spelling of this musician's surname varies widely in different sources. The most authoritative is probably "Sapparo." Tucker, Early Years, p. 203.

37. Richard Vacca, *Troy Street Observer*, February 11, 2013, https://www.troystreet.com/tspots/2013/02/11/on-february-5-1964/.

38. Deffaa, p. 42.

39. Waters, p. 29.

40. Dance, Giants, p. 7.

41. Panassié and Gautier, p. 116.

42. Dance, Giants, p. 7.

43. Waters, p 22.

44. Waters, p. 29.

45. Dance, Ellington, p. 45. If Whaley was correct that the year was 1920, Hodges would have been thirteen or fourteen.

46. Waters, p. 29.

47. Short trousers called "knickerbockers" or "knickers" (worn with long socks) were the norm instead of long pants for boys in the early twentieth century, and the transition to long pants was considered a rite of passage; hence the line in Johnny Mercer's "Blues in the Night" that says, "My momma done tol' me / when I was in knee pants." The style reduced expenditures for new pants during a boy's growth years since the length of knickers could be adjusted by buckles just below the knee. *See* Marion Sichel, *History of Children's Costume*. New York: Chelsea House, 1993.

48. Grove Dictionary, vol. 2, p. 286.

49. Lawrence, pp. 129–130.

50. Stewart, Boy Meets Horn, p. 90.

51. All Music Guide, p. 775.

52. Hershman, p. 5.

53. Prohibition ended with the ratification of the Twenty-First Amendment to the U.S. Constitution, which repealed the Eighteenth Amendment, on December 5, 1933.

54. Stewart, Boy Meets Horn, p. 208.

55. Vacca, pp. 143–145; Everett.

56. Dance, Ellington, p. 92. The Boston City Directory for 1960 shows Lincoln Drug located at 922 Tremont Street. Boston: R. L. Polk & Co., 1960.

57. Ulanov, Ellington, p. 59.

58. Dance, Ellington, p. 45.

59. Panassié and Gautier, p. 137.

60. Deffaa, p. 32. *See also* Waters, p. 29.

61. Dance, Giants, p. 12.

62. Tucker, Early Years, pp. 203–204.

63. Dance, Ellington, p. 96.

64. Stewart, Boy Meets Horn, p. 208.

65. Everett.

66. Vacca, p. 18. Nat Hentoff, Boston Boy: A Memoir, p. 203. New York: Paul Dry Books, 2001.

67. Stephan Thernstrom, *The Other Bostonians: Poverty and Progress in the American Metropolis, 1880–1970*, p. 179. Cambridge: Harvard University Press, 1973.

68. Ira Rosenwaike, *Population History of New York City*, table 69. Syracuse, NY: Syracuse University Press, 1972.

69. Gerald H. Gamm, *The Making of the New Deal Democrats: Voting Behavior and Realignment in Boston, 1920–1940*, p. 205. Chicago: University of Chicago Press, 1989.

70. Touré F. Reed, *Not Alms but Opportunity: The Urban League and the Politics of Racial Uplift*, p. 72. Chapel Hill: University of North Carolina Press, 2009. "Population of the 100 Largest Urban Places: 1940," U.S. Bureau of the Census, June 15, 1998, http://www.census.gov/population/www/documentation/twps0027/tab17.txt.

71. Jacob Goldberg, "Breaking the Color Line: African-American Musicians and the Formation of Local 802," http://www.local802afm.org/2013/02/breaking-the-color-line-2.

72. Hershman, p. 4.

73. Wendy Knight, "Playing Chef in a Little Kitchen by the Shore," *New York Times* (April 20, 2007).

74. Boston Musicians Association Oral History Project, "One Musicians' Union Where Once There Were Two," http://www.bostonmusicians.org/history/one-musicians-union-where-once-there-were-two.

75. N.Y. Code section 106.5, Provisions governing licensees to sell at retail for consumption on the premises.

76. Albert Benedict Wolfe, *The Lodging House Problem in Boston*, pp. 30–31. Cambridge: Harvard University Press, 1913.

77. Johnson, p. 324.

78. Johnson, p. 496.

79. Johnson, p. 619.

80. Ward and Burns, p. 189.

81. Hershman, p. 4.

82. Joseph Horowitz, "New Song for the New World," *Wall Street Journal* (October 29, 2014).

83. Jones, pp. 60–61; Giddins, Time-Life, p. 30.

CHAPTER 3

1. Boyer, p. 49; Dance, Giants, p. 16.

2. Philip Larkin, *All What Jazz: A Record Diary*, 2nd ed., p. 56. New York: Farrar, Straus and Giroux, 1985.

3. Segell, p. 32.

4. Stewart, Boy Meets Horn, p. 173.

5. Dance, Giants, p. 4.

6. Gleason, p. 76.

7. Richard Hadlock, liner notes to *Atlantic Jazz: New Orleans*. Rhino/Atlantic 81700, 1990.

8. Bailliett, Portraits, p. 37.

9. *See, e.g.*, Noam Chomsky, *Syntactic Structures*, 1957. Berlin: Mouton de Gruyter, 2002.

10. Whiston.

11. Dance, Mosaic, p. 1.

12. Balliett, Collected Works, p. 205.

13. Hadlock, liner notes to *Atlantic Jazz: New Orleans,* Rhino/Atlantic 81700, 1990.

14. Waters, p. 89.

15. Dance, Giants, p. 1.

16. Dance, Giants, p. 1.

17. Tomkins.

18. Handy, p. 156.

19. Ramsey and Smith, p. 141.

20. Tomkins.

21. Bigard, p. 54.

22. Balliett, Collected Works, p. 564.

23. Chilton, Bechet, p. 23.

24. Chilton, Bechet, p. 56.

25. Ward and Burns, p. 94.

26. Ward and Burns, p. 106.

27. Balliett, Collected Works, p. 564.

28. Ellington, Mistress, p. 115.

29. Teachout, p. 106–110.

30. Teachout, p. 66–67.

31. Duke Ellington, foreword to Leonard Feather's *Encyclopedia of Jazz*, p. 14. New York: Bonanza Books, 1960.

32. Id.

33. Earl Hines, quoted in Bigard, p. ix.

34. Ramsey and Smith, p. 209.

35. Friedrich Nietzsche, *The Birth of Tragedy From the Spirit of Music.* Oxford: Oxford University Press, 2000.

36. Ellison, p. 41.

37. Dance, Ellington, p. 179.

38. Chilton, Bechet, pp. 68–69.

39. Ward and Burns, p. 138.

40. Shapiro and Hentoff, p. 234.

41. Stewart, Boy Meets Horn, p. 208.

42. Ramsey and Smith, p. v.

43. Chilton, Bechet, p. 46.

44. Chilton, Bechet, p. 20.

45. Smith, p. 129.

46. Ward and Burns (p. 106) attribute the quotation to Ellington, but Stanley Dance, an earlier source, says it comes from Greer. Dance, Ellington, p. 66.

47. Chilton, Bechet, p. 70.

48. Dance, Ellington, p. 66.

49. United Press International obituary, Delaware County (PA) *Daily Times*, May 12, 1970.

CHAPTER 4

1. Uncredited liner notes to *Johnny Hodges: Rabbit's Blues*, Past Perfect Records, 205743-203, 2001.

2. DeMichael.

3. Tomkins. Hodges's memory with regard to this point indicts him, as the Sixteenth Amendment to the U.S. Constitution, authorizing a federal tax, was ratified in February 1913, and Congress enacted an income tax statute in October of that year. He would insist on being paid in cash throughout his career, an inconvenience for band managers but an aid to the avoidance of taxes.

4. Whiston.

5. Smith, p. 65.

6. Waters, p. 45.

7. O'Neal, p. 170.

8. Shapiro and Hentoff, p. 170.

9. O'Neal, p. 101.

10. Dance, Smooth One.

11. Whiston.

12. Feather, Encyclopedia, p. 133.

13. Balliett, Night Creature, p. 228.

14. Ellison, p. 59.

15. Smith, p. 159.

16. Smith, p. 159.

17. Whiston.

18. Balliett, Collected Works, p. 330.

19. John R. Tumpak, "Johnny Hodges: Sensual Musical Beauty," *Memory Lane* 172 (2011): 41–42.

20. Chilton, Bechet, p. 72.

21. Tomkins.

22. Hargrove, p. 39.

23. Shapiro and Hentoff, p. 171–172.

24. Dance, Mosaic, p. 2.

25. Panassié and Gautier, p. 114.

26. Panassié and Gautier, p. 137; Feather, Dictionary, p. 290.

27. Grove Dictionary, vol. 2, p. 434.

28. Panassié and Gautier, p. 75.

29. Richard Vacca, *The Troy Street Observer*, February 11, 2013, https://www.troystreet.com/tspots/2013/02/11/on-february-5-1964/; Tucker, Early Years, p. 203. Rex Stewart says he saw Hodges play with the Henri Sayres Orchestra, (Stewart, Boy Meets Horn, p. 208), but the bandleader was likely Sapparo, whose name has been the subject of numerous misspellings. DeMichael transcribed it as "Saytoe" in his interview of Carney and Hodges, A. H. Lawrence spells it "Saparo" (Lawrence, p. 90), and Bechet spelled it "Sapiro" (Sidney Bechet, *Treat It Gentle*, p. 129. New York: Da Capo, 1978). The records of Local 802 of the American Federation of Musicians do not include anyone by the name of Henri Sayres, nor do Panassié and Gautier; Feather, Encyclopedia; or Chilton, Who's Who.

30. Balliett, Night Creature, p. 228.

31. Whiston.

32. *See Good Morning Blues: The Autobiography of Count Basie*, Count Basie as told to Albert Murray, p. 6. New York: Primus/Donald I. Fine, 1985.

33. DeMichael.

34. Chilton, Bechet, p. 72.

35. Whiston. Hodges and Dance disagree as to the dates; Hodges says 1923 or 1924, and Dance says 1925.

36. DeMichael, p. 21.

37. Bechet, *Treat It Gentle*.

38. Chilton, Bechet, p. 251.

39. Ward and Burns, p. 155.

40. Dance, Mosaic, p. 2.

41. Conover, n.p.

42. Smith, p. 161. Again, accounts of Hodges's next stop differ. Stanley Dance says that in 1926 Hodges's first job after leaving the Bechet-Smith group was with Lloyd Scott's band at the Capitol Palace. Dance, Giants, p. 9.

43. Webb's birth year is often given as 1909 because this is the year given as his birth date on his Certificate of Death, but he was in fact born in 1905. Return of a Birth to the Office of Registrar of Vital Statistics, Board of Health, Baltimore City, February 10, 1905.

44. Richard S. Ginell, Artist Biography of Chick Webb, AllMusic, https://www.allmusic.com/artist/chick-webb-mn0000110604/biography.

45. Amin Sharif, "Chick Webb: Baltimore's Jazz Giant," *Chicken Bones: A Journal for Literary and Artistic African-American Themes*, http://www.nathanielturner.com/chickwebbbio.htm

46. Pannassié and Gautier, p. 271.

47. Burt Korall, *Drummin' Men—The Heartbeat of Jazz: The Swing Years*, p. 12. New York: Oxford University Press, 2002.

48. Chilton, Who's Who, pp. 348–349.

49. Ulanov, Ellington, p. 59.

50. Ellington, Mistress, pp. 99–100.

51. DeMichael.

52. Dance, Smooth One, p. 2.

53. Ellington, Mistress, p. 100.

54. Dance, Giants, p. 9.

55. Bigard, p. 41.

56. Bradbury, p. 6.

57. Shapiro and Hentoff, p. 194.

58. DeMichael.

59. Bradbury, p. 15.

60. DeMichael.

61. Grove Dictionary, vol. 2, p. 258.

62. Shapiro and Hentoff, p. 194.

63. According to the *New Grove Dictionary of Jazz*, vol. 2, p. 259, Webb's band also played at Rose Danceland in its early days.

64. Stewart, Boy Meets Horn, pp. 208–209.

65. New Jersey Radio Museum website, http://www.angelfire.com/nj2/piratejim/njamhistory5.html.

66. "Listening In," *Amsterdam News* (New York) (January 14, 1928), p. 9.

67. Smith, pp. 160–161.

68. J. Wilfred Johnson, *Ella Fitzgerald: An Annotated Discography, Including a Complete Discography of Chick Webb*, p. 21. Jefferson, NC: McFarland, 2001; Giddins, Time-Life, p. 30.

69. Dance, Mosaic, p. 2.

70. Ward and Burns, p. 255.

71. Dance, Giants, p. 12.

72. Dan Morgenstern, liner notes to *Ellingtonia!* Onyx Records, 1974; Dance, Smooth One.

73. Panassié and Gautier, p. 212.

74. Hajdu, p. 72.

75. Tom Roberts, *Luckey Roberts, Stride Pianist, Composer (1887–1968)*, Allaboutjazz. com. https://musicians.allaboutjazz.com/index_new.php?url=luckeyroberts&wi dth=1920.

76. Scott Yanow, Artist Biography of Rudy Jackson, AllMusic, http://www.allmusic. com/artist/rudy-jackson-mn0000363179/biography.

77. Vail I, p. 10.

78. Ellington, Mistress, p. 118.

79. DeMichael.

80. Bigard, p. 51.

81. Whiston; Giddins, Time-Life, p. 30.

82. Lawrence, p. 132.

83. Lawrence, p. 132; Dance, Mosaic, p. 2.

84. DeMichael.

85. Bigard, p. 53.

86. Ellington, Mistress, p. 118.

87. Bigard, p. 53.

88. Dance, Mosaic, p. 4.

89. O'Neal, p. 94.

90. Bigard, p. 54.

91. Dance, Mosaic, p. 4.

92. DeMichael.

93. Bigard, p. 45.

94. Bigard, p. 48.

95. Bigard, p. 54.

96. DeMichael.

97. Shapiro and Hentoff, p. 194.

98. Bigard, p. 53.

99. Dance, Mosaic, p. 2.

100. Feather, Encyclopedia, p. 108.

101. Dance, Mosaic, pp. 2–4.

102. Ellington, Mistress, p. 118.

103. Whiston.

104. DeMichael.

CHAPTER 5

1. Berger Patrick I, p. 59.

2. Grove Dictionary, vol. 2, pp. 269–270.

3. Berger Patrick I, p. 59.

4. Dance, Ellington, p. 129.
5. Balliett, Night Creature, p. 31.
6. Williams, Tradition, p. 146.
7. André Hodeir, *Toward Jazz*, p. 126. New York: Grove Press, 1962.
8. Feather, Encyclopedia, p.184.
9. Waters, p. 78.
10. Deffaa, p. 35.
11. Lawrence, p. 132.
12. Dance, Giants, p. 7.
13. Conover, n.p.
14. Berger Patrick I, p. 156.
15. Feather, Encyclopedia, 426.
16. John S. Wilson, "Billy Taylor's Big Economy Jazz Band," *New York Times* (December 20, 1970), p. 100.
17. Stewart, Jazz Masters, p. 9.
18. Stewart, Boy Meets Horn, p. 191. Stewart asserts that bassist Billy Taylor received a composing credit, but Ellington and Hodges are listed as copyright holders. Sven Eriksson, *Johnny Hodges: The Composer*, compilation, 2007, http://ellingtonweb. ca/Hostedpages/SvenEriksson-Hodges/JohnnyHodgesTheComposer.htm.
19. Berger Patrick I, p. 318.
20. Berger Patrick I, p. 316.
21. Berger Patrick I, p. 317.
22. Vail I, p. 340.
23. Berger Patrick, vol. I, p. 315.
24. Berger Patrick, vol. I, p. 316.
25. Id.
26. Stanley Dance, *Layin' on Mellow à propos de Johnny Hodges*, Bulletin du Hot Club de France no. 318 (July 1984), p. 1.
27. Berger Patrick I, p. 317.
28. Berger Patrick I, pp. 318–319.
29. Dance, Ellington, p. 93.

CHAPTER 6

1. Whiston.
2. Vail I, p. 11.
3. Stratemann, p. 9.
4. Giddins, Time-Life, p. 30.
5. Demètre Ioakimidis, "Johnny Hodges," *Jazz Hot* no. 263 (Summer 1970), p. 33.
6. Dance, Smooth One. In his 1969 liner notes to *Duke Ellington: Flaming Youth* (RCA Victor LPV-568), Dance identifies "The Mooche," recorded on October

30, 1928, as Hodges's first recording with Ellington, but this assertion is not supported by other sources and is corrected by his subsequent liner notes to *The Smooth One*.

7. Giddins, Time-Life, p. 30. G. E. Lambert says that Hodges did not fully employ "the exaggerated *glissandi*" that became his trademark until 1941. Lambert, p. 59.

8. Dance, Giants, p. 12.

9. Bigard, pp. 53–54.

10. Freddy Guy, interview by John McDonough, "Reminiscing in Tempo: Guitarist Freddy Guy's Ellington Memories," *DownBeat* (April 17, 1969), pp. 16–17.

11. Whiston.

12. Vail I, p. 75.

13. Panassié and Gautier, p. 165.

14. Boyer, p. 41.

15. Boyer, p. 41.

16. Dance, Giants, p. 13.

17. Dance, Giants, p. 13.

18. Bigard, pp. 51–52.

19. Bigard, p. 54.

20. As to the first view, *see* Dance, liner notes to *Flaming Youth: Duke Ellington*; as to the second, *see* Giddins, Time-Life, p. 30.

21. Giddins, Time-Life, p. 32.

22. Teachout, p. 89.

23. Sonny Greer, oral history interview, cited in Vail I, p. 13, and Teachout, p. 90.

24. Scott DeVeaux and Gary Giddins, *Jazz*, 2d ed., p. 9. New York: Norton, 2009.

25. Giddins, Time-Life, p. 33.

26. Lasker, 1932–1940, pp. 2–3.

27. John Hammond, "Meet John Hammond! Our New American Correspondent," *Melody Maker* (February 1932); Boyer, p. 54.

28. Mercer Ellington, p. 41.

29. Boyer, p. 49.

30. Cab Calloway and Bryant Hollins, *Of Minnie the Moocher and Me*, p. 88. New York: Crowell, 1976.

31. Teachout, p. 280.

32. Chilton, Bechet, pp. 141–142.

33. Giddins, Time-Life, p. 35.

34. Whiston.

35. Chilton, Bechet, p. 91.

36. Mercer Ellington, p. 65.

37. Tackley, p. 3.

38. Tackley, p. 4.

39. Giddins, Time-Life, p. 40.

40. Tackley, p. 194.

41. Edmund Anderson, oral history interview conducted by Valerie Archer, October 15, 1980, #550A, p. 51, Yale University Special Collections, Oral History of American Music, Irving S. Gilmore Music Library, Yale University, New Haven, CT.

42. Hasse, p. 211.

43. Tackley, p. 118.

44. Giddins, Time-Life, p. 41.

45. Oakley, OHAM, n.p.

46. Oakley, OHAM, n.p. *See also* Giddins, Visions, p. 160.

CHAPTER 7

1. State of New York Certificate and Record of Marriage no. 24297, dated July 29, 1927.

2. As far as the author has been able to determine, Bertha Pettiford was not related to Oscar Pettiford, who played bass for Ellington in the mid-to-late 1940s.

3. Dance, Giants, pp. 9, 12.

4. Mercer Ellington, p. 56.

5. Dance, Giants, p. 18.

6. State of Illinois, County of Cook Marriage License no. 1800427, returned and filed January 25, 1944.

7. Affidavit of Edith Hodges, dated July 24, 1970, in Proceeding for Letters of Administration of the Estate of John C. Hodges, file no. 4434, 1970, Surrogate's Court for the State of New York, County of New York.

8. Dance, Everybody Knows, p. 9.

9. Vail II, pp. 255, 268, 269; Dance, Giants, p. 23.

10. Renunciation of Letters of Administration and Waiver of Process, John C. Hodges, II, Proceedings for Letters of Administration, Estate of John C. Hodges, Surrogate's Court, County of New York.

11. Jones, 59–60.

12. Ulanov, Ellington, p. 271.

13. Dance, Ellington, p. 99.

14. Steve Voce, *The Independent*, 2001, www.ellingtonweb.ca/Hostedpages/Voce. The author has been unable to find any other source in which Cue Hodges is referred to as "Tootsie," leading him to view the anecdote with some skepticism.

15. Ellington, Mistress, xi.

16. Dance, Ellington, p. 266.

17. Dance, Giants, p. 23.

18. Dance, Giants, p. 20; Giddins, Time-Life, p. 47.

19. Tomkins.

20. Burman.

21. Dance, Giants, p. 6.

22. Dance, Giants, p. 23.

23. Jones's married name is Farnham; her daughter Rosa Mae's married name is Turner. Emails to the author from Jennifer Dunn dated January 29, 2014, and from Lauren Turner Morton dated May 13, 2014.

24. Unpublished interview of Mrs. Frances Vivian Farnham (née Jones) by Jennifer Dunn, her granddaughter-in-law, June 30, 1985.

25. Vail I, pp. 162–165. This was probably the 1939 tour of Sweden from April 9 through May 1.

26. Philip W. Payne, "Memo to the Subscriber," *Jazz Greats: Johnny Hodges*. Time-Life Records, TL-J19.

27. Stewart, Boy Meets Horn, p. 209.

28. Albert Murray, *South to a Very Old Place*, p. 83. New York: Modern Library, 1995.

29. Vail I, p. 320.

30. A. J. Liebling, *Between Meals: An Appetite for Paris*, p. 177. New York: Simon and Schuster, 1962.

31. Ward and Burns, p. 180.

32. Ward and Burns, p. 229.

33. Nat Hentoff, "Life Could Be a Dream When He Blew Sax," *Wall Street Journal* (February 1, 2002.

34. Stewart, Boy Meets Horn, pp. 209–210.

35. "Fattening Frogs for Snakes," Rice Miller, also known as the second Sonny Boy Williamson.

36. The most lurid account of Ellington's sexual conquests is Don George, *Sweet Man*. New York: G. P. Putnam's Sons, 1981.

CHAPTER 8

1. Jack Woker, Jazz Musician Pseudonyms, rev. July 3, 2005. http://www.jazzdiscography.com/fitzgera/pseudo.htm.

2. Dance, Giants, p. 18. The Teddy Wilson quotation is taken from an interview with *Contemporary Keyboard* (March–April, 1976).

3. *The Quintessential Billie Holiday, vol. 2*, Columbia Records CK 40790.

4. Dance, Mosaic, p. 1.

5. Vail I, p. 132.

6. *The Quintessential Billie Holiday, vol. 4*, Columbia Records CK 44252.

7. Vail I, p. 150.

8. *The Teddy Wilson Collection: 1933–1941*, Acrobat FABCD357.

9. All Music Guide, p. 52; Feather, Encyclopedia, 108.

10. According to Gunther Schuller, Hodges played on another date with Bailey and Wilson, one led by Bunny Berigan for the Parlophone label in England. Gunther Schuller, *The Swing Era* (Oxford University Press), p. 466. New York: 1989.

11. Bigard, p. 77.

12. *DownBeat*, vol. 1, no. 2 (July 1942), quoted in Bigard, p. 77.

13. *Lionel Hampton: All-Star Sessions vol. 1*, Jazztory JTD 102407, 2005.

14. Ian Carr, Digby Fairweather, and Brian Priestly, *The Rough Guide to Jazz*, p. 633. London: Rough Guides, 2004.

15. The entry in Wikipedia as of April 2019 lists thirty-four different versions of the song—including a zydeco cover by rock singer Cyndi Lauper—but none by Hodges. https://en.wikipedia.org/wiki/On_the_Sunny_Side_of_the_Street.

16. As a demonstration of the obscurity into which Hodges's treatment of the song has fallen, liner notes by Richard Loyd to a 1999 reissue of the two sessions refer to Hodges as a tenor sax player. *Lionel Hampton: All-Star Sessions vol. 1*, Jazztory JTD 102407, 2005.

17. Giddins, Time-Life, p. 39.

18. Woody Herman and Stuart Troup, *Woodchopper's Ball: The Autobiography of Woody Herman*, p. 46. New York: Dutton, 1990. Vail I, p. 250.

19. Dance, Ellington, p. 93.

20. Feather, Encyclopedia, p. 254; Panassié and Gautier, p. 110.

21. *The Chronological Eddie Heywood, 1944*, Classics 947.

22. He used the pseudonym "J. Harjes" on this recording due to contractual restrictions.

23. Balliett, Portraits, p. 101.

24. Hines would substitute for Ellington on two one-night dance engagements, the first in Washington, DC, the second in New York, and then substituted for a week at the Adams Theater in Newark, New Jersey. Vail I, p. 249.

25. Stanley Dance, liner notes to *Once Upon a Time*, Impulse A-9108.

26. Scott Yanow, *Jazz on Record: The First Sixty Years*, p. 202. San Francisco: Backbeat, 2003.

27. Dance, Smooth One.

28. Feather, Encyclopedia, p. 437.

29. Sven Eriksson, *Johnny Hodges: The Composer*, compilation, 2007, http://ellingtonweb. ca/Hostedpages/SvenEriksson-Hodges/JohnnyHodgesTheComposer.htm.   On the Mercury record label, the composer is for some reason listed as "Wayne."

30. Orrin Keepnews, liner notes to *Giants of Small Band Swing, vol. 2*, Original Jazz Classics OJC-1724, 1990.

31. Chilton, Who's Who, p. 362.

32. Orrin Keepnews, liner notes to *Giants of Small Band Swing, vol. 2*, Original Jazz Classics OJC-1724, 1990.

CHAPTER 9

1. Oakley OHAM, n.p.

2. Francis J. Dance, *Helen Oakley Dance, 1913–2001*, The Last Post, http://www. jazzhouse.org/gone/lastpost2.php3?edit=991165404.

3. Benny Goodman and Irving Kolodin, *The Kingdom of Swing*, p. 210. New York: Stackpole Sons, 1939.

4. Lasker, Small Groups, p. 4.

5. Oakley OHAM, n.p.

6. Lasker, Small Groups, p. 4.

7. Teachout, p. 163.

8. Helen Oakley Dance, liner notes to *Hodge Podge: Johnny Hodges and His Orchestra*, CBS 52587.

9. Oakley OHAM, n.p.

10. Duke Ellington Collection, Archives Center, National Museum of American History, Washington, DC. *See* Hasse, 273, for a summary of Hodges's pay for the years 1942–1943. Rex Stewart was once paid $135 per week during an engagement in Chicago, while Hodges was paid $130. Bradbury, p. 60.

11. Giddins, Time-Life, p. 41.

12. Oakley OHAM, n.p.

13. Oakley OHAM, n.p.

14. Lasker, Small Groups, p. 6.

15. Oakley OHAM, n.p.

16. Oakley OHAM, n.p.

17. Lasker, 1932–1940, p. 24.

18. Lasker, Small Groups, p. 13.

19. Oakley OHAM, n.p.

20. Nat Hentoff, *Listen to the Stories: Nat Hentoff on Jazz and Country Music*, pp. 23–24. New York: Harper Collins, 1995.

21. Stewart, Boy Meets Horn, p. 190.

22. Lasker, Small Groups, p. 13.

23. Lasker, Small Groups, p. 13.

24. Lasker, Small Groups, p. 14.

25. *Poughkeepsie Star-Enterprise*, September 18, 1938.

26. St. Clair McKelway (with A. J. Liebling), collected in *Reporting at Wit's End: Tales from The New Yorker*," p. 80. New York: Bloomsbury USA, 2010.

27. In a letter to the Editor of the *New York Times* published January 12, 1933, Mrs. Walter Graeme Eliot wrote, "The contention that Krum Elbow is or ever was on the west bank of the Hudson River is erroneous. Krum Elbow Creek winds in and out at Hyde Park and was named by early Dutch settlers Kromme Elboge, meaning Crooked Elbow."

28. *Poughkeepsie Star-Enterprise*, September 18, 1938.

29. A photo may be found at http://www.libertynet.org/fdipmm/word3/elbow.html.

30. Gary Giddins says that she was sixty-four when "Good Queen Bess" was recorded in 1940, but according to official records she would have been sixty-seven because she was born on April 7, 1873. Giddins, Time-Life, p. 47; Bureau of Vital Statistics, Births, Loudon County (Virginia) Register of Births (1854–1896), p. 173, line 14.

31. Giddins, Time-Life, p. 47.
32. Oakley OHAM, n.p.
33. Helen Oakley Dance, quoted in liner notes by Alun Morgun to *Duke Ellington and Johnny Hodges: Side by Side*. Reissue, Polygram Records, 1999.
34. Helen Oakley Dance, liner notes for *Hodge Podge*.
35. "Reminiscing With Cootie," interview by Eric Townley, *Storyville Magazine* (June–July, 1977), p. 172.
36. Conover, n.p.
37. Conover, n.p.

CHAPTER 10

1. Hajdu, pp. 11–12.
2. Hajdu, p. 19.
3. Hajdu, p. 32.
4. Hajdu, p. 49.
5. Hajdu, 50–51.
6. Leonard Feather, liner notes to *Ella at Duke's Place*, Verve Records V6-4070, 1965.
7. Leur, pp. 23–24.
8. Teachout, p. 190.
9. John S. Wilson, "Billy Strayhorn: Alter Ego for the Duke," *New York Times* (June 6, 1965).
10. The song's alternate title was "Anything You Want." Lasker, Small Groups, p. 26.
11. Hajdu, p. 60.
12. Bill Coss, "Ellington & Strayhorn, Inc.," *DownBeat* (June 7, 1962).
13. Billy Strayhorn, "The Ellington Effect," *DownBeat* (November 5, 1952), p. 4.
14. Quoted in liner notes to *Ella Fitzgerald Sings the Duke Ellington Song Book*, Patricia Willard, November, 1998, p. 14. Verve/Polygram Records, MGV 4008-2 and 4009-2, 1999.
15. Annie Kuebler, liner notes to *The Duke at Fargo 1940: Special 60ᵗʰ Anniversary Edition*, p. 6, Storyville Records STCD 8316, 8317, 2000.
16. Vail I, p. 193. Ken Dryden, Song Review: A Flower Is a Lovesome Thing, www.allmusic.com/song/a-flower-is-a-lovesome-thing-mt0012575704.
17. Alfred, Lord Tennyson, "The Lotos-Eaters," in *Seven Centuries of Verse, English & American*, p. 408. New York: Scribner's, 1967. The notion that the song was inspired by the poem is reinforced by Strayhorn's use of the term *ballade*, which in classical music refers to a narrative poem set to music.
18. Daniel Halperin, "Everything Has to Prove Something," in *Duke Ellington: His Life and Music*, ed. Peter Gammond, New York: Da Capo, 1977.
19. Hajdu, p. 121.
20. Mercer Ellington, pp. 109–110.

21. Dance, Giants, p. 6; Harvey G. Cohen, *Duke Ellington's America*, p. 319. Chicago: University of Chicago Press, 2010.

22. The phrase appears in *A Midsummer Night's Dream*, act IV, scene 1, and describes the "musical discord" that Hippolyta hears in the rumbling of the skies overhead.

23. Hajdu, p. 160.

24. Hajdu, p. 89.

25. To extend the Popeye conceit perhaps to its breaking point, Hodges and Ellington were co-composers of "Dance of the Goon." The Goons were a race of bald giants in the Popeye comic strip and cartoons, the most prominent of whom was a female, Alice the Goon.

26. Hajdu, p. 177.

27. Bill Simon, liner notes to *Duke's in Bed*, Verve Clef Series MG V-8203, 1956.

28. Stanley Dance, liner notes to *Cue for Saxophone*, London Records 820 604-2, 1988.

29. Hajdu, pp. 197–198.

30. Hajdu, pp. 198–199.

31. Hajdu, p. 120.

32. Hajdu, pp. 198–199.

33. Hajdu, p. 200.

34. Stanley Dance, liner notes to *Johnny Hodges, Soloist; Billy Strayhorn and the Orchestra*. Jazz Heritage Society 5187168, 2007.

35. The bassist was Bill Pemberton, the drummer Jimmy Grissom. Vail II, p. 65; Stratemann, p. 385.

36. Hajdu, p. 179.

37. Feather, Encyclopedia, p. 232.

38. Duke Ellington, liner notes to . . . *And His Mother Called Him Bill*, RCA 6287-2-RB, 1987.

39. "Introducing Duke Ellington," *Fortune* (August 1933), p. 9.

40. Giddins, Visions, p. 256.

41. Hajdu, p. 234.

42. Bradbury, p. 97.

43. Leur, p. 142.

44. William Butler Yeats, "Among School Children," in *The Collected Poems of W.B. Yeats*, p. 215. New York: Scribner Paperback Poetry, rev. 2d ed., 1996.

CHAPTER 11

1. While some sources give the spelling of Blanton's first name in diminutive form as "Jimmy," he used the spelling "Jimmie" in autographs. Stratemann, p. 160.

2. In his memoir Ellington says it was Webster and Blanton who went; Ellington, Mistress, p. 164. Terry Teachout, quoting unpublished research, says it was Hodges. Teachout, p. 202, quoting Ken Steiner, *On the Road and On the Air with Duke Ellington: The Blanton/Webster Era, Part One* (privately published, 2004).

3. Teachout, p. 202.

4. Vail II, p. 174.

5. Ellington, Mistress, p. 164.

6. Büchmann-Møller, p. 57.

7. Vail says it was January 8 at the Southland Café, Vail I, p. 176, and Stratemann suggests the same date, Stratemann, p. 160. Büchmann-Møller says it was probably January 26 at the Roseland State Ballroom.

8. Büchmann-Møller, p. 57.

9. According to Webster, he left because he "didn't get enough opportunities as a soloist," *Jazz Magazine* (May 1965), quoted in Valk, p. 65, and because he believed he could make more money if he had his own combo, Büchmann-Møller, p. 99. According to others, he was terminated for insubordination after either slapping Ellington in an argument or ruining one of Ellington's suits. Büchmann-Møller says that these events led to increased tensions but did not precipitate a firing. Büchmann-Møller, p. 98.

10. Jack the Bear is found in African American works as complex as Ralph Ellison's novel *Invisible Man*, and as simple as the chants of black railroad workers. Mark Tucker's liner notes for *Duke Ellington: The Blanton-Webster Band* (Bluebird, 1986) say that the inspiration for Ellington's Jack the Bear was "a Harlem bass-player who . . . had a tailor shop at the corner of St. Nicholas and Edgecombe Avenues," but the more likely antecedent is a New York stride pianist. *See* Duke Ellington, "The Most Essential Instrument," *Jazz Journal* 18/12 (December 1965), pp. 14–15, and Colin McPhee, writing as "Mercure," "The Torrid Zone," *Modern Music* 21/2 (January–February 1944).

11. "Ben Webster Speaking . . . ," *Crescendo* 3/7, 1965: 22.

12. Büchmann-Møller, p. 62.

13. Vail I, 175.

14. Büchmann-Møller, p. 98.

15. Mercer Ellington, p. 112.

16. Dance, Ellington, p. 93.

17. Lawrence Gushee, "Duke Ellington 1940," in Tucker, Reader, p. 434.

18. Stewart, Jazz Masters, p. 99. Ralph Gleason notes that when Hodges played "Things Ain't What They Used to Be," the musicians in the band who didn't have instruments in their mouths would sing along, substituting the words "All the boys in the band eat pussy" for the song's title. Gleason, p. 75.

19. Teachout, p. 209.

20. Tucker, Reader, pp. 501–502.

21. Vail I, p. 250.

22. Vail I, p. 234.

23. Tucker, Reader, p. 257.

24. Leonard Feather, "Leonard Feather Rebuts Hammond," in Tucker, Reader, p. 175.

25. Lambert, p. 59.

26. *Webster's New World Dictionary*, College Edition, p. 1304. New York: World Publishing, 1968.

27. Vail I, p. 229.

28. Vail I, p. 287.

29. Vail I, p. 307.

30. John Hammond, "The Tragedy of Duke Ellington, the Black Prince of Jazz," in Tucker, Reader, p. 119.

31. John Hammond, "Is the Duke Deserting Jazz?" in Tucker, Reader, p. 172.

32. Review of "Never No Lament," *DownBeat* (June 27, 1940), quoted in Vail I, 183.

33. Review in *DownBeat* (July 1, 1940), cited in Vail I, 184.

34. Review of "Main Stem," *DownBeat* (February 15, 1944), cited in Vail I, p. 248.

35. Review of "I Got It Bad," *DownBeat* (September 1, 1941), calling it Best Platter of the Month, cited in Vail I, p. 201.

36. Review of "Just Squeeze Me," *DownBeat* (November 18, 1946).

37. George T. Simon, "Joe Turner Star of Duke's Review!" *Metronome* (October, 1941), p. 20.

38. Ellington, Mistress, p. 175.

39. Vail I, pp. 273, 275.

40. Vail I, pp. 293, 294, 297, 339, 347.

41. Panassié and Gautier, p. 40.

42. *Esquire*, February 1, 1944, p. 28.

43. Vail I, pp. 264, 288.

44. Vail I, p. 274.

45. Vail I, p. 290.

46. Vail I, p. 297.

47. Vail I, p. 308.

48. Vail I, p. 314.

49. Vail I, p. 268.

50. Vail I, p. 289.

51. Vail I, p. 310.

52. Vail I, p. 342.

53. Vail I, p. 345.

54. Vail I, p. 355.

CHAPTER 12

1. Dance, Ellington, p. 281; Dance, Giants, p. 25.

2. Dance, Ellington, p. 266.

3. Dance, Giants, p. 25.

4. Dance, Giants, p. 28.

5. "The Duke Ellingtons—Cotton Clubbers En Masse," *Metronome* (April 1937), 19.

6. Dance, Giants, p. 25.

7. Burman.

8. Giddins, Time-Life, p. 44.

9. Ellington, Mistress, p. 118.

10. Dance, Giants, p. 26.

11. Dance, Ellington, p. 266.

12. Dance, Sportpalast.

13. John Clement, liner notes to *The Complete Verve Johnny Hodges Small Group Sessions, 1956–1961*, Mosaic Records MD6-200, 2000.

14. Nat Hentoff, *Listen to the Stories: Nat Hentoff on Jazz and Country Music*, p. 18. New York: Harper Collins, 1995.

15. Rex Stewart, "On the Sidelines: Rex Stewart Attends a Duke Ellington Recording Session," *Jazz Journal* (January 1966), p. 15.

16. Dance, Sportpalast.

17. *Duke Ellington: Copenhagen 1965, Parts One and Two*, Storyville Records ID 9548DNDVD, 2002.

18. Mercer Ellington, p. 151.

19. Mercer Ellington, p. 152.

20. Email from Gary Giddins to the author, October 9, 2014.

CHAPTER 13

1. Gitler, Jazz Masters, p. 24.

2. Giddins, Visions, p. 265.

3. Ellison, p. 66.

4. Gitler, Jazz Masters, p. 18.

5. Chuck Haddix, "Charlie Parker Finds His Musical Voice During a Stint in the Ozarks," *Kansas City Star* (September 7, 2013).

6. Ted Goia, *How to Listen to Jazz*, p. 112. New York: Basic Books, 2016.

7. Gitler, Jazz Masters, p. 20.

8. Eugene Chadbourne, *Artist Biography: William Fleet,* http://www.allmusic.com/artist/william-fleet-mn0001181637/biography.

9. Gitler, Jazz Masters, p. 20.

10. Gitler, Swing to Bop, p. 69 (emphasis in original).

11. Gitler, Swing to Bop, p. 189.

12. Valk, p. 160.

13. Büchmann-Møller, p. 94.

14. Büchmann-Møller, p. 95.

15. Mood Indigo & Beyond. *Time* (August 20, 1956).

16. Segell, p. 256.

17. Ellison, pp. 55, 74.

18. Jimmy Heath and Joseph McLaren, *I Walked With Giants: The Autobiography of Jimmy Heath*, p. 67. Philadelphia: Temple University Press, 2010.

19. Steve Voce, "Lawrence Brown and the Plastic Tooth," *Jazz Journal* (April 1964).

20. Ezra Pound, *ABC of Reading*, p. xii. New Haven: Yale University Press, 1934.

21. Ward and Burns, p. 321. Dizzy Gillespie danced solo while leading his big band, and tapes of their performances include dancers performing in an exotic fashion. *See Jivin' in Be-Bop,* Idem Home Video IDVD 1018, 2003.

22. Vail I, p. 218 (emphasis in original).

23. Vail I, p. 33.

24. Vail II, pp. 91.

25. Vail II, p. 138.

26. Ellington, Mistress, p. 31.

27. Tomkins.

28. Vail II, pp. 449--450.

29. Dance, Ellington, p. 255.

30. Booklet accompanying *The Johnny Hodges Sessions, 1951–1955,* Mosaic Records, MR6-126, 1989, p. 3.

31. *See* photographs appearing at pp. 220–221 of *Albert Murray: Stomping the Blues.* New York: McGraw-Hill, 1976

32. Jewell, p. 100.

33. Jewell, p. 210.

34. Edward Kennedy Ellington, "The Duke Steps Out," in *The Duke Ellington Reader*, ed. Mark Tucker, p. 49. New York: Oxford University Press.

35. Ward and Burns, p. 321.

36. Ellison, p. 26.

37. Ellison, p. 27.

38. Eric Felton, "How the Taxman Cleared the Dance Floor," *Wall Street Journal* (March 18, 2013).

39. Felton, "How the Taxman Cleared the Dance Floor."

40. Gitler, Swing to Bop, p. 318.

CHAPTER 14

1. Dance, Mosaic, p. 5.

2. All Music Guide, p. 985. Scott holds a unique place in the history of the Ellington orchestra because he memorialized Cootie Williams's defection to Benny Goodman in 1940 with the song "When Cootie Left the Duke." Anatol Schenker, liner notes to *Cootie Williams and His Orchestra, 1941–1944,* Classics 827, 1995, pp. 3–8.

3. Buchmann-Møller, p. 111.

4. Chilton, Who's Who, p.295.

5. Dance, Mosaic, p. 5.

6. Dance, Mosaic, p. 5.

7. John Hammond, "The Tragedy of Duke Ellington, the 'Black Prince' of Jazz," in Tucker, Reader, p. 119.

8. Teachout, p. 158.

9. Dance, Mosaic, p. 5.

10. John Hammond, "Is the Duke Deserting Jazz?" in Tucker, Reader, pp. 171–173.

11. Dance, Ellington, p. 100.

12. Dance, Ellington, p. 100; Stratemann, p. 293.

13. Vail I, p. 337, Stratemann, p. 293.

14. Dance, Mosaic, p. 20.

15. Dance, Mosaic, p. 5; Dance, Giants, p. 20; Teachout, p. 267.

16. Hajdu, p. 122.

17. Chuck Berg, liner notes to *Johnny Hodges: The Rabbit in Paris.* Inner City Records IC 7003-B, 1978; Vail II, pp. 359–360.

18. Tomkins.

19. Lawrence, p. 339.

20. Balliett, Collected Works, p. 5.

21. Hajdu, p. 140.

22. Conover, n.p.; for the dates of the 1950 European tour, *see* Stratemann, p. 322.

23. "Salute to Duke Ellington," Stratemann, p. 319.

24. Ernie Royal was added to the trumpet section, Theodore Kelly replaced Tyree Glenn on trombone, Don Byas replaced Charlie Rouse in Paris, and George "Butch" Ballard was added as a second drummer because Sonny Greer was in poor health and drinking heavily. Stratemann, p. 321.

25. Conover, n.p.

26. Don George, *Sweet Man*, p. 101. New York: G. P. Putnam's Sons, 1981.

27. Vacca, p. 136.

28. Vail II, p. 13.

29. Stanley Dance identifies all but Joe Benjamin. Dance, Mosaic, p. 5. John Edward Hasse says that Joe Benjamin was among the Ellington exiles as well. Hasse, p. 297.

30. Conover, n.p.

31. Hasse, 297; Bradbury, p. 74; Stratemann, p. 325.

32. Whiston, p. 8.

33. Jewell, p. 115.

34. Dance, Mosaic, p. 4.

35. Ellison, p. 31.

36. Hajdu, p. 140.

37. Dance, Giants, p. 6.

38. Jewell, pp. 26, 56; Teachout, p. 180.

39. Sigmund Freud, *Jokes and Their Relation to the Unconscious*, pp. 102–103. New York: Norton Library, 1960.

40. Steve Voce, "*Rabbit,*" *Jazz Journal* (January 1997).

41. George, *Sweet Man*, p. 109.

42. Oakley, OHAM, n.p.

43. Hajdu, p. 140.

44. Jewell, p. 115.
45. Stratemann, p. 394.
46. Burman.
47. Dance, Mosaic, p. 5.
48. Dance, Ellington, p. 30.
49. Lawrence, p. 15.
50. Dance, Ellington, pp. 123–124.
51. Dance, Mosaic, p. 5.
52. Jewell, p. 141.
53. Dance, Mosaic, p. 5.
54. Chilton, Who's Who, pp. 295–296.
55. Dance, Mosaic, p. 5.
56. Dance, Mosaic, p. 6.
57. Dance, Mosaic, p. 7. A vocal cover version of the song by Frank Sinatra and Harry James reached number 8 on the Billboard charts. Columbia Records DB 2934, 1951.
58. Phil Schaap, Al Sears Jazz Festival website. http://searsjazzfestival.com/about.html.
59. Dance, Mosaic, p. 6.
60. Dance, Mosaic, p. 6.
61. Coltrane, 87.
62. Thomas, p. 33.
63. Lewis Porter, "John Coltrane," in *The Oxford Companion to Jazz*, ed. Kirchner, p. 433. New York: Oxford University Press, 2000.
64. Balliett, Night Creature, p. 192.
65. Thomas, p. 33.
66. Feather, Encyclopedia, p. 372; Jones, pp. 60–61.
67. Thomas, p. 117.
68. Thomas, p. 41.
69. Thomas, p. 120.
70. Thomas, p. 116.
71. Thomas, photo images following page 88.
72. Coltrane, pp. 82–92.
73. Coltrane may have sat in with Hodges in February 1955, but this is unconfirmed. Coltrane, 95–96.
74. Coltrane, p. 76; Thomas, p. 62.
75. Thomas, p. 64.
76. Thomas, p. 66.
77. Dance, Mosaic, pp. 10, 15.
78. This is misidentified on some albums as "Sideways"; *see, e.g., Johnny Hodges: At a Dance, In a Studio, On Radio*, Enigma 1052, 1957. Coltrane, p. 405.

79. The identities of the remaining personnel are uncertain. No musicians are identified on *Johnny Hodges: At a Dance, In a Studio, On Radio* other than Hodges and Coltrane. Liner notes to *Johnny Hodges/Charlie Shavers: A Man and His Music*, Storyville SLP 4073, 1981, on which "In a Mellotone" is also heard, identify Baker and Brown on trumpet and trombone, respectively, but say "remaining personnel unknown."

80. Coltrane, p. 405.

81. Coltrane, p. 406; *Johnny Hodges: At a Dance, In a Studio, On Radio*.

82. Dance, Mosaic, pp. 15–16; liner notes to *Used to Be Duke*, Verve 849 394–2, 1991; Coltrane, p. 409.

83. Dance, Ellington, p. 91.

84. Dance, Giants, p. 22.

85. Lawrence, p. 134.

86. Jones, p. 60.

87. Thomas, p. 66.

88. Thomas, p. 155.

89. Jones, p. 60.

90. Coltrane, pp. 85–86.

91. Coltrane, p. 92.

92. Burman.

93. Conover, n.p.

94. Dance, Giants, p. 22.

95. Burman.

96. Whiston, p. 8.

97. *Los Angeles Sentinel*, June 24, 1954, sec. A, p. 11.

98. Coltrane, p. 89.

99. *Johnny's Blues (Parts I and II)*, Clef 89098; *DownBeat* (March 24, 1954).

100. Stanley Dance says that Hodges appeared on Steele's show with his group (Dance, Giants, p. 22), but Hodges contradicted this statement in his 1966 *Jazz Journal* interview with Henry Whiston, saying that he played with Cole and Jones. Whiston, p.

101. *Lewiston* (PA) *Evening Journal*, p. 3, July 30, 1959.

102. Jos Willems, *All of Me: The Complete Discography of Louis Armstrong*, p. 209. Lanham, MD: Scarecrow, 2006.

103. Gitler, Swing to Bop, pp. 318–319.

104. Whiston.

105. Duke Ellington Collection, Archives Center, National Museum of American History, Washington, DC; Stuart Nicholson, *Reminiscing in Tempo*, pp. 301–302. Boston: Northeastern University Press, 1999.

106. Dance, Giants, p. 22.

107. Oakley OHAM, n.p.

CHAPTER 15

1. Vail says that he returned on August 28 for a broadcast of an NBC radio show in New York. Vail II, p. 83. Other sources say that Hodges rejoined the band onAugust 1, 1955, which would have placed him at the Aquacade engagement for two nights. Hasse, p. 318; Bradbury, p. 80. Stratemann notes the August 28 date with a question mark. Stratemann, p. 361.

2. Raymond Horricks, *Profiles in Jazz: From Sidney Bechet to John Coltrane*, p. 71. Piscataway, NJ: Transaction, 1991.

3. Balliett, Collected Works, p. 129.

4. *Whammy* was slang for "hex or spell" that came into use in the late 1930s, and *double whammy* is attributed to boxing manager Wirt Ross, who in 1941 described it as a secret technique that would enable his fighter to defeat Joe Louis. http://www.phrases.org.uk/meanings/119750.html.

5. Balliett, Collected Works, p. 129.

6. Nat Hentoff, "Duke Ellington: Café Society, New York, *DownBeat* (January 12, 1956).

7. Duke Ellington: Ellington Showcase, Vail II, p. 89. *DownBeat* (April 4, 1956).

8. Duke Ellington: Historically Speaking—The Duke, Vail II, p. 91. *DownBeat* (May 30, 1956).

9. Hentoff, "Duke Ellington: Café Society, New York," p.

10. Hasse, p. 319.

11. Hasse, p. 319.

12. Teachout, p. 287.

13. Teachout, p. 288.

14. John Fass Morton, *Backstory in Blue: Ellington at Newport '56*, p. 129. New Brunswick, NJ: Rutgers University Press, 2008.

15. Mood Indigo & Beyond. *Time* (August 20, 1956).

16. Jewell, p. 87.

17. Hasse, pp. 327–328.

18. William Shakespeare, *A Midsummer's Night Dream*, act IV, scene 1.

19. Bill Simon, liner notes to *Duke's in Bed*, Verve Records V-8203, 1956.

20. Ben Webster, *Duke's in Bed!* Black Lion Records BL-190, 1965.

21. Quoted by Nat Hentoff in liner notes to *The Big Sound: Johnny Hodges and the Ellington Men*, Verve Records, MG V-8271, 1957 .

22. Vail II, p. 150.

23. Samuel Taylor Coleridge, *Kubla Khan*, in *Seven Centuries of Verse: English & American*, ed. A. J. M. Smith, p. 322. New York: Charles Scribner's Sons, 1967.

24. John Clement, liner notes to *The Complete Verve Johnny Hodges Small Group Sessions, 1956–61*, Mosaic Records MD6-200, p. 9, 2000.

25. Lawrence D. Stewart, liner notes to *Johnny Hodges and His Strings Play the Prettiest Gershwin*. Avid Jazz reissue, *Johnny Hodges: Three Classic Albums Plus*, 2011, AMSC 1040, 2011.

26. Vail II, p. 216.

27. Vail II, p. 225.

28. Mark Stryker, "Ellington's Score Still Celebrated," *Detroit Free Press*, January 20, 2009.

29. Stratemann, p. 406.

30. Dance, Smooth One.

31. New York Passenger Lists, 1820–1957, http://interactive.ancestry.com; Vail I, pp. 80, 87.

32. Dance, Smooth One.

33. Quoted in Dance, Mosaic, p. 12.

34. Dance, Ellington, p. 92.

35. Marcel Greene, liner notes to *Ben Webster, Johnny Hodges: The Complete 1960 Sextet Jazz Cellar Session*, Solar Records 4569895, 2011; John Clement, liner notes to *The Complete Johnny Hodges Sessions, 1956–61*, p. 12. Mosaic Records MD6-200, 2000.

36. Steve Voce, "Duke Ellington: A Cold From Little Eddie," *Jazz Journal* (March 1963).

37. Vacca, pp. 143–144.

38. Jones, p. 61.

39. Steve Voce, "One Doesn't Snap One's Fingers on the Beat," *Jazz Journal* (April 1966).

40. *Billboard* (April 28, 1962), p. 11.

41. Ellison, p. 32.

CHAPTER 16

1. *Duke With a Difference*, Riverside RLP 12-246, 1957.

2. All Music Guide, p. 1084; Feather, Encyclopedia, p. 251.

3. Don Gold, liner notes to *Taylor Made Jazz*, Argo LP 650, 1959.

4. Conover, n.p.

5. Nat Hentoff, liner notes to *Gerry Mulligan Meets Johnny Hodges*, Verve Records MG VS-68367, 1961.

6. Stratemann, p. 442.

7. *Hawkins! Eldridge! Hodges! Alive!* Verve Records 513 755-2, 1962.

8. In a coincidence for the ages, Hodges once played in a recording session with Bill "Bojangles" Robinson as a member of a disguised Ellington unit dubbed "Irving Mills and His Hotsy Totsy Gang." Vail I, p. 24.

9. Stanley Dance, liner notes to *Johnny Hodges with the Lawrence Welk Orchestra*, Ranwood Records 8246-2, 1994.

10. Duke Ellington interview conducted by Jack Cullen, October 30, 1963, #500D–E. Yale University Special Collections, OHAM.

11. *Johnny Hodges and His Strings Play the Prettiest Gershwin*, reissued as part of *Johnny Hodges: Three Classic Albums Plus*, Avid Jazz AMSC 1040, 2011.

12. Dance, Giants, p. 25.

13. Lambert, p. 59.

14. John Hammond, "Is the Duke Deserting Jazz?" in Tucker, Reader, p. 171.

15. Nat Hentoff, "Conversations Among the Elders," *Esquire* (February 1, 1960).

16. Chilton, Bechet, p. 164.

17. Leonard Feather, "Blindfold Test: Charlie Parker," *DownBeat* (March 11, 1965), p. 32.

18. Radio interview with Paul Desmond and John McLellan, unidentified Boston radio station, early 1954, www.melmartin.com.

19. Teachout, p. 346.

20. Steve Voce, "One Doesn't Snap One's Fingers on the Beat," *Jazz Journal* (April 1966).

CHAPTER 17

1. Dance, Sportpalast.

2. Stanley Dance, liner notes to *The Eleventh Hour*, Verve Records V6-8492.

3. Stanley Dance, liner notes to *Blue Pyramid*, Verve Records V6-8635.

4. Dance, Smooth One (emphasis in original).

5. Jewell, p. 115.

6. Teachout, p. 283.

7. Teachout, p. 301.

8. Leonard Feather, liner notes to *Ella at Duke's Place*, Verve Records V6-4070, 1965.

9. Will Friedwald, liner notes to *Blue Rose: Rosemary Clooney and Duke Ellington and His Orchestra*, Columbia/Legacy CK65506, 1956.

10. Bradbury, p. 85.

11. Uncredited liner notes to *Jo + Jazz*, Corinthian Records COR-108, 1960.

12. *Joya Sings Duke*, 20th-Century Fox TFM-3170, 1965.

13. Feather, Encyclopedia, p. 418.

14. Leonard Feather, "Blindfold Test: Charlie Parker," *DownBeat* (March 11, 1965), p. 32. Parker did on occasion invoke Pons in a sarcastic manner, however. In 1953 Miles Davis scolded Parker for getting drunk at a recording session. "All right, Lily Pons," Parker responded. Then he rattled off artistic clichés including "To produce beauty, we must suffer pain—from the oyster comes the pearl." Ira Gitler, *Jazz Masters*, p. 50. New York: Da Capo, 1966.

15. Dance, Giants, p. 18.

16. Nat Hentoff, *American Music Is*, pp. 84–85. New York: Da Capo, 2004.

17. Feather, Encyclopedia, p. 254.

18. Alyn Shipton, *A New History of Jazz*, p. 580. London: Continuum, 2001.

19. Jewell, p. 82.

20. Friedwald, p. 113.

21. "Sinatra Says—No Colour Bar," *Melody Maker* (October 18, 1958), p. 3.

22. Friedwald, p. 303.

23. Friedwald, p. 306.

24. Friedwald, p. 308.

25. Friedwald, p. 282.

26. Friedwald, p. 69.

27. Thomas Mann, *The Magic Mountain*, translated from the German by John E. Woods, p. 631. New York: Knopf, 1995.

28. Friedwald, p. 69.

29. J. D. Salinger, *Raise High the Roof Beam, Carpenters*, p. 78. Boston: Little, Brown, 1959.

30. Aristotle, *Poetics*, pp. 230–232. New York: Modern Library, 1954.

CHAPTER 18

1. Hargrove, p. 45.

2. "Johnny Hodges' Alto Sax," Tomoji Hirakata, https://www.youtube.com/watch?v=Ad_NFvmyPvA; "Rifftides: Doug Ramsey on Jazz and Other Matters," http://www.artsjournal.com/rifftides/2013/09/weekend-extra-johnny-hodges-saxophone.html.

3. Hargrove, p. 45.

4. Stratemann, pp. 22, 29, 73, 89, 119, 201, 227.

5. Stratemann, pp. 29–44. RKO Pictures, Inc., the studio that made the film, even required Barney Bigard, a Creole, and Juan Tizol, a Puerto Rican, to wear blackface because they were deemed too light-skinned to realistically portray members of a black jazz band. Teachout, p. 104; Ward and Burns, p. 180; Hasse, p. 129.

6. Stratemann, p. 35.

7. Stratemann, pp. 381, 395, 475, 565.

8. Stratemann, pp. 59, 119, 145.

9. *Duke Ellington: Copenhagen 1965, Parts One and Two*, Storyville ID 9548DNDVD, 2002.

10. Stratemann, pp. 555, 575.

11. Stratemann, pp. 495, 595.

12. Vail II, p. 174.

13. Steve Voce, Obituary: Stanley Dance, *The Independent* (March 1, 1999).

14. Dance, Ellington, p. 92.

15. "That the discussion of religion and politics within the Lodge shall be strictly prohibited." Basic Principle 7, United Grand Lodge of England Book of Constitutions: London: Freemasons' Hall, U.G.L. of E., 2015.

16. Stuart Nicholson, *Reminiscing in Tempo: A Portrait of Duke Ellington*, pp. 326–327. Boston: Northeastern University Press, 1999.

17. Pete Welding, "Long Day's Journey: On the Road with the Duke Ellington Orchestra," *DownBeat* (June 7, 1962), pp. 24–25, 43.

18. Duke Ellington, "Reminiscing in Tempo," *DownBeat* (July 2, 1964), pp. 8–9.

19. Dance, Giants, pp. 5–6.

20. Dance, Giants, p. 23.

21. Dance, Giants, p. 23.

22. Dance, Giants, p. 28.

23. Dance, Giants, p. 26.

24. Hargrove, p. 37.

25. Boyer, p. 27.

26. Dance, Giants, p. 23.

27. Sonny Greer, interview by Whitney Balliett, in Tucker, Reader, p. 490.

28. Dance, Giants, p. 19.

29. Jones, p. 59.

30. Dance, Giants, p. 6.

31. Dance, Mosaic, p. 4.

32. Burman.

33. Alun Morgan, liner notes to *Side by Side: Duke Ellington and Johnny Hodges Plus Others*, Verve MG VS-6109, 1959.

34. Dance, Giants, p. 12.

35. Martin Gayford, *Telegraph*, July 19, 2007.

36. Mercer Ellington, p. 137 (emphasis in original).

37. John Tynan, review in *DownBeat*, in Vail II, p. 165.

38. Harvey G. Cohen, *Duke Ellington's America*, p. 360. Chicago: University of Chicago Press, 2010.

39. Dance, Giants, p. 4.

40. Dance, Time Life, p. 26.

41. Dance, Giants, p. 5.

42. Dance, Giants, p. 15.

43. Boyer, p. 32.

44. Dance, Mosaic, p. 6.

45. Tomkins.

46. Balliett, Collected Works, p. 204.

47. Dance, Mosaic, p. 4.

48. Dance, Giants, p. 5.

49. Dance, liner notes to *Hodges & Hines: Swing's Our Thing*, Verve Records, V6-8732, 1968.

50. Nat Hentoff, "Life Could Be a Dream When He Blew Sax," *Wall Street Journal* (February 1, 2002); Nat Hentoff, "Alto Sax Was His Ax," *Wall Street Journal* (May 31, 1989).

51. Jones, p. 60.

CHAPTER 19

1. Handy, p. 238.

2. Helen Oakley, "Impressions of Johnny Hodges," *Tempo* (November 1936), pp. 10, 12.

3. Stanley Crouch, "Rooster Ben: King of Romance," *Village Voice*, Jazz Supplement (June 1986), pp. 6–7.

4. Dizzy Gillespie, with Al Fraser, *"to Be, or not . . . to Bop,"* p. 310. Garden City : Doubleday, 1979.

5. Ellison, p. 124.

6. Sidney Finkelstein, *Jazz: A People's Music*, chap. 6. New York: Citadel, 1948, cited in Lambert, p. 48.

7. Handy, pp. 13–15.

8. Handy, p. 103.

9. Francis Davis, *The History of the Blues*. New York: Hyperion, 1995.

10. Handy, p. 114.

11. Handy, p. 115.

12. Giddins, Visions, p. 29.

13. *Chicago Daily Tribune*, July 11, 1915.

14. Handy, p. 97.

15. Gunther Schuller, *Early Jazz: Its Roots and Musical Development*, p. 226. New York: Oxford University Press, 1968.

16. Panassié and Gautier, p. 185.

17. Feather, Encyclopedia, p. 131. But compare the entry in Panassié and Gautier, p. 22, which gives Bechet's date of birth as May 14, 1891.

18. *See, e.g.*, Chilton, Bechet, p. 188, quoting a 1946 review in *American Jazz Review* of a concert performance by Bechet: "[T]hen came the Blues. [Bechet] literally had the audience in his hand. . . . The audience swayed and sighed as Sidney moaned the Blues."

19. Handy, p. 103.

20. *Mississippi Juke Joint Blues—September 9, 1941*, Rhythm and Blues Records, RANDB036, 2016.

21. Ellison, p. 24.

22. Diogenes Laertius, *Lives of Eminent Philosophers*, bk. 2, pt. 36, and bk. 6, pt. 8, ed. R. D. Hicks. Cambridge: Harvard University Press, 1925.

23. On at least two occasions Hodges recorded with acoustic (unamplified) blues-style harmonica accompaniment by Buddy Lucas, producing the tracks "Rent City" and "Sneakin' Up On You" on the album *Blue Notes*, recorded in October 1966 (Verve Records VDJ-1), and "Everytime She Walks," heard on the album *Don't Sleep in the Subway*, recorded in August 1967 (Verve Records V6-8726).

24. Dance, Giants, p. 19.

25. Albert Murray, *Stomping the Blues*, p. 186. New York: McGraw-Hill, 1976.

26. James P. Johnson, interview with Tom Davin, *The Jazz Review*, cited by Albert Murray in *Stomping the Blues*, 2nd ed., p. 508. New York: Literary Classics of the United States, Inc., 2016.

27. Dan Morgenstern text, Ole Brask, photographs, *Jazz People*, p. 107. New York: Da Capo, 1993.

28. Dance, Ellington, p. 100.

29. Feather, Encyclopedia, p. 177.

30. One reference work lists Milt Herth and Glenn Hardman as swing-era organists and Fred Longshaw as an accompanist on organ for blues singer Bessie Smith. All Music Guide, p. 865.

31. Stanley Dance, liner notes to *Mess of Blues*, Verve Records V-8570, 1964.

32. Dance, Ellington, p. 242.

33. Stanley Dance, liner notes to *Blue Hodge*, Lone Hill Jazz reissue LHJ10286, 2016.

34. Jones, p. 59.

35. Stanley Dance, liner notes to *Mess of Blues*.

36. Panassié and Gautier, p. 115.

37. Dance, Ellington, p. 94.

38. Dance, Ellington, p. 99.

39. Gardner appears on *The Chant* with the Latin Jazz Quintet, Prestige/Tru Sound 670483, 1962, and a collection, *Latin Jazz Dance Classics: Volume Two,* CuBop CBCD010, 1997.

40. Esmond Edwards, quoted in Leonard Feather, liner notes to *Rippin' & Runnin': Johnny Hodges,* Verve Records V6-8753, 1969.

41. Keith Shadwick, liner notes to the Atlantic Masters reissue of *New Orleans Suite,* Atlantic Records 81227 3670-2, 2003.

CHAPTER 20

1. Stratemann, p. 597.

2. All Music Guide, p. 842.

3. All Music Guide, p. 1089.

4. Nat Hentoff, liner notes to *3 Shades of Blue: Johnny Hodges with Leon Thomas and Oliver Nelson,* Flying Dutchman Productions FDS-120, 1970.

5. Vail II, pp. 376–377.

6. Vail II, pp. 377–378.

7. Stanley Dance, liner notes to *Duke Ellington: New Orleans Suite,* Atlantic Records 81227 3670-2, 2003.

8. Id.

9. Dance, Mosaic, p. 4. He played soprano in live performances of *Jump for Joy,* Ellington's musical, in 1941. *See* George T. Simon, "Joe Turner Star of Duke's Revue!" *Metronome* (October 1941), p. 20, cited in Vail I, p. 202 ("Hodges came through with some marvelous soprano saxing").

10. Stewart, Boy Meets Horn, p. 192.

11. Jones, p. 60.

12. Dance, Mosaic, p. 4.

13. Ellington, Mistress, p. 118.

14. Lawrence, p. 385.

15. Vail II, pp. 343, 353.

16. Steve Voce, "Johnny Hodges: Everybody Knows," *Jazz Journal* (January 1970).

17. Mercer Ellington, p. 110; Vail II, p. 353; Stratemann, p. 584.

18. Stratemann, p. 584.

19. Dance, Ellington, p. 101.

20. Dance, Giants, p. 28. Ralph Gleason suggests that Hodges was stricken while in the dentist's chair and got up to go to the men's room not to relieve himself, but out of concern for the symptoms of the attack. Ralph Gleason, "The Sunlight and Beauty of Johnny Hodges," collected in *Music in the Air: The Selected Writings of Ralph J. Gleason*, p. 74. New Haven: Yale University Press, 2016. To the author's knowledge, this view has not been adopted by any other source.

21. Dance, Mosaic, p. 6.

22. Dance, Sportpalast.

23. Giddins, Time-Life, p. 47.

24. Dance, Sportpalast.

25. Ellington, Mistress, p. 119.

26. Gunther Schuller, "The Case for Ellington's Music as Living Repertory," in *Musings: The Musical Worlds of Gunther Schuller*, pp. 47–50. New York: Oxford University Press, 1986.

27. Bradbury, p. 123.

28. Raymond Carver, "Vitamins," in *Cathedral*, p. 102. New York: Knopf, 1983.

29. Howard Rosenberg, *"Hill Street," "Animal House" Beget CBS' "Public Morals,"* Los Angeles Times (October 30, 1996).

30. Balliett, Collected Works, p. 334.

31. Quoted in Stuart Nicholson, *Reminiscing in Tempo: A Portrait of Duke Ellington*, p. 208. Boston: Northeastern University Press, 1999.

32. Dance, Giants, p. 28.

33. Stanley Dance, "The Funeral Address," *Jazz Journal* 27/7 (July 1974).

34. "A Concise Biography of Johnny Hodges," http://confabwithrab.blogspot.com/2012/04/concise-biography-of-johnny-hodges.html.

35. Tomkins.

36. *See, e.g.*, Jack Chambers, "Sweet as Bear Meat: The Paradox of Johnny Hodges," *Coda* (July–August 2001), pp. 16–20.

37. Jewell, pp. 211–212.

38. "Johnny Hodges' Alto Sax," Tomoji Hirakata, https://www.youtube.com/watch?v=Ad_NFvmyPvA; "Rifftides: Doug Ramsey on Jazz and Other Matters," http://www.artsjournal.com/rifftides/2013/09/weekend-extra-johnny-hodges-saxophone.html.

39. U.S. Census Bureau, Statistical Abstract of the United States, Section 31, 20th Century Statistics, No. 1421, Expectation of Life at Birth, by Race and Sex: 1900 to 1997, 1999.

40. Dance, Giants, p. 6.

41. *Jet*, December 28, 1972.

42. Tucker, Reader, p. 340.

43. *See, e.g.,* payroll records of the Ellington orchestra for the week beginning December 12, 1963. At that time he was paid $425 while Cat Anderson was paid $300, Cootie Williams $250, and Sam Woodyard $150. Musicians were also entitled to reimbursement of some expenses. Duke Ellington Collection, Archives Center, National Museum of American History, Washington, DC.

44. Freddie Jenkins, quoted in "Reminiscing in Tempo With Freddie Jenkins," interview by Roger Ringo, *Storyville* (April–May 1973).

45. Dance, Mosaic, p. 4.

46. Duke Ellington in collaboration with Stanley Dance, "The Art Is in the Cooking," *DownBeat* (June 7, 1962), pp. 13–15.

47. Don Heckman, "The Saxophone in Jazz," in *The Oxford Companion to Jazz,* ed. Bill Kirchner, p. 603. Oxford: Oxford University Press, 2000.

48. Conover, n.p.

49. Albert Murray, *Stomping the Blues,* p. 188. New York: McGraw-Hill, 1976.

50. Gordon Jack, *Fifties Jazz Talk: An Oral Retrospective,* p. 215. Lanham, MD: Scarecrow, 2004.

51. Count Basie, as told to Albert Murray, *Good Morning Blues: The Autobiography of Count Basie,* p. 240. New York: Primus/Donald I Fine, 1985.

52. *Independent,* September 20, 1999.

53. "Phil Woods: Jazz Is Love, Hate World," *Times Recorder* (Zanesville, OH) (June 28), 1992, p. 21.

54. "Hodges," by Phil Woods, on *Flowers for Hodges,* Phil Woods/Jim McNeely. Concord Records CCD-4485, 1991.

55. "Phil Woods: Jazz Is Love, Hate World," *Times Recorder* (Zanesville, OH) June 28, 1992, p. 21.

56. Balliett, Collected Works, p. 580.

57. Jimmy Heath and Joseph McLaren, *I Walked With Giants: The Autobiography of Jimmy Heath,* p. 67. Philadelphia: Temple University Press, 2010.

58. Dance, Giants, p. 3.

59. Ira Gitler, *The Masters of Bebop: A Listener's Guide,* p. 48. New York: Da Capo, 2009.

60. Dance, Ellington, p. 179.

61. Sonny Stitt Blindfold Test, *DownBeat* (November 21, 1974), p. 27.

62. Balliett, Portraits, p. 178.

63. Dance, Sportpalast.

64. Dance, Mosaic, p. 6. *See also* Stanley Dance, liner notes to *Blues Summit,* Verve Records 2 V6S 8822, 1973.

65. Dance, Giants, p. 20.

66. Dance, Mosaic, p. 1.

67. Memorable Quotes: Paul Desmond on Ornette Coleman. Jerry Jazz Musician, January 30, 2014. http://www.jerryjazzmusician.com/2014/01/memorable-quotes-paul-desmond-ornette-coleman.

68. Dance, Giants, p. 23.

69. Dance, Ellington, p. 94.

70. Vacca, p. 284.

71. All Music Guide, p. 257.

72. Balliett, Collected Works, p. 296.

73. Cynthia Ozick, "Justice (Again) to Edith Wharton," in *Art & Ardor: Essays*, p. 3. New York: Dutton, 1984.

74. Quoted in Nat Hentoff, liner notes to *Gerry Mulligan Meets Johnny Hodges*, Verve Records MG VS-68367, 1961.

75. Homer, *The Odyssey*, bk 1, lines 404–405, trans. Robert Fagles. New York: Penguin, 1997.

76. Benny Green, liner notes to *Blues A-Plenty*, American Jazz Classics reissue 99058, 2012.

77. Id.

78. Balliett, Collected Works, p. 273.

79. Balliett, Collected Works, p. 625.

80. Cited in Lambert, p. 68.

81. T. S. Eliot, "Tradition and the Individual Talent," in *The Sacred Wood* [1921], p. 48. London: Methuen, 1960.

Bibliography and Abbreviations

All Music Guide to Jazz. Edited by Michael Erlewine, Vladimir Bogdanov, Chris Woodstra, and Scott Yanow. San Francisco: Miller Freeman Books, 1998 (All Music Guide).

Balliett, Whitney. *Collected Works: A Journal of Jazz, 1954–2000.* New York: St. Martin's, 2000 (Balliett, Collected Works).

Balliett, Whitney. *Jelly Roll, Jabbo & Fats: 19 Portraits in Jazz.* Oxford: Oxford University Press, 1983 (Balliett, Portraits).

Balliett, Whitney. *Night Creature: A Journal of Jazz, 1975–1980.* New York: Oxford University Press, 1981 (Balliett, Night Creature).

Berger, Morroe, Edward Berger, and James Patrick. *Benny Carter: A Life in American Music* (2 vols.). Metuchen, NJ: Scarecrow Press and the Institute of Jazz Studies, Rutgers University, 1982 (Berger Patrick).

Bigard, Barney. *With Louis and the Duke.* Edited by Barry Martyn. New York: Oxford University Press, 1985 (Bigard).

Boyer, Richard O. "The Hot Bach." In *Duke Ellington: His Life and Music.* Edited by Peter Gammon, pp. 22–60. New York: Da Capo, 1977 (Boyer).

Bradbury, David. *Duke Ellington.* London: Haus, 2005 (Bradbury).

Büchmann-Møller, Frank. *Someone to Watch Over Me: The Life and Music of Ben Webster.* Ann Arbor: University of Michigan Press, 2009 (Büchmann-Møller).

Burman, Maurice. "Duke's Greater Than Ever, Says Hodges: Talking to Maurice Burman." *Melody Maker* (October 18, 1958), p. 5 (Burman).

Chambers, John. "Sweet as Bear Meat: The Paradox of Johnny Hodges." *Coda* 298 (July–August, 2001), p. 16.

Chilton, John. *Sidney Bechet: The Wizard of Jazz.* New York: Oxford University Press, 1987 (Chilton, Bechet).

Chilton, John. *Who's Who of Jazz.* Rev. ed. New York: Da Capo, 1972 (Chilton, Who's Who).

Clement, John. *The Complete Verve Johnny Hodges Small Group Sessions, 1956–1961.* Mosaic Records MD6-200, 2000.

Cohen, Harvey G. *Duke Ellington's America.* Chicago: University of Chicago Press, 2010.

Conover, Willis. Interview with Johnny Hodges, audio recording, February, 1955. (digital.library.unt.edu/ark:/67531/metadc701827/. University of North Texas Music Library, digital.library.unt.edu (Conover).

Dance, Stanley. *Giants of Jazz: Johnny Hodges.* Time-Life Records, TL-J19, 1981 (Dance, Time-Life).

Dance, Stanley. Liner notes to *The Complete Johnny Hodges Sessions, 1951–1955.* Mosaic Records MR6-126, 1989 (Dance, Mosaic).

Dance, Stanley. Liner notes to *Everybody Knows Johnny Hodges.* Impulse GRD-116, 1992 (Dance, Everybody Knows).

Dance, Stanley. Liner notes to *Johnny Hodges at the Sportpalast, Berlin.* Pablo Records 2620-102, 1978 (Dance, Sportpalast).

Dance, Stanley. Liner notes to *The Smooth One.* Verve Records VE-2-2532, 1979 (Dance, Smooth One).

Dance, Stanley. *The World of Duke Ellington.* New York: Da Capo, 1970 (Dance, Ellington).

Deffaa, Chip. *Voices of the Jazz Age: Profiles of Eight Vintage Jazzmen,* p. 32. Urbana: University of Illinois Press, 1990 (Deffaa).

DeMichael, Don. "Double Play: Carney to Hodges to Ellington." *DownBeat* (June 7, 1962), p. 20 (DeMichael).

DeVito, Chris, Yasuhiro Fujioka, Wolf Schmaler, and David Wild. *The John Coltrane Reference.* Edited by Lewis Porter, p. 87. New York: Routledge, 2008 (Coltrane).

Dunn, Jennifer Daughtry. Interview with Frances Jones Hodges Farnham, June 30, 1985 (unpublished).

Ellington, Duke [Edward Kennedy]. *Music Is My Mistress.* New York: Da Capo, 1973 (Ellington, Mistress).

Ellington, Mercer, with Stanley Dance. *Duke Ellington in Person: An Intimate Memoir.* New York: Da Capo, 1979 (Mercer Ellington).

Ellison, Ralph. *Living With Music: Ralph Ellison's Jazz Writings.* Edited by Robert G. O'Meally. New York: Modern Library, 2002 (Ellison).

Everett, Tom. *Boston's Jazz: A Music With Many Faces.* Boston: Boston Jazz Society, Inc., 1994 (privately published, available for inspection at Boston Public Library, Copley Square branch) (Everett).

Feather, Leonard. *The Encyclopedia of Jazz.* New York: Bonanza, 1960 (Feather, Encyclopedia).

Friedwald, Will. *Sinatra! The Song Is You: A Singer's Art.* New York: Scribner, 1995 (Friedwald).

Gautier, Madeleine. "Johnny Hodges," Bulletin du Hot Club de France no. 198 (May 1970), p. 3.

Giddins, Gary. "Notes on the Music." *Giants of Jazz: Johnny Hodges,* Time-Life Records TL-J19 (Giddins, Time-Life).

Giddins, Gary. *Visions of Jazz: The First Century.* New York: Oxford University Press, 1998 (Giddins, Visions).

Gitler, Ira. *Jazz Masters of the Forties.* New York: Da Capo, 1966 (Gitler, Jazz Masters).

Gitler, Ira. *Swing to Bop: An Oral History of the Transition in Jazz in the 1940s.* New York: Oxford University Press, 1985 (Gitler, Swing to Bop).

Gleason, Ralph J. *Music in the Air: The Selected Writings of Ralph J. Gleason.* Edited by Toby Gleason. New Haven, CT: Yale University Press, 2016 (Gleason).

Hajdu, David. *Lush Life: A Biography of Billy Strayhorn.* New York: Farrar, Straus and Giroux, 1996 (Hajdu).

Handy, W. C. *Father of the Blues: An Autobiography.* Edited by Arna Bontemps. New York: Collier, 1970 (Handy).

Hargrove, Rich, with M. Eleanor Fisher. *Satchmo, Duke, Rabbit, & Me: Anecdotal Jazz.* Saxy Jazz Musique, 1998 (Hargrove).

Hasse, John Edward. *Beyond Category: The Life and Genius of Duke Ellington.* New York: Da Capo, 1993 (Hasse).

Hershman, Sue-Ellen. "What's in a Number? The History and Merger of Local 535." *Interlude* (January–February 1993), p. 4 (Hershman).

Ioakimidis, Demètre. "Johnny Hodges," *Jazz Hot,* 36, nos. 263 (pp. 32–33) and 264 (pp. 20–23), 1970.

Jewell, Derek. *Duke: A Portrait of Duke Ellington.* New York: Norton, 1977 (Jewell).

Johnson, James Weldon. *James Weldon Johnson: Writings.* New York: Library of America, 2004 (Johnson).

Jones, Max. *Talking Jazz.* New York: Norton, 1988 (Jones).

Lambert, G. E. *Kings of Jazz: Duke Ellington.* New York: A. S. Barnes, 1959 (Lambert).

Lasker, Steven. *The Complete 1932–1940 Brunswick, Columbia and Master Recordings of Duke Ellington and His Famous Orchestra.* Mosaic Records MD11-248, 2010 (Lasker, 1932–1940).

Lasker, Steven. *Duke Ellington: The Complete 1936–1940 Variety, Vocalion and Okeh Small Group Sessions.* Mosaic Records MD7-235, 2006 (Lasker, Small Groups).

Lawrence, A. H. *Duke Ellington and His World: A Biography.* New York: Routledge, 2001 (Lawrence).

Leur, Walter van de. *Something to Live For: The Music of Billy Strayhorn.* New York: Oxford University Press, 2000 (Leur).

The New Grove Dictionary of Jazz. 2nd ed., ed. Barry Kernfeld. New York: Grove Press, 2003 (Grove Dictionary).

Oakley, Helen. Interview by Mark Tucker, January 9, 1987, #538A, B. OHAM (Oakley OHAM).

O'Neal, Hank. *The Ghosts of Harlem: Sessions with Jazz Legends.* Nashville, TN: Vanderbilt University Press, 2009 (O'Neal).

Panassié, Hughes, and Madeleine Gautier. *Dictionary of Jazz.* London: Jazz Book Club, 1959 (Panassié and Gautier).

Ramsey, Frederic, Jr., and Charles Edward Smith, eds. *Jazzmen.* New York: Harcourt, Brace, 1939 (Ramsey and Smith).

Segell, Michael. *The Devil's Horn.* New York: Picador/Farrar, Straus and Giroux, 2005 (Segell).

Shapiro, Nat, and Nat Hentoff. *Hear Me Talkin' to Ya: The Story of Jazz as Told by the Men Who Made It.* New York: Rinehart, 1955 (Shapiro and Hentoff).

Smith, Willie "The Lion," with George Hoefer. *Music on My Mind: The Memoirs of an American Pianist.* New York: Da Capo, 1978 (Smith).

Stewart, Rex. *Boy Meets Horn.* Edited by Claire P. Gordon. Ann Arbor: University of Michigan Press, 1991 (Stewart, Boy Meets Horn).

Stewart, Rex. *Jazz Masters of the Thirties.* New York: Macmillan, 1972 (Stewart, Jazz Masters).

Stratemann, Klaus. *Duke Ellington: Day by Day and Film by Film.* Copenhagen: JazzMedia, 1992 (Stratemann).

Tackley, Catherine. *Benny Goodman's Famous 1938 Carnegie Hall Jazz Concert.* New York: Oxford University Press, 2012 (Tackley).

Teachout, Terry. *Duke: A Life of Duke Ellington.* New York, Gotham Books, 2013 (Teachout).

Thomas, J. C. *Chasin' the Trane.* New York: Da Capo, 1976 (Thomas).

Tomkins, L. "Too Late for Me to Change." *Crescendo,* 2/8 (March 1964), p. 16 (Tomkins).

Tucker, Mark, ed. *The Duke Ellington Reader.* New York: Oxford University Press, 1993 (Tucker, Reader).

Tucker, Mark. *Ellington: The Early Years.* Illini Books ed. Chicago: University of Illinois Press, 1995 (Tucker, Early Years).

Ulanov, Barry. *Duke Ellington.* New York: Creative Age, 1946 (Ulanov, Ellington).

Ulanov, Barry. *A History of Jazz in America.* New York: Viking, 1952 (Ulanov, History).

Vacca, Richard. *The Boston Jazz Chronicles: Faces, Places and Nightlife, 1937–1962.* Belmont, MA: Troy Street Publishing, 2012 (Vacca).

Vail, Ken. *Duke's Diary: The Life of Duke Ellington, 1927–1950* (Vail I), and *Duke's Diary: The Life of Duke Ellington, 1950–1974* (Vail II). Lanham, MD: Scarecrow, 2002.

Valk, J. de. *Ben Webster: His Life and Music.* Berkeley: Berkeley Hills Books, 2001 (Valk).

Ward, Geoffrey C., and Ken Burns. *Jazz: A History of America's Music.* New York: Knopf, 2000 (Ward and Burns).

Waters, Benny. *The Key to a Jazzy Life.* Toulouse, France: Benny Waters, 1985 (Waters).

Whiston, Henry. "Johnny Hodges—An interview with Henry Whiston." *Jazz Journal* 19/1, 1966, p. 8 (Whiston).

Williams, Martin. *The Jazz Tradition,* rev. ed. New York: Oxford University Press, 1983 (Williams, Tradition).

Yale University Special Collections, Oral History of American Music, Irving S. Gilmore Music Library, Yale University, New Haven, CT (OHAM).

Index